Pati's

MEXICAN TABLE

Pati's
MEXICAN
TABLE

THE SECRETS OF REAL MEXICAN HOME COOKING

PATI JINICH

Photography by Penny De Los Santos

A Rux Martin Book
HOUGHTON MIFFLIN HARCOURT
Boston   New York

Copyright © 2013 by Patricia Jinich
Photographs copyright © 2013 by Penny De Los Santos

For information about permission to reproduce
selections from this book, write to Permissions,
Houghton Mifflin Harcourt Publishing Company,
215 Park Avenue South, New York, New York 10003.

www.hmhco.com

Library of Congress Cataloging-in-Publication Data
Jinich, Pati.
Pati's Mexican table : the secrets of real Mexican home
cooking / Pati Jinich ; photographs by Penny De Los Santos.
pages cm
ISBN 978-0-547-63647-4
1. Cooking, Mexican. I. Title.
TX716.M4J56 2013
641.5972 — dc23   2012042647

Book design by Rita Sowins/Sowins Design
Food styling by Christine Albano

Printed in the United States of America
12 2021
4500844092

FOR DANIEL AND OUR BOYS,
ALAN, SAMI, AND JUJU,
CON TODO MI AMOR

CONTENTS

INTRODUCTION 8

SALSAS, PICKLES, AND GUACAMOLE ..14

SALADS 40

SOUPS 60

ANYTIME VEGETARIAN 88

SEAFOOD 114

POULTRY 136

MEAT 168

SIDES 198

DESSERTS 230

DRINKS 264

ACKNOWLEDGMENTS 280

INDEX 283

INTRODUCTION

SHOW UP IN MY KITCHEN ANY DAY OF THE YEAR, AND YOU'LL FIND SOFT CORN TORTILLAS, refried beans, at least two different salsas, the fresh Mexican cheese called queso fresco, ripe avocados, and fresh fruit—essential ingredients for countless spur-of-the-moment meals. You are always welcome to join me, because I always cook more than we can manage to eat at one sitting—not out of carelessness, but because that is the practical way of Mexican kitchens.

Salsas are the maracas of my kitchen: They shake things up whenever I need an extra kick of flavor. They can be the base of a dish or the final stroke of genius, a condiment with *mucho potencial*: not always hot, but often fruity, salty, tangy, vinegary, or crunchy. Avocados are almost equally versatile. They can be pounded into chunky guacamole, of course, but also whizzed into a silky soup; tucked into thick, crusty rolls with potatoes and chorizo for a hearty torta, a Mexican sandwich; or buzzed together with milk, cream, and lime juice for an incomparably creamy salad dressing. Soft, mild, and teasingly salty, queso fresco can be sliced into sticks, or diced, or crumbled on top of soups, salads, tostadas, tacos, and enchiladas. The beans are waiting to be slathered on a roll when my voracious boys come home from school or play. And as for tortillas, they are the building blocks for so many dishes from breakfast to dinner every day of the week: wrapped around eggs, enfolding steak for tacos, holding together a casserole. Crisp them, and they become the sturdy base for ceviche tostadas or perfect scoops for salsas. Cut them smaller, and they are a crisp garnish for soups. And with fruits of all kinds—watermelon, mango, pineapple, and more—I make some of the most refreshing drinks ever, with and without alcohol.

I'm not sure that many Americans really understand Mexican home cooking. For me, it's the everyday food I feed my family: the dishes I hanker for, the ones that make me feel at home and that, ironically, I mostly learned how to make while living away from the country where I grew up eating them. That food isn't taco salads, nachos slathered with cheese, or overstuffed burritos. Nor, for the most part, is it the complex mole sauces that take days to prepare. There are, however, other traditional dishes that I serve over and over again, because they are fabulous, as well as new dishes with creative spins that keep Mexican cooking evolving.

Mexican home cooking is beautiful in its simplicity, tremendously convenient, and wholesome. Out of our kitchens come some of the tastiest salads, soups, and cookies that you will ever find. Our food also includes a boatload of vegetarian options: casseroles of black beans and tortillas in chile sauce, plantain quesadillas stuffed with refried beans, eggs poached in delicious salsas. Not every dish has chile in it, nor is a dish necessarily spicy when it does. The best part is that this cooking fits our American lifestyle like a glove.

I didn't set out to be an obsessed food professional, but I'm a Jewish-Mexican mother, so the obsessive part comes naturally. Originally I trained as an academic and got a job in Washington, D.C., at a policy think tank, where I focused on Mexican politics and history. Eventually, though, I listened to my husband, who kept asking why I persisted in working there when all I talked about were the foods of Mexico, and all I did in my spare time was cook.

It wasn't an easy decision to switch careers. I can still hear my dad's jokes about how I wasted so many years: *quemándome las pestañas como rata de biblioteca*, which, loosely translated, means "burning the midnight oil as a bookworm" or, more literally, "burning my eyelashes as a library mouse." Yet I have no regrets. Those were not wasted years—they gave me great research skills and a deeper understanding of Mexico.

Today I'm a chef, food writer, and cooking teacher with a TV show, *Pati's Mexican Table*, on National Public Television. But most of the time, I'm an overloaded soccer mom with three kids and a powerful blender. I continually travel between the Mexican, American, and Spanglish worlds. When I say, "We are Mexican," my boys always correct me, "*Mami*, you are Mexican, we are American." So we compromise: We are Mexican-American, we speak English, and we try to hold on to the Spanish, but truthfully most of what we do is embrace a Spanglish life. Food is the natural meeting point of our cultures.

On the weekends, we start our days late so we have time for a full breakfast with one or another version of eggs, like Scrambled Egg Packets with Black Bean Sauce. *Sobre mesa,* "after table," we linger, sipping coffee and nibbling on crumbs of pound cake or cookies or slices of fruit.

We want our kids to have opinions about what they eat, and we urge them to choose their favorites. My boys always insist that their classic breaded fried chicken cutlets, *Milanesas*, be dressed with salty crumbled cheese and ground dried chile. They love green beans sprinkled with toasted pistachios and seasoned with orange. On cold days, they devour bowls of Mexican Alphabet Soup. On holidays, our table truly shows our dual cultures. Our Thanksgiving turkey gets rubbed with a pungent spicy paste from the Yucatán and roasted in fragrant banana leaves, then served with a stuffing of chorizo, pecans, apples, and corn bread.

In this book, you will find recipes and ideas that have come to my table from many paths. I have been welcomed into homes and kitchens all across Mexico over the years, and a number of the recipes you will find here have been deeply influenced by those home cooks. My go-to Passover brisket recipe, for example, is my take on Berenice Flores's *carne enchilada* from the Purépecha region in Michoacán. I grew up in Mexico City, a place that hums with food opportunities. Many of the dishes we now eat weekly, like Ancho Chile Burgers and Mexican-Style Pasta, are foods I enjoyed there at home, in restaurants, or on the street. I searched out other recipes to satisfy requests from viewers of my television show and students. I worked for months to nail down the best version of Pickled Jalapeños and Carrots, and I perfected Piggy Cookies after getting dozens of requests for this traditional recipe. Now my family can't live without them.

Thankfully, today the ingredients I use the most are widely available at the grocery store or with just a click online. Many, like tomatillos, chipotle chiles in adobo sauce, and queso fresco are used in a number of recipes, making it worthwhile to stock up. That said, I always offer substitutes for specialty ingredients when possible.

In this book, I also share Mexican cooks' tricks—simple lessons that were passed down from my grandmother to my mother and then to me. Many of the dishes in this book are even tastier when made ahead, adding to their convenience. All are magnets for bringing people to the table.

There is a saying that holds true for every meal in a Mexican home: "*Tiramos la casa por la ventana*" ("We throw the house through the window"), sparing no amount of money, time, or effort to supply a table full of soulful food. People may literally sell their furniture so they can feed an entire town for a wedding or a *quinceañera,* a daughter's fifteenth birthday party. Our food is abundant, accommodating, and much simpler than you might think. Sharing it with my new country has become my mission.

Serrano

Guajillo

Habanero

12

Pasilla

Jalapeño

Ancho

Poblano

13

SALSAS, PICKLES, AND GUACAMOLE

CHARRED TOMATO SALSA (SALSA ROJA) ...18

COOKED GREEN SALSA (SALSA VERDE) ...22

FRESH TOMATILLO AND CHIPOTLE SALSA ...24

CHUNKY POBLANO AND TOMATO SALSA ...26

TRADITIONAL TOMATO PICO DE GALLO ...28

MANGO PICO ...30

CRUNCHY RADISH PICO ...31

PICKLED ANCHO CHILE SALSA ...32

PICKLED JALAPEÑOS AND CARROTS
    (JALAPEÑOS Y ZANAHORIAS EN ESCABECHE) ...34

YUCATÁN-STYLE PICKLED RED ONIONS
    (CEBOLLAS ENCURTIDAS A LA YUCATECA) ...37

CHUNKY GUACAMOLE ...38

IT WAS A SALSA THAT SAVED THE FIRST MEAL I COOKED FOR MY HUSBAND. I'd followed step-by-step instructions from my sister Alisa for a menu I presumably couldn't mess up: grilled meat, rice, beans, and a *salsa verde*. Well, I messed up all but the salsa since it is practically impossible to ruin, and Daniel proceeded to use it to drown the entire disaster.

Daniel, like any Mexican, is wild about salsas. They flow through our veins. We've even managed to turn the word *salsa* into a verb, *salsear*, meaning "to soak, drench, drizzle, bathe, or pour," or essentially, to add salsa in any possible way to whatever you are about to eat.

There is a world of salsas that people outside of Mexico have yet to taste and understand. Workhorses in the kitchen, salsas are simple to make and come charred, fried, pureed, mashed, chopped, or raw, and with endless variations. Their common thread is the chile, since all have at least one kind, be it fresh or dried, yet they are not all spicy. Homemade salsas are also so easy, economical, and fresh tasting that after you make one or two, you will wonder why you ever bothered with jarred ones.

Take a peek in the refrigerator of any Mexican and you will find at least one of the two basic salsas: green tomatillo salsa (*salsa verde*) and a red tomato salsa (*salsa roja*). Like two arm-wrestling prizefighters battling for supremacy, green and red salsas are in an endless competition for most-favored status. Neither has managed to win, and there are even dishes that demand both, such as Divorced Eggs (page 92), where half are served with green and half with red because, really, who can make up their mind?

In this chapter, I give you the salsas you will find most often in my refrigerator: my classic charred red and two greens—one cooked and one raw. But I also want to introduce you to several other salsas that are likely to grow on you: the raw and chunky pico de gallo salsas—*pico* refers to a coarsely chopped uncooked salsa—with a Traditional Tomato Pico, a fresh Mango Pico, and an unusual Crunchy Radish Pico. Then there are the exotic pickles that serve as salsas too, like Pickled Jalapeños and Carrots, Yucatán-Style Pickled Red Onions, and Pickled Ancho Chile Salsa, all of which keep for months in the refrigerator. And, of course, no salsa chapter is complete without a guacamole. I give you my preferred version, which can be dressed up or down.

Salsas are accommodating and versatile. They can go on top, on the side, below, in between, or all over just about any dish. They can be the foundation that sets the tone of a dish, or they can be that last stroke of genius that turns it from delicious to sublime.

CHARRED TOMATO SALSA

∾ SALSA ROJA ∾

✳ MAKES ABOUT 2 CUPS ✳ PREPARATION TIME: 5 MINUTES ✳ COOKING TIME: 10 TO 12 MINUTES ✳
CAN BE MADE UP TO 5 DAYS AHEAD, COVERED, AND REFRIGERATED ✳

This is my classic red salsa, rustic and deep, with a hint of smoke that comes from charring the ingredients (see the sidebar, opposite). Infinitely accommodating and delicious on everything it touches, it is excellent served as a dip for chips; drizzled on tacos, quesadillas, and all sorts of appetizers; or used as a base for meat and vegetable dishes. Depending on how the salsa is used, it can end up tasting quite different.

1 **pound ripe tomatoes**

1 **garlic clove, unpeeled**

1 **¼-inch-thick slice large white onion (about 1 ounce)**

1 **jalapeño or serrano chile, or to taste**

¾ **teaspoon kosher or coarse sea salt, or to taste**

1. Preheat the broiler.

2. Place the tomatoes, garlic, onion, and chile on a baking sheet or in a broilerproof skillet. Broil 10 to 12 minutes, turning halfway through. Remove the tomatoes when they are mushy, their skin is charred and wrinkled, and the juices begin to run. The chile and onion should be softened and nicely charred, and the papery skin of the garlic should be burned and the clove softened. Alternatively, you can char the vegetables on a preheated *comal* or in a cast-iron or heavy nonstick skillet on top of the stove over medium heat.

3. Remove the skin from the garlic clove and discard. Place the garlic in a blender or food processor, along with the tomatoes, onion, half of the chile, the salt, and any juices. Puree until smooth. Taste for heat, and add more chile if necessary until you have the desired amount of heat.

✳ MEXICAN COOK'S TRICK: Once the tomatoes and chile are charred, you can remove the skins or leave them on. Like many cooks, I keep them for more intricate flavor and a more rustic texture.

Charring One of the signature cooking techniques in Mexico is charring, which contributes an essential flavor to a dish, concentrating and deepening it, while at the same time bringing out a subtle sweetness and a rough, out-in-the-country personality.

Traditionally ingredients like chiles, onion, garlic, spices, herbs, tomatillos, and tomatoes are charred or toasted on a *comal* (see page 111) or directly over an open flame. They can also be charred on a grill, in a skillet on the stovetop, or under the broiler, which I find the easiest and fastest way. Place the ingredients on a large baking sheet with plenty of space between them so they will not steam, and broil until they are nicely browned on one side; turn and repeat on the other side. Charring is like roasting marshmallows—you want the outside almost black and the inside cooked and transformed but not burnt.

COOKED GREEN SALSA

∿ SALSA VERDE ∿

※ MAKES ABOUT 2 CUPS ※ PREPARATION TIME: 5 MINUTES ※ COOKING TIME: 18 MINUTES ※
CAN BE MADE UP TO 5 DAYS AHEAD, COVERED, AND REFRIGERATED ※

This is my house green salsa, a piquant blend of simmered tomatillos, chiles, garlic, white onion, and cilantro. The ingredients are pureed and then given a quick cook-down to thicken and deepen the flavors. Bright and smooth, the salsa goes with nearly everything: tacos, quesadillas, sunny-side-up eggs in the morning. And just like Charred Tomato Salsa (page 18), *salsa verde* can be used as a cooking sauce for fish, chicken, shredded meat, or the vegetables of your choice.

1 **pound tomatillos, husks removed, rinsed**

1 **garlic clove**

2 **jalapeño or serrano chiles, or to taste**

⅓ **cup coarsely chopped white onion**

1 **cup cilantro leaves and top part of stems**

1 **teaspoon kosher or coarse sea salt, or to taste**

3 **tablespoons vegetable oil**

1. Place the tomatillos, garlic, and chiles in a medium saucepan and cover with water. Bring to a simmer and cook until the tomatillos change from bright to pale green and are soft but not falling apart, about 10 minutes.

2. With a slotted spoon, transfer the tomatillos, garlic, and 1 of the chiles to a blender or food processor. Add the onion, cilantro, and salt and puree until smooth. Taste for heat, and add more chile if necessary until you have the desired amount of heat.

3. Heat the oil in a medium saucepan over medium heat until hot but not smoking. Pour the salsa into the saucepan and cook, stirring occasionally, until thickened slightly, 6 to 8 minutes. Serve hot or warm.

Cilantro Although it was born in the Mediterranean, not Mexico, cilantro has put down such strong roots in our cuisine (five centuries' worth!) that it's hard to imagine cooking without it. Also known as culantro, coriander, or Chinese parsley, cilantro is sometimes confused with Italian flat-leaf parsley, which it resembles. But cilantro leaves are lacier, thinner, and more delicate, and their flavor and smell are a world apart from those of parsley: distinctive, strong, and pungent. Mexican cooks use the leaves and the thin upper part of the stems, which have a lot of flavor and a nice texture.

People have strong feelings about cilantro—they tend to love it or hate it. Those who hate it think it tastes soapy, and research shows that there may be a genetic predisposition behind that opinion. I'm in the group that loves cilantro, but I use it sparingly. A couple of sprigs are usually all that is needed.

Cilantro is a key ingredient in many salsas and guacamoles. It is also used to flavor beans, salads, stews, and rice, and the leaves are often placed in a bowl on the table as an optional garnish.

FRESH TOMATILLO AND CHIPOTLE SALSA

❋ MAKES ABOUT 4 CUPS ❋ PREPARATION TIME: 10 MINUTES ❋ CAN BE MADE UP TO 5 DAYS AHEAD WITHOUT THE OPTIONAL CHEESE AND AVOCADO, COVERED, AND REFRIGERATED ❋

1 pound tomatillos, husks removed, rinsed, and halved

1 garlic clove

2 tablespoons coarsely chopped white onion

¼ cup coarsely chopped cilantro leaves and top part of stems

1 canned chipotle chile in adobo sauce (optional), seeded if desired, plus 2 tablespoons adobo sauce

¾ teaspoon kosher or coarse sea salt, or to taste

1 large ripe Hass avocado, halved, pitted, meat scooped out, and diced (optional)

2 cups diced queso fresco, Cotija, farmer cheese, or mild feta (about 8 ounces; optional)

Talk about a magical ingredient! When used raw, tomatillos lend a considerably different character to a dish than when cooked: they're crisper, of course, but they're also more tart, with a punchy, clean flavor.

In this recipe, the smoky-sweet heat from the chipotles in adobo can be adjusted to your taste. Use just the sauce from the chipotles for a hint; for a bit more heat, add the chile without the seeds; and to really ramp it up, drop in the entire chile, including the seeds.

This salsa makes a great accent for grilled meats, fish, or chicken. Add diced avocado and cubes of cheese and you'll have a to-die-for appetizer along with a bowl of Tortilla Chips (page 66).

1. Combine the tomatillos, garlic, onion, cilantro, chipotle chile (if using), adobo sauce, and salt in a blender or food processor. Puree until smooth; it will be soupy.

2. Transfer the salsa to a serving bowl. Stir in the avocado and cheese, if desired. Taste, adjust the salt if needed, and serve.

Tomatillos are underappreciated. I don't think I have met more than a handful of people in the Washington, D.C., area who have cooked with them. People love *salsa verde*, but they don't realize that the base of that addictive salsa is this shiny green cousin of the tomato. A bit less juicy and firmer than tomatoes, with a unique tart taste, tomatillos go beautifully with the spicy, sweet, and layered flavors of Mexican cooking. They are readily available in grocery stores all across the United States.

Tomatillos are covered with papery husks, which must be removed. The fruit is a bit waxy and sticky and can have a musty smell from the moisture trapped between the fruit and the husk. Don't judge a book by its cover: Just remove the husks and give the fruit a quick rinse, and you will have shiny green gems.

When you buy tomatillos, peek inside the husks to confirm that the fruit is firm and bright green, not wrinkled or discolored. The husks should be papery and dry, not wet, but don't worry if they stick to the fruit a bit. Tomatillos will keep in the refrigerator for up to 10 days if they are fresh.

CHUNKY POBLANO AND TOMATO SALSA

❋ MAKES ABOUT 4 CUPS ❋ PREPARATION TIME: 5 MINUTES ❋ COOKING TIME: 30 MINUTES ❋
CAN BE MADE UP TO 4 DAYS AHEAD, COVERED, AND REFRIGERATED ❋

2 pounds ripe tomatoes

1 garlic clove

2 bay leaves

3 tablespoons vegetable oil

½ cup thinly sliced white onion

2 large poblano chiles (about 11 ounces), charred, sweated, peeled, stemmed, seeded, and cut into 2-inch strips (see page 27)

¼ teaspoon dried marjoram

1 teaspoon kosher or coarse sea salt, or to taste

½ teaspoon freshly ground black pepper, or to taste

A chunky base of gently browned onions and meaty strips of poblano peppers are cooked in a nicely seasoned tomato sauce. Once finished, this thick salsa is delicious with chips or as a garnish for anything from tacos or tostadas to grilled meats or chicken. I think it shines brightest as a sauce for cooking eggs—see Poached Eggs in Chunky Poblano-Tomato Salsa (page 97). It also makes a lovely poaching sauce for fish fillets.

1. Place the tomatoes, garlic, and bay leaves in a medium saucepan, cover with water, and bring to a boil over medium-high heat. Reduce the heat and simmer until the tomatoes are soft, about 10 minutes. Let cool slightly. Discard the bay leaves.

2. Transfer the tomatoes and garlic to a blender or food processor and puree until smooth.

3. Heat the oil in a large skillet over medium-high heat until hot but not smoking. Add the onion and cook, stirring now and then, until soft and translucent, 4 to 5 minutes. Stir in the poblanos and cook for 1 to 2 minutes more. Add the tomato puree, marjoram, salt, and pepper and bring to a simmer. Reduce the heat to medium and cook until the salsa has thickened and the flavors have deepened, 10 to 12 minutes. Serve hot or warm.

Poblano Chiles (see page 76) are rarely used raw in Mexican cooking. They are usually charred and peeled to bring out their best qualities. The process is simple, and you can make more than you need and freeze them for up to 6 months.

CHAR OR BROIL THEM Place the chiles under the broiler, on a hot *comal* (see page 111), in a dry skillet set over medium heat, on an outdoor grill, or directly over an open flame, which is how they are typically done in Mexico. I prefer to broil them because you can do several at a time.

Whatever method you choose, roast, turning them every 2 to 3 minutes, for 6 to 9 minutes. They should be charred and blistered on the outside, and the flesh should be cooked, not burnt—much like roasting marshmallows over a fire.

MAKE THEM SWEAT Place the chiles in a plastic bag or a bowl. Seal the bag or cover the bowl tightly with plastic wrap and allow the chiles to sweat for 10 to 20 minutes. When I was growing up, my mom always wrapped the plastic bag in a kitchen towel; I do the same.

PEEL AND RINSE Holding each chile under a thin stream of cold running water, remove the charred skin with your fingers. Then make a slit down one side of the pepper and remove the cluster of seeds and veins.

If you are using the peppers for stuffing, leave the stems intact. If using them in other dishes, remove the stems and slice the chiles.

Note: Poblano chiles vary a great deal in their level of heat. If you don't want to take any chances, you can tame them. Once the chiles are charred, peeled, and cleaned, soak them in warm water mixed with a tablespoon of brown sugar for 10 to 30 minutes, then drain.

TRADITIONAL TOMATO
PICO DE GALLO

✳ MAKES ABOUT 4 CUPS ✳ PREPARATION TIME: 15 MINUTES ✳ CAN BE MADE UP TO 1 DAY AHEAD,
COVERED, AND REFRIGERATED ✳

1 **pound ripe tomatoes, halved, cored, and chopped (about 3 cups)**

½ **cup finely chopped white onion**

1 **jalapeño or serrano chile, halved, seeded if desired, and finely chopped, or to taste**

½ **cup coarsely chopped cilantro leaves and top part of stems**

2–3 **tablespoons freshly squeezed lime juice**

2 **tablespoons olive oil (optional)**

1 **teaspoon kosher or coarse sea salt, or to taste**

There are endless variations on pico de gallo, the trademark chunky raw salsa of Mexico. As you travel throughout the country, you will find picos made from vegetables like cucumber and jicama, all kinds of fruits, and even nuts and seeds. All are delicious. This traditional version is a combination of tomatoes, onion, cilantro, and chile with a squeeze of fresh lime juice and some salt. Sometimes I add the oil, sometimes I don't. Try it both ways and see which you like best. Then consider this recipe a starting point and branch out from here.

Pico de gallo translates as "rooster's beak." Why? It's a mystery to me, and to every Mexican cook and culinary expert I've asked.

Place the tomatoes, onion, chile, cilantro, lime juice, olive oil (if using), and salt in a bowl and toss well. Let sit for at least 5 minutes before serving.

✳ MEXICAN COOK'S TRICK: Acidic fruits and vegetables taste much richer and more full-bodied when served at room temperature, so take the chill off any refrigerated salsa before serving.

Jalapeño or Serrano Chile? Many Mexican recipes call for using either jalapeño or serrano chiles. They're common and generally accepted substitutes for each other, and they have several similarities: Both are usually used before their shiny deep green skins ripen to red, and both can be used raw, cooked, charred, or fried. You can tame their heat by removing their seeds and veins, but the seeds have a lot of flavor, so most Mexican cooks, including me, would rather use less of the chile and include the seeds.

How to tell the difference between the two? See page 12 for a photo. The jalapeño, also called *cuaresmeño* in Mexico, is larger, rounder, and chubbier than the serrano. Its heat is milder and its flavor lighter. Serranos, also known simply as *chiles verdes*, are thinner than jalapeños, with a pointy tip; the Mexican cooking authority Diana Kennedy describes them as having the shape of a bullet. I think they have the bite of a bullet too. They are generally spicier and have a bolder and more fragrant flavor than jalapeños.

MANGO PICO

✳ MAKES ABOUT 4½ CUPS ✳ PREPARATION TIME: 10 MINUTES ✳ CAN BE MADE UP TO 1 DAY AHEAD, COVERED, AND REFRIGERATED ✳

⅓ cup slivered red onion

¼ cup freshly squeezed lime juice, or to taste

4 cups peeled and diced mangoes (about 2½ pounds)

1 jalapeño or serrano chile, halved, seeded if desired, and finely chopped, or to taste

2 tablespoons coarsely chopped cilantro leaves and top part of stems

2 tablespoons olive oil

1 teaspoon kosher or coarse sea salt, or to taste

The sweet bite of mango combined with the sour-and-spicy flavors of lime and chile make this versatile salsa a hit. It's a great match for seafood: Try it with grilled salmon, steamed shellfish, or Crab Cakes with Jalapeño Aioli (page 127). Eat it on its own with chips, or shatter salsa preconceptions by serving it over ice cream or sorbet or with Alisa's Marbled Pound Cake (page 251). You can substitute for the mangoes any fruit that has a sweet note and a hint of acidity, such as peaches, pineapples, or plums.

1. Toss the onion and lime juice together in a small bowl and let sit for at least 5 minutes to macerate and soften a little.

2. Place the mangoes, chile, cilantro, oil, and salt in a large bowl. Gently fold in the red onion mixture. Taste, and adjust the seasoning if needed.

✳ MEXICAN COOK'S TRICK: For this salsa, I love to use ripe Champagne mangoes, known in Mexico as *mangos ataulfos*, but any mango works. I also like the Kent variety, which is a bit meatier and firmer. You can use ripe and sweet mangoes or those that are greener and more acidic— just adjust the salt and chile as needed to balance the flavor.

Controlling Chile Heat Fresh chiles are capricious. Although you can count on different varieties of chiles to deliver different levels of heat (for instance, a habanero is a lot hotter than a jalapeño), chiles of the same variety and even those from the same plant may vary wildly in their heat level.

To get an upper hand on their mischief, it's a good practice to add chiles to recipes gradually, since it's almost impossible to tamp the heat down once you have taken it too far. (Adding water won't help.) Start with a small amount, taste, and add more until you get the level of heat you are comfortable with. Remember that, generally speaking, a salsa that contains mashed or pureed chiles will become milder as it sits in the refrigerator.

CRUNCHY RADISH PICO

✳ MAKES ABOUT 3 CUPS ✳ PREPARATION TIME: 20 MINUTES ✳ CAN BE MADE UP TO 12 HOURS AHEAD, COVERED, AND REFRIGERATED ✳

2 cups halved and thinly sliced red radishes (about 1 pound)

1 cup peeled, halved, seeded, and thinly sliced cucumber

1 jalapeño or serrano chile, halved, seeded if desired, and finely chopped, or to taste

1 tablespoon coarsely chopped cilantro leaves

3 scallions (white and light green parts only), thinly sliced

2–3 tablespoons freshly squeezed lime juice, or to taste

¼ cup vegetable oil

1 teaspoon kosher or coarse sea salt, or to taste

Peppery, pungent radishes are the stars in this unusual pico, which shows just how much they appreciate the company of citrus and salt. My late paternal grandfather was an extreme radish fan, and whenever I prepare this pico, I'm sad that I didn't know how to make it when he was alive. I first tried a similar pico on a beach on the Mexican Pacific and was instantly smitten. Extra-crunchy, it has boatloads of personality and can be made year-round. It pairs beautifully with Creamy Poblano Mahimahi (page 134), Snapper with Creamy Almond-Chipotle Pesto (page 133), or My Favorite Green Rice (page 221).

Place all the ingredients in a medium bowl; toss well. Let stand for at least 5 to 10 minutes before serving.

✳ MEXICAN COOK'S TRICK: To enhance the flavor of the cucumbers and tone down any possible bitterness, give them a nice rub. Trim the ends and rub each end with the cut piece from the opposite end. It will make the cucumber happy. Is this an old wives' tale or a savvy trick? I learned it from my maternal grandmother, and it works every time for me.

PICKLED ANCHO CHILE SALSA

* MAKES 2 CUPS * PREPARATION TIME: 15 MINUTES, PLUS MARINATING TIME * KEEPS, COVERED AND REFRIGERATED, FOR UP TO 6 MONTHS *

6–8 ancho chiles (about 3 ounces), rinsed, stemmed, and seeded

½ cup finely chopped white onion

1 garlic clove, finely chopped

½ cup vegetable oil

¼ cup unseasoned rice vinegar

¼ cup distilled white vinegar

2 teaspoons grated *piloncillo* (see page 262) or dark brown sugar, or to taste

1½ teaspoons kosher or coarse sea salt, or to taste

This marinated salsa—more like a pickle or relish—is sweet, mildly spicy, and beguiling. Versions of it are common in the northern states of Mexico. It is simple to make, since all you need to do is stem and seed the ancho chiles, cut them into strips with kitchen shears, and add the marinade.

Pair this salsa with grilled meat, chicken, or seafood. For an unusual appetizer, slather crostini or hearty crackers with soft goat cheese or cream cheese and top with the salsa. Give Tomato and Mozzarella Salad (page 56) a lift by spooning some on top, or amp up your everyday deli sandwich—especially if it has avocado—with a generous dollop right in the middle.

1. Using kitchen scissors or a sharp knife, cut the chiles lengthwise into 1-inch strips. Cut the strips into ¼-inch pieces and place them in a medium bowl. Add the onion, garlic, oil, vinegars, *piloncillo,* and salt; toss to mix well. Transfer to a container with a tight-fitting lid and refrigerate for at least 8 hours.

2. Serve chilled or at room temperature.

* MEXICAN COOK'S TRICK: Don't worry if the chiles seem stiff and brittle at first; they will soften as they sit in the marinade.

White Onions My paternal grandfather loved white onions so much that he would peel them and take bites from them like an apple, alternating with plain bread smeared with butter and sprinkled with salt. My grandmother used to complain that he depleted her necessary weekly provisions.

Onions are used in Mexican cooking in practically every meal, and white onions rule, except in the Yucatán Peninsula, where the red onion is queen. Other options throughout the country are scallions and an onion variety I have a hard time finding in the U.S., called the Texas scallion.

Lower in sulfur than yellow onions, white onions have a bright, clean, pleasant flavor that barely bites. Vidalia and Walla Walla onions are too sweet for the Mexican palate. Crisp and fresh when raw, the flavor of white onions flows to a warmer dimension when they are cooked or charred. Choose onions that show no signs of moisture, and peek into the outer layer to check for any signs of mold—which means they are likely rotten inside.

PICKLED JALAPEÑOS AND CARROTS

∾ JALAPEÑOS Y ZANAHORIAS EN ESCABECHE ∾

⁕ MAKES ABOUT 5 CUPS ⁕ PREPARATION TIME: 25 MINUTES, PLUS MARINATING TIME ⁕
COOKING TIME: 20 MINUTES ⁕ KEEPS, COVERED AND REFRIGERATED, FOR UP TO 2 MONTHS ⁕

1 pound jalapeño chiles,
   halved and seeded

1 pound carrots, peeled and
   cut on the diagonal into
   ¼-inch slices

2 tablespoons kosher or
   coarse sea salt

2 cups distilled white vinegar

1 cup unseasoned rice
   vinegar

10 bay leaves

2 teaspoons dried oregano,
   preferably Mexican

1 teaspoon dried thyme

1 teaspoon cumin seeds

1 teaspoon black peppercorns

5 whole cloves

1 teaspoon dark brown sugar

¾ cup vegetable oil

8 ounces pearl onions,
   peeled, or large scallions,
   trimmed to the white and
   light green parts

4 garlic cloves

There's not a day that I don't eat pickled jalapeños and carrots. In Mexico, many restaurants place a bowl of them in the middle of the table for people to nibble on with their meal, and they are a standard accompaniment to take-out pizza. I usually prefer mine homemade, but should I run out, there are always a couple of store-bought cans in the pantry as insurance against an emergency. They are a necessity for tortas (see page 142) and are delicious in quesadillas or as a side to scrambled eggs, grilled meats, or rice.

Some cooks add boiled baby potatoes, green beans, mushrooms, cauliflower, and/or cactus paddles. The options are endless, and all are terrific.

1. Place the chiles and carrots in a large bowl, sprinkle with the salt, and toss to coat. Let sit for 30 minutes to macerate and release some of their juices. Drain, reserving the juices.

2. In a blender or food processor, combine the vinegars, bay leaves, oregano, thyme, cumin seeds, peppercorns, cloves, and brown sugar. Blend until smooth, at least 1 minute.

3. Heat the oil in a large skillet over medium-high heat until hot but not smoking. Add the onions and cook for 2 to 3 minutes, stirring occasionally, until they begin to soften. Stir in the garlic and cook for another minute, or until it barely begins to color. Add the carrots and jalapeños and cook for 3 to 4 minutes, giving them a couple of stirs. Pour in their reserved

In jar: Pickled Jalapeños and Carrots; in foreground: Yucatán-Style Pickled Red Onions

juices, along with the vinegar mixture, and simmer briskly for 10 minutes, or until the vegetables soften. Let cool.

4. Pack the mixture into glass containers with tight-fitting lids and refrigerate. Let the vegetables pickle for at least 4 hours before serving.

✳ MEXICAN COOK'S TRICK: I don't recommend using gloves when working with chiles, since washing your hands afterward with soapy water works fine. In fact your hands are essential to feeling the varying degrees of heat. But since there are quite a few chiles to prepare in this recipe, you may want to use gloves if you are not used to working with them. If you don't, just remember not to touch your eyes for a while.

   If you want your pickled chiles hotter, use serranos instead of jalapeños. Or, if you are really brave, leave the chiles whole, seeds intact, and just snap off the stems.

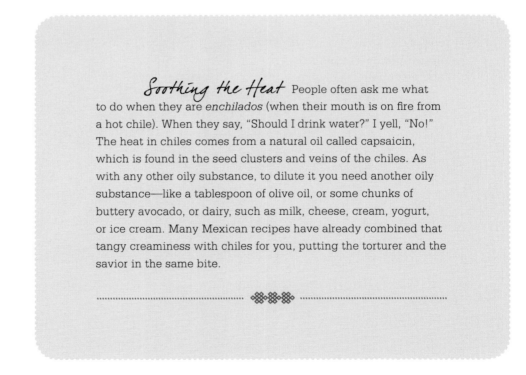

Soothing the Heat People often ask me what to do when they are *enchilados* (when their mouth is on fire from a hot chile). When they say, "Should I drink water?" I yell, "No!" The heat in chiles comes from a natural oil called capsaicin, which is found in the seed clusters and veins of the chiles. As with any other oily substance, to dilute it you need another oily substance—like a tablespoon of olive oil, or some chunks of buttery avocado, or dairy, such as milk, cheese, cream, yogurt, or ice cream. Many Mexican recipes have already combined that tangy creaminess with chiles for you, putting the torturer and the savior in the same bite.

YUCATÁN-STYLE PICKLED RED ONIONS

∾ CEBOLLAS ENCURTIDAS A LA YUCATECA ∾

❋ MAKES ABOUT 2 CUPS ❋ PREPARATION TIME: 10 MINUTES, PLUS MARINATING TIME ❋
KEEPS COVERED AND REFRIGERATED FOR UP TO 1 MONTH ❋

1 cup bitter orange juice
(see page 166) or a mixture
of ¼ cup *each* grapefruit
juice, orange juice, lime
juice, and distilled white
vinegar

¼ teaspoon ground allspice

½ teaspoon kosher or coarse
sea salt, or to taste

¼ teaspoon freshly ground
black pepper

1 large red onion, thinly
sliced (2 cups)

2 bay leaves

1 banana pepper or jalapeño
or serrano chile

Mildly spicy, tangy, and surprisingly crunchy, these pickled onions are a permanent fixture on every table in the Yucatán Peninsula and will be a revelation at your table. At my home, they find their way into toasted sandwiches, or turn up atop rice, alongside tacos, quesadillas, enchiladas, and scrambled eggs, and they're a refreshing topping for refried beans. They are also a faithful companion to anything that contains achiote paste (see page 166), like my Mexican Thanksgiving Turkey (page 164). The best part? The pickles take only 10 minutes to make and they keep for weeks in the refrigerator.

1. Place the bitter orange juice, allspice, salt, and pepper in a medium bowl and mix well. Stir in the red onion and bay leaves.

2. Char or broil the banana pepper under the broiler, on a hot *comal,* in a dry skillet over medium heat, or on an outdoor grill, turning once or twice, until the skin is lightly charred, 3 to 6 minutes.

3. Add the pepper, without removing the charred skin, to the onion mixture and toss well. Let marinate at room temperature for at least 30 minutes, or up to 2 hours, before serving.

❋ MEXICAN COOK'S TRICK: Pickled red onions are traditionally made with banana peppers, also called *güeros* (slang for "blonde") or *x'catic,* in the Mayan language. You can substitute a jalapeño or serrano chile.

CHUNKY GUACAMOLE

✳ MAKES A GENEROUS 1 CUP ✳ PREPARATION TIME: 10 MINUTES ✳ CAN BE MADE UP TO 12 HOURS AHEAD, COVERED, AND REFRIGERATED ✳

2 ripe Hass avocados, halved, pitted, meat scooped out, and coarsely mashed or diced

3 tablespoons chopped white onion

2 tablespoons coarsely chopped cilantro (leaves and top part of stems)

2 tablespoons seeded (if desired) and finely chopped jalapeño or serrano chile, or to taste

2 tablespoons freshly squeezed lime juice, or to taste

1 teaspoon kosher or coarse sea salt, or to taste

Guacamole is a funny word. It comes from a combination of two words in Náhuatl (the original language of the Aztecs): *ahuacátl,* which means "avocado," and *mulli,* which means "mashed."

Avocados are revered in Mexico, where they have been combined with chiles and herbs for centuries. It was only after the Spaniards arrived that the mix began to include onion and citrus, which they brought along in their galleons. The citrus helps the avocado stay fresh and green for hours.

There are countless versions of guacamole, but this one, chunky rather than smooth, is my favorite. We eat it every way we can: with chips and quesadillas, inside tortas, or the ultimate for me, simply spread on a warm corn tortilla.

When I have extra time, I dress the guacamole up. In the fall, I sprinkle pomegranate seeds on top. When my boys want something heartier, I top it with crisp bacon pieces, crumbled *chicharrones* (fried pork skin, readily available at Latin or international markets), or cooked crisp pieces of Mexican chorizo. In the summer, I spoon some chopped crabmeat over it and drizzle it with more lime juice and a sprinkling of salt.

Gently mix all the ingredients in a bowl or mash in a *molcajete* (a Mexican mortar and pestle; see page 154), taste and adjust the seasonings, and serve.

SALADS

EVERYDAY GREEN SALAD ...44

RED LEAF, AVOCADO, AND GRAPEFRUIT SALAD
WITH OLIVE-MINT VINAIGRETTE ...45

AVOCADO AND HEARTS OF PALM SALAD ...46

SPINACH–GOAT CHEESE SALAD WITH CARAMELIZED PECANS AND JAMAICA
VINAIGRETTE ...48

CARAMELIZED PECANS OR PEANUTS (GARAPIÑADOS) ...49

BOSTON LETTUCE SALAD WITH AVOCADO DRESSING, CANDIED PINEAPPLE,
AND SPICY PUMPKIN SEEDS ...50

SPICY PUMPKIN SEEDS (PEPITAS ENCHILADAS) ...51

WATERMELON AND TOMATILLO SALAD WITH FETA CHEESE ...53

JICAMA, BEET, ORANGE, AND CARAMELIZED PEANUT CHRISTMAS SALAD
(ENSALADA DE NAVIDAD) ...54

TOMATO AND MOZZARELLA SALAD WITH PICKLED ANCHO CHILE VINAIGRETTE ...56

PICKLED CHAYOTE SALAD ...58

ALTHOUGH THE UNITED STATES SHARES AN IMMENSE BORDER WITH MEXICO, Mexican food is often misunderstood here. Take salads, for example. Most Americans don't think of them as part of our cuisine, but we eat them all the time. And no, we don't have "taco salads"! We use seasonal, fresh ingredients found in the daily markets and the *mercados sobre ruedas* ("markets on wheels") that roll through our neighborhoods and are similar to farmers' markets in the United States. Mexicans have shopped "local" for centuries.

Not every Mexican dish is full of chiles and heat, and that is true of salads too. What's more, our everyday salads have a generous share of international elements. They are often dressed with vinaigrettes that include soy sauce, Maggi Sauce (see page 211), one or another mustard, and Worcestershire sauce, all standard ingredients in Mexican pantries.

At the same time, we lean toward what may seem to you exotic or unusual, using ingredients like *Jamaica*, here in the vinaigrette that dresses the Spinach–Goat Cheese Salad with Caramelized Pecans, or the combination of mint and jalapeño that spikes the Watermelon and Tomatillo Salad with Feta Cheese. We give salads texture and crunch by sprinkling nuts, such as the Caramelized Pecans or Peanuts, or Spicy Pumpkin Seeds, as in the Boston Lettuce Salad with Avocado Dressing.

Salads can be party food too. It isn't December if I'm not walking into a Christmas party with my take on Mexico's traditional *Ensalada de Navidad*, which bathes jicama, beets, oranges, and caramelized peanuts in a honey vinaigrette.

However varied our salads may be, they always have an underpinning of simplicity and ease. The French use a whisk or fork to emulsify a vinaigrette, but we just shake it up in a jar or whir it in a blender, and we add ingredients *a ojo de buen cubero* ("with good judgment," or "a wise eye"): *un tanto de vinagre, un tanto de aceite, y la puntita de una cucharita de mostaza*—"up to here of vinegar, up to here of oil, and the tip of a teaspoon of mustard."

EVERYDAY GREEN SALAD

✳ MAKES ABOUT 1 CUP VINAIGRETTE; SALAD SERVES 6 ✳ PREPARATION TIME: 20 MINUTES ✳ VINAIGRETTE CAN BE MADE UP TO 1 WEEK AHEAD, COVERED, AND REFRIGERATED (MIX WELL BEFORE USING) ✳

The recipe for this vinaigrette uses basic staples with stunning results. I like to make it ahead, doubling or tripling the recipe, and keep it handy in the refrigerator to toss with whatever I have on hand, from salad greens to cooked green beans or asparagus.

It loves a good rest in the refrigerator, where the ingredients marry and the onion pickles as the hours go by.

VINAIGRETTE

⅓ cup distilled white vinegar

⅓ cup vegetable oil

⅓ cup olive oil

½ teaspoon Dijon mustard

1 garlic clove, minced or pressed

⅓ cup slivered red onion

1½ teaspoons kosher or coarse sea salt, or to taste

¼ teaspoon freshly ground black pepper, or to taste

½ teaspoon sugar, or to taste

1 head butter or red leaf lettuce, leaves separated, rinsed, dried, and torn into pieces

4 carrots (about 12 ounces), peeled and thinly sliced on the diagonal

1 large cucumber (about 12 ounces), peeled, halved lengthwise, seeded, and thinly sliced

2 ripe tomatoes (about 12 ounces), quartered, seeded, and thinly sliced crosswise

1 large ripe Hass avocado, halved, pitted, meat scooped out, and thinly sliced

1. In a jar or a plastic container with a lid, combine the vinegar, oils, mustard, garlic, onion, salt, pepper, and sugar. Cover tightly and shake for 10 seconds, or until the vinaigrette is well emulsified. Alternatively, combine all the ingredients in a small bowl and mix with a whisk or fork, or blend in a blender or food processor.

2. Place the lettuce, carrots, cucumber, and tomatoes in a large salad bowl. Pour in a generous amount of the vinaigrette and toss; the salad should be coated with the vinaigrette but not drenched. Arrange the avocado slices on the top, drizzle on a bit more vinaigrette, and serve.

✳ MEXICAN COOK'S TRICK: For chunky bites of onion, you can simply mix all the ingredients for the vinaigrette in a container, or you can puree them, including the onion and garlic, in a blender for a smoother texture.

RED LEAF, AVOCADO, AND GRAPEFRUIT SALAD WITH OLIVE-MINT VINAIGRETTE

* SERVES 6 * PREPARATION TIME: 15 MINUTES * VINAIGRETTE CAN BE MADE UP TO 2 DAYS AHEAD, COVERED, AND REFRIGERATED (MIX WELL BEFORE USING) *

1 teaspoon red wine vinegar

3 tablespoons freshly squeezed lime juice

1 garlic clove, minced or pressed

½ teaspoon kosher or coarse sea salt, or to taste

¼ teaspoon freshly ground black pepper, or to taste

3 tablespoons olive oil

¼ cup vegetable oil

¼ cup pitted and chopped kalamata olives

2 tablespoons chopped fresh mint

1 head red leaf lettuce, leaves separated, rinsed, dried, and thickly sliced

1 large ripe Hass avocado, halved, pitted, meat scooped out, and cut into chunks

1 pink grapefruit, peeled and cut into suprêmes (see Mexican Cook's Trick)

When I was in college, one of my haunts was a hole-in-the-wall Greek restaurant in Mexico City with food to die for. They served a lemony-minty green salad, and I always tossed in some of the kalamata olives on the table and squeezed fresh limes over it when I ordered it. This recipe is my homage to those flavors. The dressing, flecked with savory olives, makes a perfect companion to the creaminess of the avocado. Add grapefruit, and you have a winner.

1. Combine the vinegar, lime juice, garlic, salt, and pepper in a small bowl. Slowly add the oils in a thin, steady stream, mixing with a whisk or a fork until the vinaigrette is emulsified. Stir in the olives and mint.

2. Put the lettuce in a large salad bowl and toss with half of the dressing. Arrange the avocado and grapefruit pieces on top, pour more dressing on top, and serve.

* MEXICAN COOK'S TRICK: Though it may seem daunting, cutting citrus fruit into segments—called suprêmes, or *supremas* in Spanish—is easy. And since citrus pith and membranes are bitter, you're better off without them. Cut off the top and bottom of the fruit so it has a stable base, and with a sharp knife, cut away the skin in wide strips, following the shape of the fruit. Try to remove all the pith as you cut, but take as little of the flesh as possible. Then, holding the fruit over a bowl, cut down along the sides of each membrane, releasing the segments into the bowl. Don't discard the juice: Either drink it or pour it into the vinaigrette.

AVOCADO AND HEARTS OF
PALM SALAD

✳ SERVES 6 TO 8; SERVES 4 AS A MAIN ✳ PREPARATION TIME: 15 MINUTES ✳ COOKING TIME: 5 MINUTES ✳
VINAIGRETTE CAN BE MADE UP TO 5 DAYS AHEAD, COVERED, AND REFRIGERATED (MIX WELL BEFORE USING); SALAD
CAN BE ASSEMBLED UP TO 12 HOURS AHEAD, COVERED, AND REFRIGERATED ✳

3 tablespoons hulled raw
  pumpkin seeds

1 cup fresh or thawed frozen
  corn kernels

2 teaspoons apple cider
  vinegar

1 tablespoon freshly
  squeezed lime juice

½ teaspoon dried oregano,
  preferably Mexican, or
  1½ teaspoons finely
  chopped fresh oregano

¼ teaspoon dark brown sugar

¾ teaspoon kosher or coarse
  sea salt, or to taste

¼ teaspoon freshly ground
  black pepper

2 tablespoons olive oil

2 tablespoons vegetable oil

1 14-ounce can hearts of
  palm, rinsed, drained, and
  cut into ½-inch-thick slices

1 cup halved cherry tomatoes
  (about 6 ounces)

1 tablespoon chopped red
  onion, or to taste

3 large Hass avocados,
  halved, pitted, meat
  scooped out, and cut into
  bite-sized chunks

Pairing buttery avocados with tender hearts of palm is a tradition in my family for special occasions. Cherry tomatoes and corn make the salad even more alluring, and pumpkin seeds add a nutty crunch. Serve as a main dish with a side of toast or pita bread, or serve as a side dish to chicken, meat, or fish. No one who has tried it at my home or in my class has ever left without the recipe.

1. Heat a small heavy skillet over medium-low heat. Add the pumpkin seeds and toast, stirring often, until you hear popping sounds, like popcorn, and they begin to brown lightly, 3 to 4 minutes; take care not to burn them. Transfer to a small bowl.

2. Bring a small saucepan of water to a simmer over medium-high heat. Add the corn and cook for 1 to 2 minutes, to heat through. Drain and set aside.

3. Combine the vinegar, lime juice, oregano, brown sugar, salt, and pepper in a small bowl. Slowly add the oils in a thin, steady stream, mixing with a whisk or a fork until emulsified.

4. In a large salad bowl, combine the hearts of palm, corn, cherry tomatoes, and red onion. Add the vinaigrette and toss gently to combine. Gently fold in the avocados, taking care not to mash them.

5. Sprinkle the salad with the toasted pumpkin seeds and serve.

✳ MEXICAN COOK'S TRICK: Hearts of palm—*palmitos,* or "little palm trees," in Spanish—are readily available canned or jarred. Be sure to rinse them before using to rid them of any canned flavor or graininess from the preserving liquid.

SPINACH–GOAT CHEESE SALAD WITH CARAMELIZED PECANS AND JAMAICA VINAIGRETTE

* SERVES 6 * PREPARATION TIME: 20 MINUTES, PLUS MACERATING TIME * VINAIGRETTE CAN BE MADE UP TO A WEEK AHEAD, COVERED, AND REFRIGERATED (SHAKE WELL BEFORE USING) *

JAMAICA VINAIGRETTE

- ½ cup dried *Jamaica* flowers (see page 183), any small twigs or stems removed
- 1 garlic clove
- ⅓ cup vegetable oil
- ⅓ cup olive oil
- 1 tablespoon red wine vinegar
- 1 teaspoon sugar, or to taste
- 1 teaspoon kosher or coarse sea salt, or to taste
- ½ teaspoon freshly ground black pepper, or to taste

- 8 cups (about 10 ounces) fresh spinach leaves, rinsed, dried, and roughly chopped
- 4 cups (about 8 ounces) watercress, rinsed, dried, and lower part of stems removed
- 6 scallions (white and light green parts only), thinly sliced
- 6 ounces fresh goat cheese, crumbled or cut into chunks (¾ cup), or more to taste
- 1 cup Caramelized Pecans (recipe follows) or store-bought caramelized or honey-roasted pecans, coarsely chopped

Fresh spinach and spicy watercress are tossed with a thick, tart vinaigrette made with *Jamaica* flowers, which contribute an almost cranberry-like flavor. Crumbles of fresh goat cheese and a generous sprinkling of sweet and crunchy caramelized pecans top off the salad.

Dried *Jamaica*, or hibiscus, flowers are now readily available in the Latin or international aisle of larger grocery stores and health food stores—luckily for me, as I no longer have to stuff them into my suitcase every time I come home from Mexico and then explain them to airport security.

When you're on the go, tuck a portion of this salad into crusty bread, and you'll have a sandwich to brag about.

1. Combine the *Jamaica* flowers, garlic, oils, vinegar, sugar, salt, and pepper in a small bowl. Mix well and let stand for at least 2 hours, or up to 12 hours, so the flowers soften and release their flavor.

2. Pour the flower mixture into a blender or food processor and puree for 1 minute. The vinaigrette will be thick. It will not be smooth, since the flowers aren't completely pureed, but that's what you want.

3. Combine the spinach and watercress in a large salad bowl. Toss with an ample amount of the vinaigrette until the leaves are coated. Sprinkle with the scallions, goat cheese, and pecans and serve.

* MEXICAN COOK'S TRICK: The longer the vinaigrette sits, the better it gets, since the flowers keep on giving more flavor. Taste as the days go on, and adjust the dressing with salt and sugar as needed.

CARAMELIZED PECANS OR PEANUTS

∿ GARAPIÑADOS ∿

✳ MAKES A GENEROUS 1 CUP ✳ PREPARATION TIME: 5 MINUTES ✳ COOKING TIME: 20 MINUTES ✳
CAN BE STORED IN AN AIRTIGHT CONTAINER IN A COOL PLACE FOR UP TO 2 WEEKS ✳

1 cup unsalted pecans or peanuts

½ cup real maple syrup

½ tablespoon cold unsalted butter, diced

Garapiñados, or candied nuts, are sold on the street all over Mexico in paper cones or plastic bags. They are a wildly popular snack, and they're spectacular sprinkled on salads. The traditional way of making caramelized pecans or peanuts is somewhat laborious. I've grown very fond of my sister Alisa's shortcut recipe, which doesn't require a candy thermometer.

1. Preheat the oven to 375°F. Line two baking sheets with parchment paper.

2. Place the nuts in a bowl, pour the maple syrup over them, and toss to coat. Spread the nuts evenly on one of the baking sheets and scatter the butter pieces on top. Bake for 10 minutes. Stir to make sure all the nuts are coated with syrup and bake for 10 more minutes, or until they are browned and the syrup is bubbling and has darkened and thickened to the consistency of caramel.

3. Immediately, before the caramel hardens, scoop the nuts off the baking sheet with a metal spatula or slotted spoon and place them on the other lined baking sheet, keeping the pieces as separate as you can; they will try to clump and stick together. Cool completely.

BOSTON LETTUCE SALAD WITH AVOCADO DRESSING, CANDIED PINEAPPLE, AND SPICY PUMPKIN SEEDS

❋ SERVES 6 ❋ PREPARATION TIME: 10 MINUTES ❋ DRESSING CAN BE MADE UP TO 12 HOURS AHEAD, COVERED, AND REFRIGERATED ❋

2 ripe Hass avocados, halved, pitted, meat scooped out, and cut into chunks

½ cup milk

½ cup Mexican crema (see page 135), crème fraîche, or sour cream

1 garlic clove

3 tablespoons freshly squeezed lime juice

½ teaspoon kosher or coarse sea salt, or to taste

2 heads Boston lettuce, leaves separated, washed, dried, and torn into pieces

½ cup chopped candied pine-apple

½ cup Spicy Pumpkin Seeds (recipe follows)

In Mexico there is a long tradition of transforming fruits and vegetables like pineapple and even sweet potatoes by candying them, which cloaks them in an irresistible sugar casing and also helps preserve them. Here tender leaves of Boston lettuce are bathed in a thick and creamy avocado dressing and studded with sweet-tart candied pineapple, as well as crunchy spiced pumpkin seeds. You can use other candied fruits in this salad, such as papaya or mango. The dressing can be made ahead, but the salad should be tossed right before it is served.

1. Combine the avocados, milk, cream, garlic, lime juice, and salt in a blender or food processor and puree until smooth.

2. Place the lettuce in a large salad bowl. Toss with the dressing until the leaves are lightly coated. Sprinkle with the pineapple and pumpkin seeds and serve.

SPICY PUMPKIN SEEDS

∾ PEPITAS ENCHILADAS ∾

* MAKES 1½ CUPS * PREPARATION TIME: 2 MINUTES * COOKING TIME: 5 MINUTES * CAN BE STORED IN A PLASTIC BAG OR JAR UP TO 1 WEEK *

1 tablespoon vegetable oil

1½ cups hulled raw pumpkin seeds

1 teaspoon ground dried chile, such as piquín, or a Mexican mix, such as Tajín

1½ teaspoons kosher or coarse sea salt, or to taste

1½ teaspoons sugar, or to taste

Pumpkin seeds are an irresistible nibble any time, and this version is one of the most addictive in my arsenal. Their crisp nuttiness is enhanced by a combination of salt, sugar, and ground chile.

And pumpkin seeds are good for you. Full of nutrients and healthy fats, they're a great thing to sneak into your kids' food. Sprinkle them on salads or grilled chicken or fish, toss them with popcorn, or munch them straight from the bowl.

1. Heat the oil in a small skillet over medium-low heat until hot but not smoking. Add the pumpkin seeds and toast, stirring often, until you hear popping sounds, like popcorn, and they begin to brown, 3 to 4 minutes; take care not to burn them. Remove with a slotted spoon and transfer to a medium bowl.

2. While they are still hot, sprinkle the seeds with the chile, salt, and sugar and toss to coat. They will become crunchier as they cool.

Pumpkin Seeds (Pepitas) have been eaten for centuries in Mexico. You find them in all kinds of variations: raw, hulled, roasted, salted, and my favorite, spiced. Traditionally they are used raw to thicken and flavor sauces and stews, often called *pipianes* (see Shrimp in Red Pipián, page 122, and Lamb Chops in Green Pipián, page 195).

Since Mexicans are world-class snackers, we also eat pepitas out of hand from little packages sold at street stands and nibble them alongside popcorn at the movie theater. And talk about versatile! Pepitas also go for sweet spins on many traditional candies, cookies, and cakes. Mexican confectioners even make marzipan out of them.

Pepitas are also delicious toasted and tossed with ground dried chile, salt, and sugar. Make plenty, as they are perfect with an ice-cold *Michelada* (page 277) or sprinkled on top of salads like Boston Lettuce Salad with Avocado Dressing (opposite).

Pepitas can be found alongside the nuts in the health food section of most grocery stores.

WATERMELON AND TOMATILLO SALAD WITH FETA CHEESE

✳ SERVES 6 ✳ PREPARATION TIME: 20 MINUTES ✳ VINAIGRETTE CAN BE MADE UP TO 3 DAYS AHEAD, COVERED, AND REFRIGERATED (MIX WELL BEFORE USING); SALAD CAN BE ASSEMBLED WITHOUT THE CHEESE AND MINT GARNISH UP TO 12 HOURS IN ADVANCE, COVERED, AND REFRIGERATED ✳

You know those photos of kids with big slices of watermelon in their hands and juice dripping down their chins? Consider this salad a neater version of that image. Essentially summer in a bowl, this salad features an unexpected combination of ingredients. The exotic companions of mint, feta, and tart tomatillos take watermelon to a new dimension. Green tomatoes can stand in for the tomatillos in a pinch.

- 2 teaspoons chopped fresh mint, plus more for garnish
- 1 tablespoon seeded (if desired) and finely chopped jalapeño chile, or to taste
- 3 tablespoons freshly squeezed lime juice
- 1½ teaspoons distilled white vinegar
- 1 teaspoon kosher or coarse sea salt, or to taste
- 3 tablespoons olive oil
- 3 tablespoons vegetable oil
- 6 cups seeded and cubed ripe watermelon
- About 12 ounces tomatillos, husks removed, rinsed, quartered, and thinly sliced crosswise (3 cups)
- About 4 ounces feta cheese or queso fresco, crumbled or cut into small dice (¾ cup), or to taste

1. In a small bowl, combine the mint, jalapeño, lime juice, vinegar, and salt. Slowly add the oils in a thin, steady stream, mixing with a whisk or a fork until emulsified. Let sit for at least 5 minutes before using, so the mint and jalapeño flavors can marry and infuse the vinaigrette.

2. Place the watermelon and tomatillos in a large salad bowl. Toss gently with enough vinaigrette to lightly coat. Sprinkle the cheese on top, garnish with mint, and serve.

JICAMA, BEET, ORANGE, AND CARAMELIZED PEANUT CHRISTMAS SALAD

∾ ENSALADA DE NAVIDAD ∾

* SERVES 6 * PREPARATION TIME: 15 MINUTES * COOKING TIME: 30 TO 35 MINUTES * VINAIGRETTE CAN BE MADE UP TO 5 DAYS AHEAD, COVERED, AND REFRIGERATED (MIX WELL BEFORE USING); JICAMA, BEETS, AND ORANGES CAN BE PREPPED 1 DAY AHEAD, SEPARATELY COVERED AND REFRIGERATED *

3 tablespoons red wine vinegar

1 teaspoon honey

1 teaspoon kosher or coarse sea salt, or to taste

½ teaspoon freshly ground black pepper, or to taste

¼ cup extra-virgin olive oil

2 tablespoons vegetable oil

1 medium jicama (about 1¼ pounds), peeled and cut into ½-inch-thick sticks

3 pounds beets, cooked (see Mexican Cook's Trick), peeled, and quartered

3 oranges, peeled and cut into ½-inch-thick slices

1 cup coarsely chopped Caramelized Peanuts (page 49)

This festive salad is a mainstay on Mexican Christmas tables. It vibrates with the different colors of the ingredients and contrasting flavors and textures. You get the watery crunch of raw jicama, the freshness of juicy oranges, and the sweetness of tender cooked beets, slicked with a vinaigrette sweetened with a bit of honey and topped with crunchy peanuts.

There are many versions, some including other fruits such as bananas, apples, or grapes; add or subtract as desired.

Also known as Mexican yam or turnip, jicama is a root vegetable that tastes similar to a fresh water chestnut, but sweeter and juicier. Look for jicama that is rock hard, with no sign of mold or moisture on the skin. Peel away the thin, beige-colored fibrous skin before using. The meat should be crisp and milky white. If it is beginning to brown, its time has passed, and rather than tasting glorious, it will be unpleasantly sour.

1. Combine the vinegar, honey, salt, and pepper in a small bowl. Slowly add the oils in a thin, steady stream, mixing with a whisk or a fork until emulsified.

2. Place the jicama, beets, and oranges in separate bowls and toss each with about one third of the vinaigrette. Arrange the ingredients in a pattern on a large platter. I like to do parallel stripes, and I often start with beets in the center, placing jicama on one side and oranges on the other. Sprinkle on the caramelized peanuts and drizzle any remaining vinaigrette on top.

* MEXICAN COOK'S TRICK: To cook beets, cut off the greens and most of the stems, leaving about 1 inch. Don't scrub them or cut off the thin root, or they will bleed their juices, sweetness, and color as they cook. Place them in a pot, cover with cold water, and bring to a boil, then lower the heat, cover, and cook until tender. Medium beets (about 2 inches in diameter) cook in 30 to 35 minutes. For this salad, you want them crunchy, so don't overcook. Drain, let cool completely, then peel and cut.

PICKLED CHAYOTE SALAD

* SERVES 6 * PREPARATION TIME: 30 MINUTES * COOKING TIME: 30 MINUTES * VINAIGRETTE CAN BE
MADE UP TO 5 DAYS AHEAD, COVERED, AND REFRIGERATED (MIX WELL BEFORE USING); SALAD CAN BE ASSEMBLED
UP TO 12 HOURS AHEAD, COVERED, AND REFRIGERATED *

3 pounds (3–4) chayotes

3 tablespoons distilled white
vinegar

¾ teaspoon kosher or coarse
sea salt, or to taste

¼ teaspoon freshly ground
black pepper, or to taste

½ teaspoon dried oregano,
preferably Mexican, or
1½ teaspoons finely
chopped fresh

Pinch of sugar, or to taste

¼ cup vegetable oil

3 tablespoons olive oil

½ cup slivered red onion

Chayote tastes like a combination of cucumber and zucchini, with the firmness of an unripe pear and a whisper of sweetness. As odd as that description may sound, give this light, bright salad a try; I bet you will love it.

The trick with chayotes is not to overcook them, leaving them firm to the bite. They are delicious simply boiled and served with salt and butter, and they're ideal candidates for the simple oil and vinegar treatment they get here. This salad is great alongside Crispy Chicken Milanesa (page 156) and Chipotle Mashed Potatoes (page 212).

Growing up, my sisters and I used to fight over the seeds from chayotes (each squash has only one soft seed). Steaming-hot with a sprinkle of salt, they are a treasure. Don't discard them—I'll fight you for them!

1. Place the chayotes in a large pot, cover with water, and bring to a boil over high heat. Reduce the heat to medium and simmer for 25 to 30 minutes, or until the chayotes can be pierced easily with a knife but are still firm. Drain and let cool.

2. Combine the vinegar, salt, pepper, oregano, and sugar in a large bowl. Using a whisk or a fork, slowly beat in the oils in a thin, steady stream until emulsified. Stir in the onion and let sit for at least 10 minutes.

3. Peel the chayotes, cut them in half, and remove the seeds (and eat them!). Cut into ½-inch-thick slices or ½-inch sticks.

4. Toss the chayote with the vinaigrette and taste for seasonings. Let sit for at least 10 minutes and serve lukewarm or at room temperature, or refrigerate and serve cold.

* MEXICAN COOK'S TRICK: When making oil-based salad dressings, I often opt for combining a vegetable oil with olive oil. On its own, olive oil can sometimes be overpowering in a vinaigrette.

Chayote, also called *choko*, vegetable pear, mirliton, or christophene, is a beautiful pear-shaped squash whose texture is similar to an unripe pear but less grainy. It is typically used in soups; as a side vegetable, often stuffed with both sweet and savory fillings; and in salads. It is best cooked al dente, unless you plan to stuff it, in which case it should be cooked until soft.

In Mexico some chayotes are dark green, even purple, with a thick, thorny skin. Here the most commonly available variety is light green with thin, smooth skin. They are available in many large supermarkets. Avoid any that are wrinkled or have brown spots. Chayotes keep for a couple of weeks in the refrigerator.

SOUPS

CLASSIC AVOCADO SOUP (*SOPA DE AGUACATE*) ...64
  TORTILLA CHIPS, CRISPS, OR TOSTADAS (*TOTOPOS, TIRITAS, O TOSTADAS*)...66
CREAMLESS CREAM OF ZUCCHINI SOUP (*CREMA DE CALABACITA*)...67
CREAMY CORN SOUP ...68
HEARTY PINTO BEAN SOUP (*SOPA TARASCA*) ...70
  DRIED CHILE CRISPS (*TIRITAS DE CHILE SECO*)...72
SQUASH BLOSSOM SOUP (*SOPA DE FLOR DE CALABAZA*) ...75
WEEKNIGHT POTATO AND LEEK SOUP (*SOPA DE PORO Y PAPA*)...77
TOMATO-ZUCCHINI SOUP WITH MELTY CHEESE (*MINGUICHI*) ...78
ALPHABET SOUP (*SOPA DE LETRAS*) ...80
WHITE POZOLE (*POZOLE BLANCO*) ...81
RED POZOLE (*POZOLE ROJO*) ...84
MEXICAN CHICKEN BROTH (*CALDO DE POLLO*) ...87

SHORTLY AFTER MOVING TO THE UNITED STATES, I BEGAN HAVING RECURRING DREAMS. They had a consistent theme: Coming home from work, I would open the door to our apartment in Texas. There would be Sara Martínez, aka Tochito, my childhood nanny from Oaxaca, simmering *Caldo de Pollo* (Mexican Chicken Broth) in my mother's gorgeously aged soup pot. I would wake up disoriented and homesick and cover my eyes with my hands and blankets, trying to keep the dreamy aromas from flying away.

I was lonesome in my new married life in the middle of who-would-have-ever-imagined Texas, with my husband, Daniel, eternally traveling. I was working during the day and finishing my thesis by night, and I didn't know how to cook anything more than scrambled eggs and quesadillas. Taking a cue from those night messages, I began hunting down familiar ingredients, searching for cookbooks, and transcribing directions from anyone with the tiniest notion of how to prepare the foods I craved. That's when I started my own weekly *caldo* production and began to learn to cook.

Caldo has become my painter's palette, from which come all manner of soups. I often make the ones I miss from my Mexican childhood, like Alphabet Soup, and classics like Avocado Soup and Squash Blossom Soup. Some soups are those that I've fallen in love with on my travels, like Hearty Pinto Bean Soup and Tomato-Zucchini Soup with Melty Cheese, and are now staples in our home. I celebrate with Red Pozole, a signature of my mother's parties, which was served at my wedding. And I've also dreamed up my own concoctions, like Creamy Corn Soup, which is laced with vanilla and smoky chipotle. Every single one of these soups has the depth of flavor of the *caldo* that appeared in my dreams.

CLASSIC AVOCADO SOUP

∾ SOPA DE AGUACATE ∾

✳ SERVES 6 ✳ PREPARATION TIME: 10 MINUTES ✳ COOKING TIME: 20 MINUTES ✳ CAN BE MADE UP TO 12 HOURS AHEAD, COVERED, AND REFRIGERATED ✳

2 tablespoons vegetable oil

2 tablespoons unsalted butter

1½ cups coarsely chopped white onions

¾ cup loosely packed cilantro leaves

3 large ripe Hass avocados, halved, pitted, meat scooped out, and cut into chunks

6 cups broth from Mexican Chicken Broth (page 87) or canned chicken or vegetable broth

1 tablespoon freshly squeezed lime juice, or to taste

¾ teaspoon kosher or coarse sea salt, or to taste

1½ cups Tortilla Crisps (page 66) or croutons

1 cup diced queso fresco, Cotija, farmer cheese, or mild feta

I have tasted many avocado soups, but this one, based on a recipe from Doña María Rosa Marmolejo, the former cook at the Mexican ambassador's residence in Washington, D.C., is creamier, lighter, and yet more luxurious than any other I've had. With just a handful of ingredients and no more than 20 minutes of cooking time, you will have an elegant soup that can be served chilled in the summer or at room temperature in cooler months.

Follow María Rosa's lead and garnish the soup depending on your mood and the weather. If it's rainy, opt for croutons; when it's sunny, use Tortilla Crisps. Rain or shine, María Rosa always serves the soup with diced queso fresco on top.

1. Heat the oil and butter in a medium skillet over medium-low heat until the butter melts and begins to foam. Add the onions and cook, stirring occasionally, until completely softened and lightly browned, 15 to 20 minutes. Stir in the cilantro and cook until it wilts, about 30 seconds. Remove from the heat.

2. Working in batches if necessary, place the avocados in a blender or food processor, along with the onion mixture, broth, lime juice, and salt, and puree until smooth. Taste for seasoning.

3. Serve the soup at room temperature, or chill and serve cold. Top each serving with some of the tortilla crisps or croutons and cheese, or pass the garnishes in bowls at the table and let your guests customize.

✳ MEXICAN COOK'S TRICK: Once you've cut an avocado open, if you will not be using it all immediately, cover it tightly with plastic wrap and store it in the refrigerator. It will stay fresh for up to 12 hours. If it is mashed with freshly squeezed lime juice, its color, flavor, and texture will hold even better. It's often said that storing the avocado meat with the pit in it keeps it from darkening, but this is a myth. The pit merely protects part of the meat so it will not oxidize. Plastic wrap does the trick—and better.

How to Buy an Avocado I prefer the Mexican Hass variety of avocado because it is meatier and creamier, with a richer flavor than varieties like El Fuerte, which can be stringy and watery. The Mexican Hass avocado tree blooms four times a year, so it is always in season. You can recognize Hass avocados by their thick and pebbly skin, which changes from dark green to almost black as it ripens. But color is not enough to tell when an avocado is ripe. You have to hold it in your hand and give it a gentle squeeze. If it gives a little, it's ready. If it feels more like a rock, it's not. On the other hand, if it is squishy, it is overripe—and can't be used.

To ripen avocados at home, leave them out on the counter. If you want to speed up their ripening, wrap them in newspaper or put them inside a paper bag for a couple of days. Once they are ripe, use right away or refrigerate for up to 5 days.

TORTILLA CHIPS, CRISPS, OR TOSTADAS

∾ TOTOPOS, TIRITAS, O TOSTADAS ∾

✳ MAKES ABOUT 48 TORTILLA CHIPS, 1²/₃ CUPS CRISPS, OR 6 TOSTADAS ✳ PREPARATION TIME: 2 MINUTES
✳ COOKING TIME: IF FRIED, 6 MINUTES; IF BAKED, 20 MINUTES ✳ CAN BE STORED IN A TIGHTLY
COVERED CONTAINER FOR UP TO A WEEK ✳

Yes, you can get tortilla chips at the store, but if you make your own they will be fresher and more alluring. You can use homemade or store-bought corn tortillas, and they can be fried (the traditional way to prepare them) or baked. For chips, cut each tortilla into 8 triangles; for crisps, cut them into smaller square or rectangular bites; for tostadas, leave them whole.

Vegetable oil

6 **corn tortillas (5–6 inches in diameter), store-bought or homemade (page 94), cut into wedges or shapes for chips or crisps, left whole for tostadas**

¼ **teaspoon kosher or coarse sea salt, or to taste**

TO FRY: In a deep 12-inch skillet, heat ½ inch of oil over medium-high heat until hot but not smoking—a tortilla piece dipped in the oil should bubble around the edges. Add the tortilla pieces in small batches and fry, turning once, until they are a rich golden brown and nicely crisped. For crisps and chips, cook for 20 to 30 seconds per side; cook tostadas one at a time for 1½ to 2 minutes per side. Remove with a slotted spoon and drain on paper towels. Sprinkle immediately with salt so it will stick to the surface.

TO BAKE: Preheat the oven to 350°F. Lightly grease a baking sheet. Place the tortilla pieces (or whole tortillas) on the baking sheet. Gently brush the tops with oil and sprinkle with salt. Bake for about 20 minutes, stirring and flipping them occasionally, until golden brown and crispy. Let cool.

CREAMLESS CREAM OF ZUCCHINI SOUP

~ CREMA DE CALABACITA ~

* SERVES 6 * PREPARATION TIME: 15 MINUTES * COOKING TIME: 25 MINUTES * CAN BE MADE UP
TO 2 DAYS AHEAD, COVERED, AND REFRIGERATED *

2 tablespoons unsalted butter

1 tablespoon vegetable oil

1 cup coarsely chopped white onion

1 cup sliced leeks (white and light green parts only)

1 jalapeño or serrano chile, halved, seeded if desired, and coarsely chopped

8 cups diced or coarsely chopped zucchini or other summer squash (about 3 pounds)

6 cups broth from Mexican Chicken Broth (page 87) or canned chicken or vegetable broth

1 teaspoon kosher or coarse sea salt, or to taste

½ teaspoon freshly ground black pepper, or to taste

Creamless cream soup? How can that be?

Pureeing gently cooked onion, leeks, and chile with zucchini simmered in chicken broth yields the deceiving silky texture. And though the soup looks elegant and refined, it definitely has some sass. I serve it with slices of crusty bread or with Tortilla Crisps (page 66) on top.

1. Heat the butter and oil in a large pot over medium-low heat until the butter melts and begins to foam. Stir in the onion, leeks, and jalapeño and cook, stirring occasionally, until the onion softens and the edges begin to brown lightly, about 15 minutes.

2. Raise the heat to medium, add the zucchini, and cook for 4 to 5 minutes. Add the broth, salt, and pepper and bring to a simmer. Simmer for 10 minutes, or until the zucchini is tender. Remove from the heat.

3. Working in batches, puree the soup in a blender or food processor until smooth. Reheat if necessary and serve.

CREAMY CORN SOUP

✳ SERVES 6 ✳ PREPARATION TIME: 15 MINUTES ✳ COOKING TIME: 25 MINUTES ✳ CAN BE MADE UP TO
4 DAYS AHEAD, COVERED, AND REFRIGERATED ✳

I created this simple-to-make soup to celebrate the historic role of vanilla in Mexico. In it, three of Mexico's culinary darlings—corn, vanilla, and chipotle—intermarry, creating delicate layers of flavors. The sweet heartiness of the corn plays against the fragrance of the vanilla and the rich, spicy smokiness of the chipotle.

2 tablespoons vegetable oil

2 tablespoons unsalted butter

⅔ cup coarsely chopped white onion

⅔ cup thinly sliced leeks (white and light green parts only)

4 cups fresh or thawed frozen corn kernels

5 cups broth from Mexican Chicken Broth (page 87) or canned chicken or vegetable broth

1 canned chipotle chile in adobo sauce (optional), seeded if desired, plus 2 tablespoons adobo sauce

½ vanilla bean, sliced open

1 cup milk

1 teaspoon kosher or coarse sea salt, or to taste

¼ teaspoon freshly ground black pepper, or to taste

Slices of toasted crunchy bread, such as baguette, *bolillo*, or *telera* (optional; see page 142)

1. Heat the oil and butter in a large pot over medium heat until the butter melts and starts to foam. Add the onion and leeks and cook for 5 to 6 minutes, stirring now and then, until softened. Add the corn and cook for 4 to 5 minutes, stirring occasionally, until it softens and deepens in color.

2. Add the broth, chipotle chile (if using), and adobo sauce, bring to a gentle simmer, and cook for 5 to 6 minutes. Remove from the heat and let cool.

3. Working in batches, transfer the soup into a blender or food processor and puree until smooth. Or, if you want the soup to have a smoother texture, pass it through a strainer, using a spoon to press on the solids. (If you want a more rustic texture, don't strain it; I never do.) Return the soup to the pot.

4. Scrape the seeds from the vanilla bean and add them to the soup, along with the bean. Gently heat the soup over low heat until hot, then add the milk. Season with the salt and pepper, stir, and allow the soup to steep gently over low heat, 8 to 10 minutes. Remove the vanilla bean and serve, with bread if desired.

Vanilla: A Love Story Second only to the discovery in Latin America of the cacao bean was the discovery of vanilla, one of the most romantic and sensual fragrances in the world. Contrary to what some people think, vanilla didn't originate in Madagascar, but instead in the lush state of Veracruz in Mexico. The vanilla plant, a flowering orchid, grew wild on the lands of the Totonac Indians. Being astonishingly resourceful, they figured out that if cured and dried, the pods of the plant had an exceptional aroma. The Totonac revered vanilla pods and used them in their sacred rituals and as tributes in times of war.

According to legend, the flower sprang from the doomed love of a prince and princess who were murdered as they tried to run off together, unable to consummate their forbidden love with even a kiss. A vanilla orchid sprouted where their blood fell, at the foot of a tree, and grew to look like lovers suspended in an eternal embrace.

HEARTY PINTO BEAN SOUP

∽ SOPA TARASCA ∽

✳ SERVES 6 TO 8 ✳ PREPARATION TIME: 10 MINUTES ✳ COOKING TIME: 25 MINUTES ✳ CAN BE MADE UP TO
4 DAYS AHEAD, COVERED, AND REFRIGERATED (YOU MAY NEED TO ADD SOME CHICKEN BROTH OR WATER TO THIN THE
SOUP OUT WHEN YOU REHEAT IT); CAN ALSO BE FROZEN FOR UP TO 3 MONTHS ✳

I tasted this soup from the state of Michoacán a couple of years ago while on a culinary research trip in Morelia, the capital. I fell so madly in love with it that I promised every cook I met that I would try anything as long as I could, please, have some *sopa tarasca* first. It gets its name from Michoacán's predominant indigenous group, the Tarascos (also called the Purépechas).

Thick and rich, it's perfect for the cold fall and winter months. Served with garnishes including fresh cheese, diced avocado, and Mexican crema, along with dried chile crisps if you like, it becomes a hearty one-bowl meal.

1 **ancho chile, rinsed, stemmed, and seeded**

1½ **pounds ripe tomatoes**

3 **tablespoons vegetable oil**

4 **cups Simple Beans from the Pot (page 216) made with pinto beans, pureed with 1 cup cooking liquid, or two 15.5-ounce cans pinto beans, drained and pureed with 1½ cups water**

4 **cups broth from Mexican Chicken Broth (page 87) or canned chicken or vegetable broth**

½ **teaspoon kosher or coarse sea salt, or to taste**

1 **cup crumbled queso fresco, Cotija, farmer cheese, or mild feta**

½ **cup Mexican crema (see page 135), crème fraîche, or sour cream**

1½ **cups Tortilla Crisps (page 66)**

½ **cup Dried Chile Crisps (page 72) made with ancho chiles (optional)**

1 **ripe Hass avocado, halved, pitted, meat scooped out, and diced**

1. Place the ancho chile and tomatoes in a medium saucepan, cover with water, bring to a simmer, and simmer over medium-high heat for 10 to 12 minutes, until the chile has softened and plumped and the tomatoes are soft. Let cool slightly.

2. Working in batches if necessary, transfer the chile, tomatoes, and ½ cup of the cooking liquid to a blender or food processor and puree until smooth.

3. Heat the oil in a large pot over medium-high heat. Add the chile-tomato puree and cook for 6 to 8 minutes, stirring occasionally, until it darkens in color and thickens. Reduce the heat to medium, stir in the bean puree, broth, and salt, and bring to a simmer. Simmer for 12 to 15 minutes, or until the soup deepens in flavor and has a creamy consistency. Taste for seasoning and remove from the heat (the soup will thicken quickly).

4. Ladle the soup into bowls and sprinkle each serving with about a tablespoon of cheese, some cream, a handful of tortilla crisps, a few dried chile crisps (if using), and some diced avocado—or pass the garnishes at the table and let your guests customize.

DRIED CHILE CRISPS

∾ TIRITAS DE CHILE SECO ∾

✳ MAKES ABOUT ½ CUP ✳ PREPARATION TIME: 5 MINUTES ✳ COOKING TIME: 5 MINUTES ✳ CAN BE MADE UP TO
1 WEEK AHEAD AND STORED, TIGHTLY COVERED, AT ROOM TEMPERATURE ✳

**2–3 ancho or pasilla chiles
(about 1 ounce), stemmed
and seeded
Vegetable oil**

Crunchy and uniquely Mexican, dried chile crisps are typically made with ancho or pasilla chiles. Try both to see if you have a preference. The crisps are a great accompaniment to soups, salads, and even guacamole, but unlike tortilla chips, they are not a snack on their own—they are meant to complement a dish by providing a robust hit of flavor.

1. Slice each chile lengthwise into strips about 1 inch wide, then slice the strips crosswise into ½- to 1-inch pieces. (They don't all have to be equal.)

2. Heat ¼ inch of oil in a small skillet over medium heat until it sizzles when you drop in a piece of chile. Gently add the chile pieces and stir for just 2 to 3 seconds—be cautious, as they can easily burn and become bitter. Remove the crisps with a slotted spoon and drain on paper towels.

Ancho Chiles are the most popular dried chile in Mexico. They are adored, and rightly so, as their flavor is unmatched.

An ancho is a poblano chile (see page 76) that has been ripened to an intense red and then dried to concentrate its fruitiness. The ancho is a charmer, inside and out: Wide, chubby, and wrinkled but still pliable, with dark red-brown skin, it looks very different from other dried chiles (see the photograph on page 13). Its flavor is deep, rich, and sharp, with a hint of bittersweet chocolate and the fruitiness of prunes. It is not hot, and has a somewhat sweet fragrance.

To use anchos, rinse them or dust them off with a kitchen towel, remove the stems, slit lengthwise, and remove the seeds and veins. Depending on the cook and the recipe, sometimes they are toasted, sometimes not. Usually they are rehydrated. To do so, cover them with boiling water and let them sit until plump and softened, 10 to 15 minutes, then drain and use as indicated. Or place them in a pan, cover with water, and simmer gently for about 10 minutes, until plump and rehydrated. In many cases, the simmering liquid is also used, as it holds much of the color and flavor of the chile.

SQUASH BLOSSOM SOUP

∾ SOPA DE FLOR DE CALABAZA ∾

* SERVES 6 * PREPARATION TIME: 20 MINUTES * COOKING TIME: 30 MINUTES * CAN BE MADE UP
TO 5 DAYS AHEAD, COVERED, AND REFRIGERATED *

2 **tablespoons unsalted butter**

2 **tablespoons vegetable oil**

1 **cup finely chopped white onion**

12 **ounces (about 8 cups) fresh squash blossoms, rinsed, drained, and chopped, or two 7-ounce cans squash blossoms, rinsed, drained, and chopped**

¼ **teaspoon freshly ground black pepper, or to taste**

1½ **teaspoons kosher or coarse sea salt, or more to taste**

2 **poblano chiles (about 11 ounces), charred, sweated, peeled, stemmed, seeded, and cut into 1-x-½-inch strips (see page 27)**

2 **cups fresh or thawed frozen corn kernels**

4 **cups diced zucchini (about 1½ pounds)**

4 **cups broth from Mexican Chicken Broth (page 87) or canned chicken or vegetable broth**

1 **cup milk**

This soup pairs the subtle flowery flavors of squash blossoms with the fruitiness of poblanos. Add the sweet crunch of fresh corn and a splash of milk to finish, and you have a summertime hit. After you taste it, you'll understand why the combination of poblanos, squash, and corn appears in so many Mexican dishes.

You can often find squash blossoms in farmers' markets—grab them when you see them. In Mexico squash blossoms are found fresh only during the rainy season. Since the demand for squash blossoms extends far beyond those months, companies offer them in cans and jars, available year-round. Though the color, flavor, and texture of fresh blossoms are nicer, bottled or canned blossoms are a reasonable substitute in this recipe if you can find them.

1. Heat 1 tablespoon each of the butter and oil in a large pot over medium heat until the butter melts and bubbles. Add the onion and cook until soft and translucent, 5 to 6 minutes, stirring occasionally. Stir in the squash blossoms, sprinkle with the pepper and ½ teaspoon of the salt, and cook until the blossoms have wilted and are tender, 3 to 4 minutes. Transfer to a medium bowl and set aside.

2. Heat the remaining 1 tablespoon butter and 1 tablespoon oil in the same pot over medium heat until the butter melts. Stir in the poblanos and cook for 2 to 3 minutes. Add the corn and zucchini and cook for another 3 minutes, stirring occasionally, or until softened but not mushy.

3. Add the broth and the remaining 1 teaspoon salt, bring to a gentle simmer, and cook for 12 to 15 minutes.

4. Meanwhile, place half of the cooked squash blossoms and the milk in a blender or food processor and puree until smooth.

(recipe continues)

5. Reduce the heat under the pot to low and stir the squash blossom puree into the soup (keep the heat low, or the milk may appear to curdle). Stir in the remaining squash blossoms and heat gently for 3 to 4 minutes. Taste and add more salt if needed. Serve hot.

✳ MEXICAN COOK'S TRICK: To use fresh squash blossoms, remove the lower part of the stem and rinse them thoroughly. (Little insects appreciate their fragrance as much as we do.) Although some cooks remove the green sepals, I like their crunch. Be sure to rinse canned or jarred blossoms thoroughly.

Poblano Chiles, which are the fresh versions of anchos, are stars in Mexican kitchens, used in a broad range of ways and dishes. Large and wide-shouldered, with a curvy body ending in a finely chiseled tip (see the photo on page 13), they are meaty and beguilingly flavorful: flowery and fruity. Think of them less as spicy chile peppers and more as vegetables with a boatload of personality.

Mexicans stuff, pickle, and puree poblanos and use them to flavor soups, creams, and sauces. Poblanos are most famous as *rajas* (see Creamy Poblano Rajas, page 209), where they are charred, sweated, peeled, and cut into strips or squares. Be warned, though: The poblanos are capricious. Their heat can range from mild to hot. To tame them, see the note on page 27.

WEEKNIGHT POTATO AND LEEK SOUP

∾ SOPA DE PORO Y PAPA ∾

✳ SERVES 6 ✳ PREPARATION TIME: 15 MINUTES ✳ COOKING TIME: 30 TO 40 MINUTES ✳ CAN BE MADE UP TO 4 DAYS AHEAD, COVERED, AND REFRIGERATED ✳

3 tablespoons unsalted butter

2 tablespoons vegetable oil

4 cups thinly sliced leeks (white and light green parts only)

8 cups broth from Mexican Chicken Broth (page 87) or canned chicken or vegetable broth

4 cups peeled and cubed (½ inch) potatoes (about 1½ pounds)

¾ teaspoon kosher or coarse sea salt, or to taste

Freshly ground black pepper

On rushed cold nights, this is my go-to soup. Wholesome and satisfying, it is made from staples that I think of as workhorse ingredients: leeks and potatoes.

The soup could not be more flexible. Serve it in its humble form with chunks of potato and leek, which is the way my boys like it best, or fancy it up by pureeing it and topping it with chopped fresh chives.

The trick to getting the most flavor from the leeks is cooking them long and slow. They cannot be rushed—they need time to let loose their sweetness and build depth as they nearly caramelize in the butter. The rest takes care of itself: good chicken broth, potatoes, salt, and freshly ground pepper.

1. Heat the butter and oil in a large pot over medium-low heat until the butter melts and begins to foam. Add the leeks and cook leisurely for 15 to 20 minutes, stirring occasionally, until completely soft and beginning to brown.

2. Stir in the broth, potatoes, salt, and pepper to taste. Increase the heat to medium-high, bring to a simmer, and cook until the potatoes are tender and the flavors have come together, 15 to 20 minutes.

3. If you want a thicker soup, scoop out 1 cup (making sure you have at least ½ cup potatoes) and puree in a blender, then return to the pot. Or, if you want a "cream" of potato and leek soup, puree the entire batch. Serve hot.

✳ MEXICAN COOK'S TRICK: Leeks harbor a lot of dirt between their layers. To remove it, slice the leeks lengthwise and rinse under a stream of cool running water, gently separating the layers with your fingers and letting the water flow through until no sand and grit remain. There is no need to entirely separate the layers—keep them intact after rinsing and the leeks will be easier to slice.

TOMATO-ZUCCHINI SOUP WITH MELTY CHEESE

∾ MINGUICHI ∾

* SERVES 6 TO 8 * PREPARATION TIME: 15 MINUTES * COOKING TIME: 35 MINUTES * CAN BE MADE UP TO 5 DAYS AHEAD, COVERED, AND REFRIGERATED *

This tomato broth, sparked with the flavors of onion, garlic, and the complex poblano chile, is combined with delicate bites of zucchini and crisp corn. The magic happens when it is poured over chunks of mild cheese, turning it into a gooey queso party. Kids and adults alike find it irresistible. Be sure to serve with additional cheese on the table, because, frankly, more is more.

2 tablespoons vegetable oil

1 tablespoon unsalted butter

½ cup chopped white onion

1 garlic clove, finely chopped

2½ cups fresh or thawed frozen corn kernels

1½ pounds ripe tomatoes, quartered and pureed, or one 28-ounce can tomato puree or crushed tomatoes

1 tablespoon kosher or coarse sea salt, or to taste

¼ teaspoon freshly ground black pepper, or to taste

4 cups broth from Mexican Chicken Broth (page 87) or canned chicken or vegetable broth

2 poblano chiles (about 11 ounces), charred, sweated, peeled, stemmed, seeded, and cut into 1-x-½-inch strips (see page 27)

2 cups diced zucchini

2 cups diced queso fresco, Cotija, mozzarella, or Monterey Jack (8 ounces), plus more for serving

1. Heat the oil and butter in a large pot over medium heat until the butter melts and begins to foam. Add the onion and cook until it softens and becomes translucent, 5 to 6 minutes. Stir in the garlic and cook until just fragrant, about 1 minute. Add the corn and cook for 2 to 3 minutes, until warmed.

2. Increase the heat to medium-high, add the tomato puree, salt, and pepper, bring to a simmer, and simmer for 7 to 8 minutes, or until the puree thickens and darkens. Add the broth, bring to a simmer, and simmer for 10 to 12 more minutes.

3. Stir in the poblanos and cook for 2 minutes, so they begin to share their flavor with the soup. Add the zucchini and cook for another 5 minutes, or until just cooked through.

4. Divide the diced cheese among individual soup bowls. Pour the hot soup over the cheese and serve.

* MEXICAN COOK'S TRICK: Tomato puree is a linchpin of Mexican cuisine, showing up everywhere. You can buy it, but you can also make your own and keep it for weeks. Quarter ripe tomatoes and puree in a blender or food processor until smooth. Pour the puree into a covered container and refrigerate, or pop into the freezer: Done. It will keep for 2 weeks refrigerated or for 2 months frozen.

ALPHABET SOUP

∿ SOPA DE LETRAS ∿

✴ SERVES 6 ✴ PREPARATION TIME: 5 MINUTES ✴ COOKING TIME: 20 MINUTES ✴ CAN BE MADE 5 DAYS AHEAD, COVERED, AND REFRIGERATED ✴

1½ **pounds ripe tomatoes, quartered, or one 28-ounce can tomato puree or crushed tomatoes**

¼   **cup coarsely chopped white onion**

1   **garlic clove**

3   **tablespoons vegetable oil**

2   **cups (12 ounces) alphabet-shaped pasta or other small pasta**

1   **teaspoon kosher or coarse sea salt, or to taste**

8   **cups broth from Mexican Chicken Broth (page 87) or canned chicken or vegetable broth**

MEXICAN COOK'S TRICK: You can determine how strong you want the flavor of the soup to be by adjusting the amount of time you fry the pasta. If you want it mild, fry the pasta just until it starts to change color. If you want a more robust flavor, let the pasta brown more deeply, which is how it is typically done in Mexico. The time needed to fry the pasta changes depending on the pasta shape, so judge by color. Whatever choice you make, stir often and don't let the pasta burn.

Just like American kids, my sisters and I grew up eating alphabet soup. In Mexico however, the soup is made with a tomato base and the pasta is browned before any liquid is added. It's a wonderful technique, because it is impossible to wind up with a bland-tasting soup when you treat pasta this way. The soup is also known as *sopa aguada*, which translates to "thin or wet soup"—in Mexico pasta and rice that aren't presented in a soup are sometimes called *sopa seca*, or "dry soup."

Any small pasta will work nicely here, like stelline (stars), farfalle (bow ties), or conchiglie (shells). The soup is also commonly made with broken pieces of vermicelli or angel hair, which are called *fideo* in Mexico. Now that I have my own kids to cook for, I vary the pasta shapes depending on their whims.

1. Place the tomatoes, onion, and garlic in a blender or food processor and puree until smooth.

2. Heat the oil in a large pot over medium-high heat until hot but not smoking. Add the pasta and fry, stirring constantly, for 2 to 3 minutes; it will change in color from deep white to a light toast to a golden brown. Take care not to burn it: You want to cook it until it smells toasty—not like burned toast.

3. Pour the tomato puree over the pasta, sprinkle in the salt, and stir. The puree will want to splatter all over your burners, so it's a good idea to cover the pot partially. Let the puree cook for about 6 minutes, stirring often, until it thickens and becomes a deeper red. Keep stirring so the pasta doesn't stick to the bottom of the pot. You will begin to see the bottom of the pot as you stir, but the sauce should not be completely dry. (Cooking the tomato puree to this point gives the soup a nice depth of flavor.)

4. Stir in the broth and bring to a boil, then reduce the heat to medium and simmer for 10 minutes. Taste for seasoning and serve.

WHITE POZOLE

∾ POZOLE BLANCO ∾

✳ SERVES 12 ✳ PREPARATION TIME: 20 MINUTES ✳ COOKING TIME: 4 TO 4½ HOURS IF USING DRIED HOMINY;
1 HOUR IF USING CANNED ✳ CAN BE MADE UP TO 4 DAYS AHEAD, COVERED, AND REFRIGERATED ✳

1 **pound dried hominy (see page 83; also called *maíz mote pelado* or giant white corn) or three 29-ounce cans hominy, drained and rinsed**

1 **head garlic, papery outer layers removed (if using dried hominy)**

2 **3-pound chickens, cut into serving pieces**

1 **white onion**

5 **cilantro sprigs**
Kosher or coarse sea salt

ACCOMPANIMENTS, AS DESIRED

5–6 **limes, halved**

10 **radishes, halved and thinly sliced**

1 **head romaine lettuce, leaves separated, rinsed, dried, and thinly sliced**

½ **cup chopped white onion**
Dried ground chile, such as piquín, or a Mexican mix, such as Tajín
Dried oregano, preferably Mexican
Tortilla Chips or Tostadas (page 66)
Refried beans, homemade (page 220) or store-bought

Pozole is one of Mexico's most famous meals in a bowl, and it's perfect for entertaining, since it is even better when prepared a day ahead of time. It has many variations, and whether they are white, green, or red, or made with chicken or pork or both, you can be certain that whoever had a hand in the dish will tell you that her version is the very best.

All pozoles begin with a white version to which a cooked sauce, red or green, may be added. For me, white pozole speaks of cold rainy days in the company of family and friends, while red pozole means music, parties, and friends gone wild. I encourage you to taste both versions.

As with most Mexican dishes, you can customize your bowl with garnishes: pozole tends to be served with a large number of them. Add lettuce, onion, and radishes as you like and serve the refried beans on the side with chips. Please do squeeze some lime juice into your pozole; a shot of citrus takes it to where it should be.

1. If using dried hominy, place it in a large pot, add water to cover by at least 4 inches, and add the head of garlic. (If using precooked hominy, start with step 2.) Don't add salt now, or the hominy will toughen. Bring to a boil, then simmer over medium-low heat, partially covered, for 4 to 4½ hours, or until the hominy has "bloomed," or opened (it will be chewy). Add 2 teaspoons salt. Skim the foam from the top as the hominy cooks and check the level of water occasionally, adding more if needed.

2. Meanwhile, place the chicken in a large pot and add water to cover by at least 2 inches. Add the onion, cilantro, and 1 tablespoon salt and bring to a boil. Reduce the heat and simmer, partially covered, until the chicken is cooked through and tender, about 40 minutes. Drain, reserving the cooking broth.

(recipe continues)

3. When the chicken is cool enough to handle, remove the skin and bones and shred the meat into bite-sized pieces.

4. In the pot, combine the cooked hominy and its broth or the canned hominy and 2 cups water with the shredded chicken and its broth. Taste for salt, add more if necessary, and cook for 10 minutes more; the pozole should be soupy.

5. Serve the pozole in soup bowls, with the garnishes in bowls on the table.

✳ MEXICAN COOK'S TRICK: The word *pozole*, from the Náhuatl, means "foam." When hominy, the main ingredient of pozole, is cooked, it opens up in such a way that it appears to bloom and forms a bit of foam on the surface—that's how you know when it is ready. If you use precooked hominy from a can, or from the refrigerated bags found in many Latin or international markets, rinse and drain well before using.

Pozole can also be made with pork, and many cooks use a combination of pork and chicken. Substitute 3 pounds chicken parts and 3 pounds pork shoulder (butt) for the 2 whole chickens used here and cook as directed in step 2. Just keep in mind that the pork takes twice as long to cook. Reserve the broth to add to the pozole.

Hominy, or *maíz cacahuacintle*, also known as giant white corn or *maíz mote pelado*, looks like corn kernels on steroids. White, superthick, and meaty, these giant kernels are an excellent choice for stews and soups. They are also used to make masa as well as some traditional sweets and drinks. And the cobs are eaten street-style, grilled and dressed with crema or mayo, chile, and lime (for a recipe adapted for sweet corn, see page 202).

The dried hominy available in stores has already been peeled and "beheaded," or *descabezado*—lightly cooked in water with slaked lime to soften and remove the outer skin and tougher part of the kernels.

Cooking dried hominy is simple: Just throw it in a pot, cover it with water, bring to a simmer, and wait for it to "bloom"—it will open like a flower, in 4 hours or longer. (Soaking the hominy for 2 to 12 hours will reduce the cooking time.) As with dried beans, don't add salt until the end, or it will toughen the kernels.

In Mexico, and sometimes in the United States, you can find plastic bags of fully cooked hominy and its broth in the refrigerated section of markets, which is even more convenient and much better than canned. You can also purchase canned cooked hominy, which will do in a pinch. Just be sure to drain and rinse it well before using.

RED POZOLE

~ POZOLE ROJO ~

✳ SERVES 12 ✳ PREPARATION TIME: 20 MINUTES (PLUS MAKING WHITE POZOLE) ✳ COOKING TIME: 30 MINUTES ✳
CHILE PUREE CAN BE MADE UP TO 5 DAYS AHEAD, COVERED, AND REFRIGERATED; POZOLE CAN BE MADE
UP TO 4 DAYS AHEAD, COVERED, AND REFRIGERATED ✳

Red pozole is a Mexican party in a bowl. Following tradition, when Daniel and I married, we served our guests *pozole rojo*—which comes from the state of Jalisco, where it is known as *tapatío*—at our *tornaboda*, or "after-wedding party." A Mexican wedding can go on for hours. Day turns into night as people eat, sing, and dance, and sometimes the night turns into day, and there are always many guests barely standing toward the end. Right before the party finally winds down, steaming bowls of pozole are brought out to make everyone right.

This is a version of our wedding party pozole, garnished with the same options as for the white pozole on page 81. And as with the white version, please do serve it with a generous squeeze of lime.

Conveniently, the soup tastes even better made ahead and reheated.

CHILE PUREE

2 ancho chiles, rinsed, stemmed, and seeded

3 guajillo chiles, rinsed, stemmed, and seeded

¼ cup chopped white onion

3 garlic cloves

Pinch of ground cumin

2 whole cloves

1 teaspoon kosher or coarse sea salt, or to taste

3 tablespoons vegetable oil

White Pozole (page 81)
Kosher or coarse sea salt

ACCOMPANIMENTS, AS DESIRED

5–6 limes, halved

10 radishes, halved and thinly sliced

1 head romaine lettuce, leaves separated, rinsed, dried, and thinly sliced

½ cup chopped white onion

Dried ground chile, such as piquín, or a Mexican mix, such as Tajín

Dried oregano, preferably Mexican

Tortilla Chips or Tostadas (page 66)

Refried beans, homemade (page 220) or store-bought

1. TO MAKE THE CHILE PUREE: Place the chiles in a medium saucepan, cover with water, and bring to a boil over medium-high heat. Simmer for 10 minutes, or until softened and rehydrated.

2. Place the chiles, along with ¾ cup of their cooking liquid, the onion, garlic, cumin, cloves, and salt in a blender or food processor and puree until smooth. Pass the puree through a fine-mesh strainer into a bowl, pressing on the solids with the back of a wooden spoon to extract as much liquid as possible.

3. Heat the oil in a medium saucepan over medium heat until hot but not smoking. Add the chile puree and bring to a boil, then simmer for 6 to 8 minutes, partially covered with a lid, stirring occasionally, until thickened. Remove from the heat.

(recipe continues)

4. Heat the white pozole in a large pot over medium-high heat until it is simmering. Stir in the chile puree and cook for 20 minutes. Taste and adjust the salt.

5. Serve the pozole in soup bowls, with the garnishes in bowls on the table so your guests can customize their pozole.

Guajillos, one of the most commonly used dried chiles throughout Mexico, are widely available in the United States. This chile is a crowd-pleaser, as it has an amiable, savory flavor without a big punch of heat at the end—guajillos are not spicy. Their look and flavor are quite refined: elegantly long and pointy, with a gorgeous maroon color and a smooth, shiny skin (see the photograph on page 12). But they are also sturdy and tough, so much so that they are commonly strained out when used in sauces.

Mexicans use guajillos in many ways: in table sauces, in stews and meat dishes, in moles and soups. The chiles can be ground or simmered and then pureed or mashed. Sometimes they are pickled and stuffed.

To get them ready to use, rinse or clean with a dry towel and remove the stems, seeds, and veins. Toast the chiles on a hot *comal* or in a heavy skillet for 10 to 15 seconds per side, until the skin is brownish and opaque, taking care not to burn them, or they will taste bitter. Once toasted, proceed with the recipe, rehydrating the chiles as directed. As with anchos, the simmering or cooking liquid that the chiles are rehydrated in is used both for color and flavor.

MEXICAN CHICKEN BROTH

∽ CALDO DE POLLO ∽

✳ MAKES ABOUT 8 CUPS BROTH AND 6 CUPS SHREDDED CHICKEN ✳ PREPARATION TIME: 15 MINUTES
✳ COOKING TIME: 50 MINUTES ✳ BROTH CAN BE REFRIGERATED FOR UP TO 4 DAYS OR FROZEN FOR UP TO 6 MONTHS;
CHICKEN CAN BE COVERED AND REFRIGERATED FOR UP TO 3 DAYS ✳

1 **3-pound chicken, cut into
serving pieces, or 2–3
pounds mixed chicken
parts**

3 **carrots, peeled and cut into
large chunks**

1 **white onion, halved**

3 **celery stalks, cut into large
chunks**

1 **garlic clove**

5–6 **black peppercorns**

5–6 **fresh Italian parsley sprigs**

½ **teaspoon dried marjoram**

½ **teaspoon dried thyme**

2 **bay leaves**

1 **tablespoon kosher or coarse
sea salt, or to taste**

3½ **quarts water**

I like to make *caldo de pollo* every Sunday, because it sets the right affectionate tone in the house as it wraps the entire place in its aroma, and it's also the backbone of a streamlined week of eating. You get a batch of rich-tasting chicken broth that can be used in soups, stews, rice, and pasta dishes, plus generous amounts of moist cooked chicken that can be shredded or cut up for salads, sandwiches, tacos, tortas, casseroles, or Chicken Tinga (page 140). Drop everything into the pot, cover with water, and go.

1. Place all the ingredients in a large pot and bring to a boil. Reduce the heat to medium-low, skim off any foam, and simmer, partially covered, for 50 minutes. Turn off the heat and let cool.

2. With a slotted spoon, transfer the chicken pieces to a bowl. Strain the broth into a container, cool, and refrigerate. Remove the skin and bones from the chicken. Shred or cut the meat into chunks for future use and refrigerate if not using right away.

✳ MEXICAN COOK'S TRICK: *Caldo de pollo* cooks for less than an hour, much less time than a typical French stock. The Mexican way brings you a gentle, tasty broth, but most important, it allows the chicken meat to have a life of its own, since the briefer cooking doesn't suck out all the flavor, texture, and nutrients.

ANYTIME
VEGETARIAN

DIVORCED EGGS (*HUEVOS DIVORCIADOS*) ...92
    HOMEMADE CORN TORTILLAS ...94
POACHED EGGS IN CHUNKY POBLANO-TOMATO SALSA
    (*HUEVOS RABO DE MESTIZA*) ...97
SCRAMBLED EGG PACKETS WITH BLACK BEAN SAUCE
    (*HUEVOS ENVUELTOS BAÑADOS EN FRIJOL*) ...98
MEXICAN FRITTATA WITH POBLANOS, POTATOES, AND FETA ...100
PLANTAIN AND REFRIED BEAN QUESADILLAS ...103
CHILAQUILES IN RED SALSA (*CHILAQUILES EN SALSA ROJA*) ...105
OAXACA-STYLE MUSHROOM AND CHEESE QUESADILLAS ...106
TORTILLA AND BLACK BEAN CASSEROLE ...110
GRILLED CHEESE AND BEAN HEROES (*MOLLETES*) ...113

I AM STUBBORN—REALLY STUBBORN. Like a mule. When I began to think about this book and talk to friends who watch my TV show, read my blog, and take my classes, I kept getting requests to include more meatless and vegetarian options. I kept on saying, "No. No. No!"

You see, for me, and for most Mexicans I know, there is no "vegetarian" in Mexican cuisine—no compartmentalizing labels. But slowly, like a mule turning around on a steep path, I began to realize that many of my favorite dishes are in fact vegetarian. We just don't call them that.

We have beautiful sauces based on nuts, seeds, and chiles; countless bean and rice dishes; vegetable stews and casseroles; an infinite number of corn-based dishes— tacos, tostadas, and tamales; and many pozoles and moles made with potatoes, cactus paddles, mushrooms, or zucchini, no meat. What's more, a simple switch from chicken broth to vegetable broth or water can take many of the nonvegetarian dishes in this book into vegetarian territory.

When I finally came around, I pulled together some of my favorite vegetarian meals that are good for eating just about any time. They include exquisitely simple egg dishes for breakfast, brunch, or best of all, at midnight after a night out, such as Mexican Frittata with Poblanos, Potatoes, and Feta and Poached Eggs in Chunky Poblano-Tomato Salsa. There are also one-dish meals, like Tortilla and Black Bean Casserole, which will tempt any carnivore; exotic and festive Plantain and Refried Bean Quesadillas; addictive Chilaquiles in Red Salsa; and the irresistibly homey *Molletes*, Grilled Cheese and Bean Heroes. Hats off to everyone trying to eat simpler and closer to the ground, and a big thank-you especially to all those who urged me to look at my native cuisine a little differently.

DIVORCED EGGS

~ HUEVOS DIVORCIADOS ~

* SERVES 4 * PREPARATION TIME: 5 MINUTES * COOKING TIME: 15 MINUTES *

Vegetable oil

8 corn tortillas, store-bought or homemade (page 94)

8 large eggs, at room temperature

Kosher or coarse sea salt

2 cups *salsa verde,* homemade (page 22) or store-bought, heated

2 cups charred tomato salsa, homemade (page 18) or store-bought, heated

2 cups refried beans, homemade (page 220) or store-bought, heated

¼ cup crumbled queso fresco, Cotija, farmer cheese, or mild feta

Not for nothing are Mexicans known to be witty and sarcastic during life's downturns. Consider the name given to these eggs: "divorced." They are perfect for people who can't decide between red sauce and green sauce, or for voracious types like me, who want them both at the same time.

Eat these eggs for breakfast, for lunch, or at 2:00 A.M., but eat them. Traditionally the eggs should be served sunny-side up so the yolks break into both sauces and turn the divorce into an even bigger mess.

1. Heat ¼ inch of oil in a medium skillet over medium-high heat until hot but not smoking. The oil is ready if when you dip the edge of a tortilla into it, it bubbles happily around the edges without going wild. Using tongs, dip the tortillas one at a time in the oil for 10 to 15 seconds per side. The tortillas will first appear to soften and then begin to crisp. Drain on paper towels and cover with aluminum foil or an inverted plate to keep warm. (Alternatively, you can lightly toast the tortillas on a well-heated *comal* or in a skillet over medium heat for 30 seconds per side.)

2. Pour off all but 2 tablespoons of the oil you used for the tortillas if you fried them. If you toasted the tortillas, add 2 tablespoons oil. Heat the oil over medium heat. Crack 2 eggs into the pan, sprinkle with salt to taste, and cook to your preferred doneness. Keep warm while you repeat with the remaining eggs.

3. To serve, place 2 of the warmed tortillas on four plates and top with 2 eggs. Ladle a generous amount of green sauce over one of the eggs on each plate and red sauce over the other. Serve with the refried beans on the side and a sprinkling of the cheese.

* MEXICAN COOK'S TRICK: I like my eggs with the whites cooked and the yolks still runny. I crack the eggs into the hot skillet and then cover with a lid or a plate to let the steam help cook the whites from above.

HOMEMADE CORN TORTILLAS

✳ MAKES TWELVE TO FIFTEEN 5-INCH TORTILLAS ✳ PREPARATION TIME: 10 TO 12 MINUTES ✳
COOKING TIME: 20 MINUTES ✳ CAN BE WRAPPED IN A TOWEL, SEALED IN A PLASTIC BAG, AND REFRIGERATED
FOR UP TO 3 DAYS OR FROZEN FOR UP TO 2 MONTHS ✳

2 cups corn tortilla flour or instant corn masa flour, such as Maseca

Pinch of kosher or coarse sea salt

About 1¾ cups water

Tortillerías Few things compare to freshly made corn tortillas. Having grown up in Mexico City, I am utterly spoiled. I ate fresh corn tortillas that we bought every couple days at a *tortillería,* a tortilla factory of sorts, like a bakery. Even better were the ones brought by the tortilla lady who came by our house certain days of the week with a big basket filled to the brim. Here in the United States, there are not many *tortillerías,* and I have not yet seen a tortilla lady, but I continue to hope!

I didn't start making corn tortillas at home until I moved to Washington, D.C. And though I made good tortillas, it wasn't until I met Doña Rosa Arroyo, a lovely woman from Oaxaca with an even lovelier *sazón* (roughly, a talent for using just the right amount of seasoning) who works with me at the Mexican Cultural Institute, that I learned how to make pretty darn amazing ones. It took just a short time for Doña Rosa to straighten me out: *"No, señora Pati, su masa esta seca y tiene que voltear las tortillas dos veces hasta que se inflen."* My dough was too dry: adding the right amount of water was the easy fix. But I still could not get them to puff up. So Doña Rosa taught me the double-flip method, which, though it takes a bit of patience, makes the tortillas puff beautifully once you get the rhythm.

If you want to make the tortillas ahead, they can be kept, wrapped in a clean kitchen towel or cloth, at room temperature. Reheat them on a hot *comal* or in a heavy skillet set over medium heat for at least 30 seconds on each side, until they are pliable again, before eating.

1. Set a *comal*, a flat griddle, or a cast-iron skillet over medium heat until thoroughly heated. (If the pan isn't hot enough, the tortillas will stick to it.)

2. Meanwhile, cut two circles about the size of the tortilla press plates (or at least 6 inches in diameter if using a rolling pin) out of thin plastic bags, such as produce bags from the grocery store; do not use plastic wrap.

3. In a large bowl, mix together the flour, salt, and water and then knead in a circular motion until the dough feels smooth and without lumps. It shouldn't be wet or sticky but nice and moist. If it feels coarse when you gather the dough together, add a bit more water. Masa dries out fast, so keep it covered while you make the tortillas.

(recipe continues)

4. Roll a piece of the dough in the palm of your hand into a ball about 1½ inches in diameter. Place one of the plastic circles on the bottom of the tortilla press and place the ball on top. Place the other plastic circle on top of the ball and clamp down the press to make a flat disk, jiggling the press a little as you get to the bottom (this makes for a rounder tortilla). It should be about 5 inches in diameter and about ⅛ inch thick. Alternatively, you can place a ball between plastic sheets or parchment paper and roll out the tortillas with a rolling pin.

5. Open the press, check the tortilla for dryness (see Mexican Cook's Trick), and add water to the dough if needed. Remove the plastic on top of the tortilla, then lift up the bottom piece of plastic and the tortilla with one hand and peel the tortilla away from the plastic with the other hand. Keep at least half of the tortilla off your hand to make it easier to transfer it swiftly to the hot pan.

6. Place the tortilla on the hot surface and don't touch it for 30 seconds—even if it doesn't lie completely flat, resist the temptation to fiddle with it! Cook until you can easily lift it with a spatula, 40 seconds to 1 minute; it should be opaque on the cooked side. Flip and cook for about a minute longer, until it has begun to get brown freckles. Flip once more. After 10 to 15 seconds, the tortilla should puff like pita bread, if not all over, at least in one area. If it is not puffing, gently tease it along by poking it in the center with the tip of your finger. Once it puffs, let the tortilla continue cooking for another 15 to 20 seconds, so that it cooks all the way through. That extra cooking is what makes the difference between stiff tortillas and those that are toothy, tender, and pliable.

7. Transfer the cooked tortilla to a clean kitchen towel or a cloth-lined *tortillero* (a tortilla basket, which looks just like a bread basket) and cover to keep warm while you make the rest of the tortillas.

✻ MEXICAN COOK'S TRICK: The masa has to be as soft and smooth as Play-Doh. This has less to do with the kneading—which takes under a minute—than with the amount of water. The measurement given on most bags for corn tortilla flour is too low. Here I give you the measurement that works for me. Things will vary, however, according to climate and ingredients. One way to tell if your masa needs more water is to take a look at the first tortilla after you have pressed it out. If the edges seem cracked and rough, you need more water. The tortilla should be smooth and even along the edges, not at all ridged.

POACHED EGGS IN CHUNKY POBLANO-TOMATO SALSA

∿ HUEVOS RABO DE MESTIZA ∿

❋ **SERVES 4** ❋ **PREPARATION TIME: 5 MINUTES** ❋ **COOKING TIME: 10 MINUTES** ❋

**Chunky Poblano and
Tomato Salsa (page 26)**

8 **large eggs, at room temperature**

Kosher or coarse sea salt

1 **cup crumbled queso fresco,
Cotija, farmer cheese, or
mild feta**

**Warm corn tortillas, store-
bought or homemade
(page 94), or toast
(optional)**

Rather than poaching eggs in plain old water, in Mexican recipes the eggs are cooked in a sauce, multiplying the flavor. Here they are nestled in a rich poblano chile and tomato salsa that thickens as the eggs cook. You end up with an entire meal in one savory casserole.

Rabo de mestiza means "ragged clothes," or in slang, the ponytail of a mixed-heritage woman—which most Mexican women are. This dish of humble origin can be traced back to colonial times and still shows up everywhere, from the simplest to the fanciest restaurants.

1. Bring the salsa to a simmer in a 12-inch skillet over medium heat. Lower the heat to medium-low and make 8 nests in the sauce with the back of a spoon. (Alternatively, you can do this in batches of 4 eggs in a smaller skillet.) Crack the eggs, one at a time, into the nests. Sprinkle a bit of salt on top of each egg, cover the pan, and let the eggs poach until cooked to your liking. I prefer the whites set and the yolks runny, which takes about 5 minutes.

2. Serve the eggs sprinkled with the crumbled cheese, with warm corn tortillas (or toast) on the side, if desired.

❋ MEXICAN COOK'S TRICK: For poached eggs that keep a nice, compact shape, add them to gently simmering sauce by cracking them, one at a time, into a small bowl or cup, then sliding them into the sauce. If the sauce is chunky, as in this recipe, first make nests in the sauce with the back of a spoon and slip the eggs into the nests.

SCRAMBLED EGG PACKETS WITH BLACK BEAN SAUCE

∾ HUEVOS ENVUELTOS BAÑADOS EN FRIJOL ∾

✳ SERVES 4 ✳ PREPARATION TIME: 10 MINUTES ✳ COOKING TIME: 20 MINUTES ✳ ROLLED TORTILLAS CAN BE MADE AHEAD AND KEPT COVERED IN A WARM (250°F) OVEN FOR UP TO 2 HOURS ✳

Vegetable oil

8 corn tortillas, store-bought or homemade (page 94)

4 cups Simple Beans from the Pot (page 216) made with black beans and pureed with 1 cup cooking liquid, or two 15.5-ounce cans black beans, drained and pureed with 1½ cups water

Kosher or coarse sea salt

⅓ cup chopped white onion

1 jalapeño or serrano chile, halved, seeded if desired, and minced, or to taste

8 large eggs, beaten until foamy

¼ cup Mexican crema (see page 135), crème fraîche, or sour cream

½ cup crumbled queso fresco, Cotija, farmer cheese, or mild feta

1 ripe Hass avocado, halved, pitted, meat scooped out, and sliced (optional)

Salsa of your choice (optional)

Tender soft-scrambled eggs get special treatment when slowly cooked with onion and a fresh chile. Wrap them in warm soft corn tortillas, ladle on an earthy black bean sauce, and they're transformed into a hearty main course.

When we have a group of friends over for a late weekend brunch, I make a double recipe ahead of time and keep it warm in the oven, ready to come out as soon as I hear a knock on the door. In addition to serving it with ripe avocado, Mexican crema, and crumbled cheese, I like to have a side of Fresh Tomatillo and Chipotle Salsa (page 24) to ladle on top.

1. Heat ¼ inch of oil in a medium nonstick skillet over medium-high heat until hot but not smoking. The oil is ready if when you dip the edge of a tortilla in the oil, it bubbles happily around the edges without going wild. Using tongs, dip the tortillas one at a time in the oil for 10 to 15 seconds per side. The tortillas will first appear to soften and then begin to crisp. Drain on paper towels and cover with aluminum foil or an inverted plate to keep warm. Set the pan aside. (Alternatively, you can lightly toast the tortillas on a well-heated *comal* or skillet over medium heat for about 30 seconds per side.)

2. Heat the bean puree in a medium saucepan over medium-low heat, stirring occasionally, until very hot. The puree will have the consistency of heavy cream. Taste for salt, adding more if need be. Reduce the heat to the lowest setting and keep warm.

3. Pour off all but 3 tablespoons of oil from the pan you used to cook the tortillas if you fried them. If you toasted the tortillas, add 3 tablespoons oil. Heat the oil over medium heat. Add the onion and cook until translucent and beginning to brown lightly, 3 to 4 minutes. Add the chile and cook until softened, about 2 more minutes. Reduce the heat to medium-low, pour in the beaten eggs, sprinkle with ½ teaspoon salt, and cook,

stirring often and gently, to your desired doneness. I like my eggs still soft, not dry, which takes 4 to 5 minutes. Remove from the heat.

4. To assemble the packets, place a tortilla on a plate and spoon about 3 tablespoons of the scrambled eggs onto it. Roll it up and place in a serving dish, seam side down. Continue with the remaining tortillas and eggs. When all the tortillas are rolled and in the dish, pour the bean puree on top.

5. Drizzle on the cream, sprinkle the cheese over all, and bring to the table. Serve with the slices of avocado and your favorite salsa, if you'd like.

* MEXICAN COOK'S TRICK: To get the fluffiest scrambled eggs, beat them with a fork or whisk until they are a bit foamy, then cook them slowly and gently, stirring, until they're fluffy and creamy. Don't let them dry out by overcooking them.

Queso Fresco, literally "fresh cheese"—is a firm, white, moist, slightly tangy, milky-tasting cheese that is teasingly salty. It has a lovely texture: hard enough to cut into cubes or blocks but easily crumbled between your fingers. It's similar to a mild young feta or farmer cheese, queso blanco, or Cotija, all of which are great substitutions if you can't find queso fresco.

MEXICAN FRITTATA WITH POBLANOS, POTATOES, AND FETA

✳ SERVES 4 TO 6 ✳ PREPARATION TIME: 10 MINUTES ✳ COOKING TIME: 30 MINUTES ✳ CAN BE MADE UP TO 2 HOURS AHEAD AND KEPT, COVERED, AT ROOM TEMPERATURE ✳

¼ cup vegetable oil

1 cup chopped white onion

2 poblano chiles (about 11 ounces), charred, sweated, peeled, stemmed, seeded, and cut into 1-x-½-inch strips (see page 27)

8 large eggs

3 tablespoons milk

¾ teaspoon kosher or coarse sea salt, or to taste

1 pound red potatoes, peeled, diced, cooked in salted boiling water for 5 minutes, and drained

Pinch of freshly ground black pepper, or to taste

½ teaspoon ground allspice

¾ cup diced feta cheese (about 4 ounces)

Few things are as adaptable as a frittata. This one goes on a luxurious ride with seasoned potatoes, poblano chiles, feta cheese, and a surprising nip of allspice to pull it all together.

When I serve it for breakfast or brunch, I pass a loaf of crusty bread. For lunch or dinner, I like to accompany the frittata with Everyday Green Salad (page 44). Frittatas are delicious hot, warm, or lukewarm—though my husband happens to love them stone cold, tucked between slices of rustic bread for a torta.

1. Preheat the broiler.

2. Heat the oil in a 10- to 12-inch broilerproof skillet over medium heat until hot but not smoking. Add the onion and cook, stirring occasionally, until soft and barely beginning to brown, 6 to 8 minutes. Add the chiles and cook until they begin to brown lightly, about 3 minutes.

3. Meanwhile, in a medium bowl with a whisk or a fork, beat the eggs with the milk and ¼ teaspoon of the salt until foamy.

4. Toss the potatoes into the onion mixture, stir in the remaining ½ teaspoon salt, the pepper, and allspice, and cook, stirring occasionally, until the potatoes are completely softened, about 6 to 8 minutes.

5. Pour the egg mixture on top of the potato mixture and stir gently as the eggs begin to cook along the edges and bottom of the pan, 2 to 3 minutes. Sprinkle the cheese on top.

6. Place the skillet under the broiler and broil until the frittata is puffed and lightly browned on top, 3 to 4 minutes. Remove from the oven, cut into wedges, and serve. Or let cool and serve at room temperature.

✳ MEXICAN COOK'S TRICK: Despite a frittata's versatility, it does not reheat well. If you want to make it ahead to serve warm, place the pan on top of the stove and cover it with a lid or a clean kitchen towel. It will stay warm for at least an hour.

PLANTAIN AND REFRIED BEAN QUESADILLAS

❋ MAKES 6 TO 8 QUESADILLAS ❋ PREPARATION TIME: 20 MINUTES ❋ COOKING TIME: 20 MINUTES ❋
CAN BE ASSEMBLED AHEAD, COVERED, AND REFRIGERATED FOR UP TO 2 DAYS OR FROZEN,
TIGHTLY COVERED, FOR UP TO 3 MONTHS ❋

DOUGH

1 pound yellow plantains

1 tablespoon sugar, or to taste

1–2 tablespoons rice flour (see page 206) or all-purpose flour, if needed

1 cup refried beans, home-made (page 220) or store-bought

Vegetable oil

Salsa of your choice

Although quesadillas get their name from the words *queso*, Spanish for "cheese," and *illas*, from the word *tortillas*, in Mexico not all quesadillas are made with both—or either—ingredients. In fact, the word *quesadilla* simply refers to its turnover shape.

In this traditional version from the Gulf of Mexico, refried beans are tucked into a dough made from plantains and fried until crisp. Carmen Titita, one of Mexico's leading cooks and restaurateurs, does an excellent version at El Bajio, her restaurant in Mexico City.

This recipe is very easy, and it's worth making a big batch, as you can freeze the quesadillas for months and then cook them as you please. I like to serve them with Charred Tomato Salsa (page 18) or Pickled Ancho Chile Salsa (page 32).

1. TO MAKE THE DOUGH: Place the unpeeled plantains in a large pot of boiling water and simmer, partially covered, until they are soft to the touch, 20 to 25 minutes. Remove from the water with tongs and let them cool slightly, until they can be handled.

2. Trim off the ends of the plantains. Make a lengthwise slit in the skin of each one, peel off the skin, and slice. Place in a blender or food processor, along with the sugar, and process until smooth. If the dough seems too soft and runny, add some flour to thicken it a bit. (You can also let the dough sit in the refrigerator, covered, for 30 minutes to make it more manageable.)

3. TO MAKE THE QUESADILLAS: Meanwhile, cut two circles about the size of the tortilla press plates (or at least 6 inches in diameter if using a rolling pin) out of thin plastic bags, such as produce bags from the grocery store.

(recipe continues)

4. Roll a piece of the dough in the palm of your hand into a ball about 1 inch in diameter. Place one of the plastic circles on the bottom of the tortilla press and place the ball on top. Place the other plastic circle on top of the ball and clamp down on the press to make a flat disk about ¼ inch thick, jiggling the press a little as you get to the bottom (this makes for a rounder tortilla). Alternatively, you can place the ball between plastic sheets or parchment paper and roll out with a rolling pin.

5. Remove the top piece of plastic and place a generous tablespoon of the refried beans in the center of the dough. Use the bottom piece of plastic to fold the dough over the filling like a turnover. Firmly pinch the edges of the turnover together. Gently lift the quesadilla off the plastic and set aside. Continue with the remainder of the dough and beans.

6. Heat 1 inch of oil in a 12-inch skillet over medium heat until hot but not smoking, 3 to 4 minutes. Dip the tip of a quesadilla into the oil; if the oil is ready, it will bubble around the edges but not be too wild. Fry the quesadillas a few at a time until golden and lightly crisp, about 2 minutes. Turn and cook the quesadillas on the other side, about 2 more minutes. They should be soft and tender. Don't let them brown too much, or they will burn. Drain on paper towels.

7. Serve with your favorite salsa.

* MEXICAN COOK'S TRICK: To make this dough, you need slightly underripe plantains (see page 250). Unlike bananas, plantains are still underripe when they are yellow and only fully ripe when they are jet-black. For this dough, you want them to be yellow, when the sugars are starting to come out but the plantains aren't too soft.

CHILAQUILES IN RED SALSA

∿ CHILAQUILES EN SALSA ROJA ∿

✳ SERVES 6 ✳ PREPARATION TIME: 10 MINUTES ✳ COOKING TIME: 5 MINUTES ✳

2 recipes Charred Tomato Salsa (page 18)

3 recipes Tortilla Chips (page 66)

½ cup thinly sliced white onion

½ cup crumbled queso fresco, Cotija, farmer cheese, or mild feta

½ cup Mexican crema (see page 135), crème fraîche, or sour cream

There are two kinds of people in Mexico: those who like their chilaquiles crispy and those who like them soft. Count me in the first group.

Chilaquiles are triangles of fried or baked corn tortillas drenched in a seasoned sauce and topped with crumbled fresh cheese, crunchy raw onions, and a drizzle of Mexican crema. If you want your chilaquiles crispy, get them to the table as soon as possible; if you prefer them soaked and soft, let the crisp chilaquile–loving people like me get their servings first. It takes no more than 10 minutes for them to soften at the table.

Chilaquiles are revered as a breakfast or brunch food. Serve alongside Refried Beans (page 220) or Simple Beans from the Pot (page 216) and eggs any way you like them.

1. Heat the salsa in a large skillet over medium heat. When it is hot, add the tortilla chips, quickly stirring them in so that they are fully coated.

2. Turn out onto a large platter and garnish with the sliced onion, crumbled cheese, and drizzle the cream over. Serve immediately.

OAXACA-STYLE MUSHROOM AND CHEESE QUESADILLAS

❋ MAKES 12 QUESADILLAS ❋ PREPARATION TIME: 15 MINUTES ❋ COOKING TIME: 20 MINUTES ❋
FILLING CAN BE MADE UP TO 24 HOURS AHEAD, COVERED, AND REFRIGERATED ❋

MUSHROOM FILLING

- 1 tablespoon vegetable oil
- 1 tablespoon unsalted butter
- ½ cup chopped white onion
- 1 jalapeño or serrano chile, finely chopped and seeded if desired, or to taste
- 2 garlic cloves, minced or pressed
- 1 pound mushrooms, such as white buttons, creminis (baby bellas), or others of your choice, cleaned and thinly sliced
- 1½ teaspoons kosher or coarse sea salt, or to taste
- 2 tablespoons fresh epazote leaves or cilantro leaves, chopped

- 2 cups instant corn masa flour, such as Maseca, or 12 store-bought corn tortillas
- 1¾ cups water if making homemade tortillas
- 2 cups shredded mild cheese, such as mozzarella or Monterey Jack (about 8 ounces)
- Vegetable oil if making homemade tortillas
- Salsa of your choice

During the rainy months in Oaxaca, market stands are filled with baskets of mushrooms picked by women before sunrise. They are always sold out before noon. Food stands also sell mixed-mushroom quesadillas, most of them made in the simple way, with a base of onion, garlic, fresh chile, and a fresh green herb like cilantro or epazote, a combination that brings out the earthy flavors of the mushrooms.

I use this technique with whatever mushrooms I find. Standard button mushrooms work great, but the quesadillas pack more punch when those are combined with more flavorful varieties such as creminis (baby bellas) or shiitakes.

Fresh quesadillas are incredibly easy to make with instant corn masa. That said, don't hesitate to use ready-made corn tortillas. Either way, these are heavenly. Serve them hot with a salsa of your choice: Try Charred Tomato Salsa (page 18) or Cooked Green Salsa (page 22).

1. TO MAKE THE MUSHROOM FILLING: Heat the oil and butter in a large skillet over medium-high heat until the butter melts and starts to foam. Add the onion and cook until soft and translucent, 3 to 4 minutes. Add the chile and cook until softened, 1 to 2 minutes. Add the garlic and cook until just fragrant, less than a minute; do not let it brown. Add the mushrooms and salt and cook, stirring occasionally, until the mushrooms release their juices and the liquid begins to evaporate, about 5 minutes. Add the epazote and cook for 1 minute, or until the mushrooms are just slightly moist, neither wet nor dry. Remove from the heat.

2. IF MAKING HOMEMADE TORTILLAS: Cut two circles about the size of the tortilla press plates (or at least 6 inches in diameter if using a rolling pin) out of thin plastic bags, such as produce bags from the grocery store.

(recipe continues)

Epazote is a deeply Mexican ingredient that has no substitute. It is used both as a culinary herb and for medicinal purposes, and its leaves have a unique, clear, deep flavor. It contributes an intangible character that is difficult to pin down but can be described as slightly astringent. It has an equally distinctive smell, penetrating and pungent—some people think it smells like a petroleum product. It is best used judiciously and added in the last stages of cooking so that it doesn't take over.

Epazote is also known as the "poor man's herb," since it grows wild almost everywhere in Mexico. Its long leaves are a lovely dark green with serrated edges. You can sometimes find epazote fresh in markets, as well as dried in packets; the dried version is much milder. In some dishes, epazote is used interchangeably with cilantro, though they have very different flavors.

Epazote is most commonly used with beans; in fact some cooks consider it essential in bean dishes, not only because the flavor combination is divine but also because the herb is said to aid digestion and reduce gas.

When you are using fresh epazote, 2 or 3 sprigs are usually more than enough for any dish. If you can't find it fresh, substitute 1 teaspoon crumbled and dried epazote for 3 to 4 leaves.

3. In a large bowl, mix the masa flour with the water and knead for a couple of minutes, until soft. Roll a piece of the dough in the palm of your hand into a ball about 1 inch in diameter. Place one of the plastic circles on the bottom of the tortilla press and place the ball on top. Place the other plastic circle on top of the ball and clamp down on the press to make a flat disk about ¼ inch thick, jiggling the press a little as you get to the bottom (this makes for a rounder tortilla). (Alternatively, you can place the ball between plastic sheets or parchment paper and roll the tortillas out with a rolling pin into 5-inch-diameter circles.)

4. Remove the top piece of plastic and place a generous 2 tablespoons of the cheese and about 1½ tablespoons of the mushroom filling in the center of the dough. Use the bottom piece of plastic to fold the tortilla over the filling like a turnover. Firmly pinch the edges of the turnover together. Gently lift the quesadilla off the plastic and set aside. Continue with the remainder of the dough, cheese, and mushroom filling.

5. Heat 1 inch of oil in a 12-inch skillet over medium heat until hot but not smoking. The oil is ready if when you dip the edge of a quesadilla into the oil, it bubbles happily all around it without going wild. Add the quesadillas a few at a time, making sure not to crowd the skillet, and cook for 2 to 4 minutes per side, or until golden brown and lightly crisp. With a slotted spoon, transfer to a paper-towel-lined platter to drain. Keep warm while you repeat with the remaining quesadillas.

6. IF USING STORE-BOUGHT TORTILLAS: Heat a *comal*, a flat griddle, or a 12-inch skillet over medium heat for 8 to 10 minutes, or until thoroughly heated. (If the pan isn't hot enough, the tortillas will stick to it.) Lay a tortilla on the *comal* and heat for about 20 seconds on each side, until it softens and becomes pliable. Add about 2 tablespoons cheese and about 1½ tablespoons of filling in the center of the tortilla. Fold the tortilla over, press down lightly, and let cook until the cheese has melted and the tortilla has begun to crisp lightly, 2 to 3 minutes. Turn and continue cooking until the second side begins to crisp lightly, another 2 to 3 minutes. Transfer to a platter, cover to keep warm, and repeat with the remaining tortillas, cheese, and filling.

7. Serve the quesadillas hot, with the salsa.

TORTILLA AND BLACK BEAN CASSEROLE

✳ SERVES 6 TO 8 ✳ PREPARATION TIME: 20 MINUTES ✳ COOKING TIME: 1 HOUR ✳ CAN BE ASSEMBLED UP TO 12 HOURS AHEAD, COVERED, AND REFRIGERATED (THE BAKING TIME WILL BE LONGER) ✳

6–8 pasilla chiles (2 ounces), rinsed, stemmed, and seeded

6 garlic cloves, unpeeled

3 cups vegetable broth

Vegetable oil

¾ teaspoon kosher or coarse sea salt, or to taste

2 teaspoons sugar, or to taste

12 corn tortillas, store-bought or homemade (page 94)

3 cups Simple Beans from the Pot (page 216), made with black beans, or two 15.5-ounce cans, drained

12 ounces Monterey Jack or mozzarella cheese, shredded (about 3 cups)

¾ cup Mexican crema (see page 135), crème fraîche, or sour cream

I got this impossibly good Mexican casserole from my dear friend Sally Swift, the co-creator of public radio's *The Splendid Table*, who grew up in the sticks of Wisconsin with nary a tortilla or chile in sight. She has been fascinated with Mexican flavors ever since she was a child, when she tried to make tortillas out of any flour she found in her mother's pantry.

Sally's food is generous, big-hearted, and meant to be shared around a large boisterous table. This casserole layers tortillas, black beans, cheese, Mexican crema, and a simple but sophisticated pasilla chile sauce. It is an often-requested favorite at my house.

You can also make this casserole with pinto beans.

1. Heat a *comal* or large skillet over medium heat until hot. Lay the chiles flat in the pan and toast them for 10 to 15 seconds per side, until they become fragrant and pliable and their color darkens. Take care not to let them burn, or they will turn bitter. Transfer the chiles to a large bowl, cover with hot water, and let soak for 10 to 30 minutes, until softened.

2. Meanwhile, char the garlic, in its skin, on the *comal* or skillet, until nicely browned and very tender, about 10 minutes. Set aside to cool, then peel.

3. When the chiles are softened, transfer them to a blender or food processor, along with ½ cup of the soaking liquid, the garlic, and 2 cups of the broth. Puree.

4. Heat 1 tablespoon oil in a medium saucepan over medium-high heat until hot but not smoking. Add the chile puree, bring to a simmer, and simmer vigorously, stirring often, until the sauce has started to thicken and darken in color, about 5 minutes (partially cover the pan if the sauce splatters). Add the remaining 1 cup broth, the salt, and sugar, reduce the heat to medium, and simmer, stirring often, until the sauce is reduced to about 2 cups, about 20 minutes. Remove from the heat and set aside.

(recipe continues)

Comales are flat plates or griddles designed to be used over a fire, although today they are used on stovetops. For centuries they were made from clay. You can still see those in homes in the Mexican countryside, where there will likely be two *comales*, one for making tortillas and corn masa–based foods and another for charring or toasting vegetables and spices. These days you can find aluminum and even nonstick *comales*, but my preference, and that of most cooks I know, is cast iron.

In Mexico *comales* pass from generation to generation, and they are treasured. Mine is around fifty years old and came to me from my mother. It is seasoned, blackened, banged-up, and chipped, and it speaks its history every time I cook with it.

You can find *comales* in international, Asian, and Latin stores as well as online. Clean a *comal* as you would a wok, with warm water, a little soap, and a gentle sponge, taking care not to remove the seasoning you are building every time you cook. If you don't have a *comal*, use a cast-iron or other heavy skillet.

5. Meanwhile, heat ¼ inch of oil in a medium skillet over medium-high heat until hot but not smoking. The oil is ready if when you dip the edge of a tortilla in the oil, it bubbles happily around the edges without going wild. Using tongs, dip the tortillas in the oil one at a time for 10 to 15 seconds per side. The tortilla will first soften and then begin to crisp. Drain the tortillas on paper towels. Alternatively, lightly toast the tortillas on a well-heated *comal* or skillet over medium heat for about 30 seconds per side. Cover with aluminum foil or an inverted plate to keep warm.

6. Preheat the oven to 350°F.

7. Spread one third of the sauce over the bottom of a 9-x-13-inch baking dish. Place half of the tortillas over the sauce, then cover with a layer of half the black beans and one third of the cheese. Cover with another layer of the remaining tortillas, one third of the sauce, one third of the cheese, and the remaining beans. Finish with the remaining sauce and cheese, and the cream.

8. Cover the dish tightly with aluminum foil and bake for 15 to 20 minutes. Uncover and continue baking until the casserole is bubbly around the edges and the cheese is nicely melted, about 20 minutes longer. Remove from the oven and let rest for 5 to 10 minutes, then serve.

GRILLED CHEESE AND BEAN HEROES

∽ MOLLETES ∽

✳ SERVES 4 TO 6 ✳ PREPARATION TIME: 5 MINUTES ✳ COOKING TIME: 10 MINUTES ✳ CAN BE ASSEMBLED UP TO 2 HOURS IN ADVANCE AND KEPT COVERED AT ROOM TEMPERATURE ✳

4 *teleras*, *bolillos*, Portuguese buns, or petite baguettes, or 1 large baguette cut into 4 pieces

2 cups refried beans, homemade (page 220) or store-bought

2 cups shredded Manchego, mozzarella, Monterey Jack, or mild cheddar cheese (about 8 ounces)

Traditional Tomato Pico de Gallo (page 28) or other salsa of your choice

The reason you will always find refried beans, melty cheese, and crusty bread in my kitchen is *molletes.* We eat them anytime, day or night, just as we did in my childhood home. My eldest likes crisp bacon or crumbled fried chorizo on top. My youngest wants avocado and sauce from chipotles in adobo on top, and my middle one likes them, just as I do, in their purest form: crusty bread slathered with a thick layer of refried beans and a generous amount of shredded cheese. Pop them in the oven to melt the cheese for your tastiest quick meal. Eat them open-faced. Most people like them topped with pico de gallo.

1. Preheat the oven to 350°F.

2. Slice the bread or rolls lengthwise in half. Spread each piece with 3 generous tablespoons refried beans and top with 3 generous tablespoons cheese and place on a baking sheet. If you want to add more toppings (see the headnote), sprinkle them on top of the cheese.

3. Bake the *molletes* until the cheese has melted and the edges of the bread are nicely toasted, 8 to 10 minutes. Serve hot, topped with the salsa or with it on the side.

SEAFOOD

CEVICHE TOSTADAS PUERTO VALLARTA ...118
SHRIMP COCKTAIL PACÍFICO (*CÓCTEL DE CAMARÓN DEL PACÍFICO*) ...120
SHRIMP IN RED PIPIÁN (*CAMARONES EN PIPIÁN ROJO*) ...122
SHRIMP CROQUETTES IN TOMATO BROTH ...124
CRAB CAKES WITH JALAPEÑO AIOLI ...127
    JALAPEÑO AIOLI ...128
RODRIGO-STYLE FISH (*PESCADO RODRIGO*) ...131
SWEET AND SALTY SALMON ...132
SNAPPER WITH CREAMY ALMOND-CHIPOTLE PESTO ...133
CREAMY POBLANO MAHIMAHI ...134

IF FOOD HAS THE CAPACITY TO TRANSPORT US,

it seems to me that seafood can take us the farthest of all. Cooking fresh fish and shellfish has always felt like a luxury to me, rife with possibilities. The moment I walk into a seafood store, the options sparkle, whether I'm in Washington, D.C., or Mexico City.

My dad and my grandfather, who immigrated to Mexico in the early 1900s, used to rise early on Sunday mornings to go to the old Mercado San Juan, a huge labyrinthian market in Mexico City which sells the freshest seafood—and just about anything else that's edible. They went before dawn so they could procure the biggest, plumpest, freshest shrimp. If I begged enough, they would let me tag along. As we went, my grandfather would tell us the story of how his Polish family survived in the middle of the Eastern European farmland. Salted herring would come from faraway Nordic lands in immense wooden barrels. They pickled the herring and sold them to passersby. On special occasions, they ate the fish themselves, battering and frying them, and serving them with boiled potatoes, bread, and vodka. What a feast!

After hearing that tale so many times, I always feel immensely lucky to be able to choose from so much abundance at my local seafood shop. Seafood is so versatile that it gives you the freedom to travel anywhere you like on Mexico's coast. With shrimp alone, you can visit a breezy beach on the Pacific Coast with a Mexican Shrimp Cocktail, or the Yucatán with Shrimp Croquettes in slightly spicy and rich tomato broth, or southern Mexico with velvety Shrimp in Red Pipián.

In this chapter, you'll find plenty of ideas on how to put a Mexican spin on the gifts from the sea.

CEVICHE TOSTADAS PUERTO VALLARTA

❋ MAKES 10 TOSTADAS ❋ PREPARATION TIME: 15 MINUTES, PLUS MARINATING TIME ❋ CEVICHE CAN BE MADE UP TO 12 HOURS AHEAD, COVERED, AND REFRIGERATED ❋

1 **pound very fresh mackerel fillets or other saltwater fish fillets, such as grouper, halibut, striped bass, red snapper, or fluke, skinned, rinsed, and cut into 1- to 2-inch pieces**

1 **cup peeled and coarsely chopped carrots**

⅔ **cup freshly squeezed lime juice**

1 **jalapeño or serrano chile, halved, seeded if desired, and finely chopped, or to taste**

2 **tablespoons finely chopped white onion**

3 **tablespoons chopped cilantro leaves**

½ **teaspoon dried oregano, preferably Mexican**

1 **teaspoon kosher or coarse sea salt, plus more to taste**

Pinch of freshly ground black pepper, or to taste

10 **tostadas, homemade (page 66) or store-bought**

1 **large ripe tomato, thinly sliced**

1 **ripe Hass avocado, halved, pitted, meat scooped out, and sliced**

Many years ago, I ate a version of this ceviche at the Camino Real Hotel in Puerto Vallarta. At noon, right when the sand was starting to really burn your feet, waiters appeared on the beach, passing ceviche tostadas on big black trays. I loved the tostadas so much I would skip breakfast (very unusual behavior for me) to leave room for them.

As with most ceviches, the fish is marinated in freshly squeezed lime juice, which flavors as well as "cooks" the fish. This recipe is distinguished from other ceviches as the fish is not considered "wet" by Mexicans but called "dry," since it's thoroughly drained after marinating. It's also different because the fish is finely chopped rather than cut into bite-sized pieces.

Two things are crucial: fresh fish and fresh lime juice. Bottled juice won't do.

1. Place the fish fillets and carrots in a food processor and pulse 5 or 6 times, or until the mixture is finely chopped, taking care not to turn it into a puree. Alternatively, mince with a sharp knife.

2. Place the fish mixture in a large bowl, pour the lime juice over it, and gently toss. Cover and marinate at room temperature for 30 to 45 minutes. (The fish will "cook" more quickly in the citrus if it is not refrigerated.)

3. Drain the fish thoroughly in a fine-mesh strainer, pressing out as much liquid as possible with the back of a spoon. Return the fish to the bowl and stir in the chile, onion, cilantro, oregano, salt, and pepper. Mix well. Cover and refrigerate for at least 30 minutes, or up to 12 hours, so all of the flavors come together.

4. When ready to serve, taste the ceviche for salt and add more if necessary. Mound 2 to 3 tablespoons of ceviche on top of each tostada. Top each with a slice or two of tomato and avocado and a final sprinkling of salt.

* MEXICAN COOK'S TRICK: I can't emphasize enough the importance of using fresh, not thawed-from-frozen, fish to make ceviche. Fish loses much of its taste and texture if frozen and thawed and this is especially noticeable in ceviche. Fresh fish has a shelf life of about 3 days, but for ceviche, as fresh as possible is best. Choose your fish wisely. The flesh should be moist and firm; a good, clean saltwater smell is crucial too. The fish should transport you to the ocean—don't settle for less.

SHRIMP COCKTAIL PACÍFICO

∿ CÓCTEL DE CAMARÓN DEL PACÍFICO ∿

∗ SERVES 6 ∗ PREPARATION TIME: 15 MINUTES, PLUS MARINATING TIME ∗ COOKING TIME: 5 MINUTES ∗
CAN BE MADE UP TO 12 HOURS AHEAD, COVERED, AND REFRIGERATED ∗

1 pound medium shrimp,
    peeled and deveined

1 cup ketchup

¾ cup freshly squeezed lime
    juice

1 tablespoon Worcestershire
    sauce

1 teaspoon Maggi sauce (see
    page 211) or soy sauce

2 tablespoons olive oil

¼ cup finely chopped white
    onion

1 jalapeño or serrano chile,
    halved, seeded if desired, and
    finely chopped, or to taste

½ cup coarsely chopped
    pimiento-stuffed olives

½ cup seeded and chopped ripe
    tomato

2 tablespoons chopped fresh
    Italian parsley

2 tablespoons chopped
    cilantro leaves

1 teaspoon dried oregano, pref-
    erably Mexican, or ¼ tea-
    spoon finely chopped fresh

¼ teaspoon kosher or coarse sea
    salt, or to taste

1 ripe Hass avocado, halved,
    pitted, meat scooped out,
    and cubed

Tortilla chips, store-bought
    or homemade (page 66), or
    saltine crackers

Every time I make this dish, I'm transported back to childhood family vacations on the Mexican Pacific Coast. As I spoon it into my mouth, I feel the salty breeze and hear my grandfather shout, *"Bandida!"*—a recurring comment on how fast I could eat a grown-up serving. If only he could see how fast my kids—true *"bandidos"*—eat it.

The shrimp are quickly cooked until just tender, then marinated in a tomato, cilantro, chile, and lime marinade, with a handful of salty green olives for balance. Serve with tortilla chips or saltines.

1. Bring a large pot of salted water to a rolling boil over high heat. Add the shrimp and cook for 1 minute. Immediately drain the shrimp, and let cool.

2. In a large bowl, combine the ketchup, lime juice, Worcestershire sauce, Maggi sauce, and olive oil. Add the shrimp and toss to combine. Add the onion, chile, olives, tomato, parsley, cilantro, oregano, and salt and mix gently until well blended. Cover and refrigerate for at least 30 minutes, or up to 12 hours.

3. When ready to serve, stir the avocado into the shrimp cocktail. Serve with tortilla chips.

∗ MEXICAN COOK'S TRICK: Fresh shrimp are always tastier, but most shrimp is sold frozen or frozen thawed. The good news is that shrimp freezes well and comes out of the thawing process in great shape. However, once thawed, it should be used as soon as possible. Shrimp should look plump and firm and have no "fishy" smell. If you buy them with the shell and tail on, they hold their texture better and you can use the shells to make a lively broth. Thaw frozen shrimp under a stream of cold running water or in the refrigerator—never thaw them with hot water, in the microwave, or at room temperature.

SHRIMP IN RED PIPIÁN

~ CAMARONES EN PIPIÁN ROJO ~

❋ SERVES 6 TO 8 ❋ PREPARATION TIME: 25 MINUTES ❋ COOKING TIME: 1 HOUR ❋ PIPIÁN SAUCE CAN BE MADE UP TO 5 DAYS AHEAD, COVERED, AND REFRIGERATED ❋

Pipián is one variety of Mexico's many mole sauces. A hefty base of toasted and ground pumpkin seeds gives the sauce a velvety edge. This red *pipián*, from the southern states of Mexico, combines pumpkin seeds with peanuts and sesame seeds and then adds a rich layer of charred tomatoes, garlic, and onion along with cloves, cinnamon, and dried mild chiles. The nutty richness is the perfect foil for the briny shrimp.

Serve with Blissful Corn Torte (page 204), My Favorite Green Rice (page 221), or plain white rice.

If you buy shrimp without shells, you can substitute clam juice or water for the shrimp broth.

- **2 pounds medium shrimp, peeled and deveined, shells reserved (see head-note)**
- **2½ teaspoons kosher or coarse sea salt, or to taste**
- **6 guajillo chiles (about 2 ounces), rinsed, stemmed, and seeded**
- **2 ancho chiles (about 1 ounce), rinsed, stemmed, and seeded**
- **½ cup hulled raw pumpkin seeds**
- **3 tablespoons sesame seeds**
- **4 whole cloves**
- **1 pound ripe tomatoes, left whole**
- **3 garlic cloves, unpeeled**
- **1 thick slice white onion**
- **½ cup unsalted roasted peanuts**
- **½ teaspoon ground cinnamon**
- **½ teaspoon freshly ground black pepper**
- **2 teaspoons dark brown sugar**
- **1 tablespoon apple cider vinegar**
- **3 tablespoons vegetable oil**

1. Place the shrimp shells in a large pot, cover generously with water, add ½ teaspoon of the salt, and bring to a simmer over medium heat. Cook for 20 minutes. Strain the broth; discard the shells.

2. Heat a *comal* or a 12-inch skillet over medium-low heat until hot. Lay the chiles flat in the pan and toast them for 10 to 15 seconds per side, until they become fragrant and pliable and their color darkens.

3. Transfer the toasted chiles to a medium saucepan and cover with water. Bring to a simmer over medium heat and cook for 10 minutes. Set aside.

4. Toast the pumpkin seeds in the *comal* or skillet over medium-low heat, stirring often, until you hear popping sounds, like popcorn, and they begin to brown lightly, 3 to 4 minutes; take care not to burn them. Set aside. Add the sesame seeds and toast until light brown, 2 to 3 minutes; set aside. Toast the cloves, stirring often, until they turn darker and are fragrant, 30 to 40 seconds. Set aside.

5. Char the tomatoes, garlic, and onion under the broiler, on the hot *comal*, in a dry skillet, or on an outdoor grill at medium heat (see page 19), turning occasionally, until nicely charred and softened, 10 to 12 minutes. Remove from the heat.

6. When the garlic is cool enough to handle, peel it and place in a blender or food processor along with the tomatoes, onions, and the chiles, with 1 cup of their cooking liquid. Add the pumpkin seeds, sesame seeds, cloves, peanuts, cinnamon, the remaining 2 teaspoons salt, the pepper, brown sugar, and vinegar and puree until smooth.

7. Heat the oil in a large pot over medium heat until hot but not smoking. Add the puree and 4 cups of the shrimp broth and simmer, partially covered, for about 45 minutes, stirring often so the sauce doesn't stick to the bottom, until thickened and deepened in color.

8. Raise the heat to medium-high, add the shrimp, and simmer for 2 to 3 minutes, then turn off the heat. Let the shrimp finish cooking in the sauce, about 5 more minutes, then serve.

SHRIMP CROQUETTES IN TOMATO BROTH

❋ MAKES ABOUT 10 CROQUETTES; SERVES 5 AS MAIN COURSE, 8 TO 10 AS AN APPETIZER ❋ PREPARATION
TIME: 15 MINUTES ❋ COOKING TIME: 50 MINUTES ❋ CROQUETTES AND BROTH CAN BE MADE UP TO 2 HOURS AHEAD ❋

3 tablespoons olive oil

¼ cup chopped white onion

1 garlic clove, minced or
   pressed

1 pound ripe tomatoes,
   chopped

4 cups water

1 serrano or jalapeño chile,
   left whole

2 bay leaves

1½ teaspoons kosher or coarse
   sea salt, or to taste

½ teaspoon freshly ground
   black pepper, or to taste

1 pound shrimp, peeled,
   deveined, and coarsely
   chopped (about 2 cups)

2 tablespoons freshly
   squeezed lime juice

¼ teaspoon ground cumin

½ teaspoon dried oregano,
   preferably Mexican

3 large eggs, separated

1 cup all-purpose flour
   Vegetable oil

Crispy on the outside, fluffy on the inside, and studded with pieces of tender shrimp, these patties are irresistible—especially when you serve them in a slightly spicy tomato broth. Every time I make them, I wonder how something that sounds so fancy, looks so beautiful, and tastes so good can be so easy.

Cumin, judiciously combined with oregano, takes me on a trip to Campeche, a state in the Yucatán Peninsula where I've tasted similar dishes. If you find Mexican oregano, use it. It is stronger, more fragrant, and less sweet than the Mediterranean kind. If you can't find it, Mediterranean works too.

The croquettes can be served as appetizers in a small bowl with broth on top or on their own. If you are having them as a main course, serve them over rice with sauce on top.

1. Heat the olive oil in a medium saucepan over medium-high heat. Add the onion and cook for 4 to 5 minutes, or until soft and translucent. Stir in the garlic and cook until just fragrant, less than a minute. Add the tomatoes and cook, stirring frequently, until the tomatoes break down and thicken, about 10 minutes.

2. Add the water, chile, bay leaves, 1 teaspoon of the salt, and ¼ teaspoon of the pepper and bring to a boil. Reduce the heat to medium and simmer for 12 to 15 minutes, until the broth has thickened slightly but is still soupy. Set aside.

3. Place the shrimp in a medium bowl and add the lime juice, cumin, oregano, the remaining ½ teaspoon salt, and the remaining ¼ teaspoon pepper; toss to combine.

4. In a large bowl, beat the egg whites with an electric mixer at medium speed for about 3 minutes, or until they hold firm peaks. Reduce the speed to low and add the egg yolks, one at a time. Add in the flour ¼ cup at a time, mixing until combined. With a spatula, gently fold in the shrimp and any liquid in the bowl, being careful not to deflate the egg whites.

(recipe continues)

5. Heat ¾ inch of vegetable oil in a large skillet over medium-high heat until hot but not smoking. Test by dropping a bit of batter into the oil—if it bubbles happily around the batter, the oil is ready. Gently drop in heaping tablespoons of the shrimp batter (they can be as large as you want, just make sure not to crowd them in the pan) and fry for about 2 minutes per side, until cooked through and nicely browned and crusty. Drain on paper towels and continue with the rest of the batter.

6. Bring the tomato broth to a simmer in a 12-inch skillet. Fish out the chile and bay leaves. Drop in the shrimp croquettes, turn the heat to low, and simmer until the croquettes are heated through and have absorbed some of the broth, about 2 minutes. Serve.

CRAB CAKES WITH JALAPEÑO AIOLI

❋ MAKES 6 CRAB CAKES ❋ PREPARATION TIME: 15 MINUTES ❋ COOKING TIME: 15 MINUTES ❋ CAKES CAN BE SHAPED UP TO 2 DAYS AHEAD, COVERED, AND REFRIGERATED ❋

1 habanero, jalapeño, or serrano chile, seeded and finely chopped, or to taste

2 teaspoons freshly squeezed lime juice

2 teaspoons chopped cilantro leaves and top part of stems, plus (optional) coarsely chopped leaves for garnish

3 tablespoons dried bread crumbs

1 large egg

2 teaspoons mayonnaise

½ teaspoon kosher or coarse sea salt, or to taste

¼ teaspoon freshly ground black pepper, or to taste

1 pound jumbo lump crabmeat, any shells and cartilage removed and meat broken into smaller pieces

1 tablespoon unsalted butter

1 tablespoon olive oil

Jalapeño Aioli (recipe follows)

1 lime, cut into 6 wedges (optional)

If I had a chance to cook for Moctezuma, the famed Aztec emperor with a reputation for being a ravenous eater, this is what I would serve him. These crab cakes are so perfect I've officially retired all my other versions. Mexican chef Alfredo Solis, a charming man who started as a dishwasher and worked his way up the restaurant ladder to become chef de cuisine at Ceiba in Washington, D.C., devised the recipe. When he decided to add my Snapper with Creamy Almond-Chipotle Pesto (page 133) to his menu, I nabbed his crab cake recipe in return.

1. In a medium bowl, combine the chile, lime juice, cilantro, bread crumbs, egg, mayonnaise, salt, and pepper and mix well. Gently fold in the crabmeat just until blended and the mixture holds together.

2. Shape the crab mixture into six 3-inch-wide cakes about 1 inch thick.

3. Heat the butter and oil in a 12-inch skillet over medium-high heat until the butter begins to foam. Cook in batches, adding only as many crab cakes as will fit without crowding, and cook for 2 to 3 minutes per side, or until lightly browned outside and still moist inside. Transfer to a platter or plates and keep warm in a low (250°F) oven.

4. Sprinkle with cilantro if desired. Top each cake with a dollop or two of the aioli, and serve with the lime, if you like.

❋ MEXICAN COOK'S TRICK: Chef Solis uses habanero chiles, the spiciest of the fresh Mexican chiles, to balance the sweetness of the crab. If you use them, be sure to wash your hands with warm soapy water after handling them—and whatever you do, don't touch your eyes before you do so. If you want less heat, opt for serranos or jalapeños.

JALAPEÑO AIOLI

✳ MAKES A GENEROUS 1 CUP ✳ PREPARATION TIME: 5 MINUTES ✳ CAN BE MADE UP TO 2 DAYS AHEAD, COVERED, AND REFRIGERATED ✳

This punchy aioli is delicious not only with the crab cakes but also spooned on top of grilled fish, alongside Baby Potatoes with Lime and Parsley (page 210), or scooped up with pieces of crusty bread.

1 jalapeño or serrano chile, halved and seeded if desired, or to taste

1 tablespoon freshly squeezed lime juice

1 cup mayonnaise

¼ cup cilantro leaves

¼ teaspoon kosher or coarse sea salt, or to taste

Pinch of freshly ground black pepper, or to taste

Place all the ingredients in a blender or food processor and process until smooth.

RODRIGO-STYLE FISH

∿ PESCADO RODRIGO ∿

✻ SERVES 6 ✻ PREPARATION TIME: 10 MINUTES, PLUS MARINATING TIME ✻ COOKING TIME: 10 MINUTES ✻ SAUCE CAN BE MADE UP TO 24 HOURS AHEAD, COVERED, AND REFRIGERATED (MIX WELL BEFORE USING) ✻

Pescado Rodrigo is a beloved dish in Mexico City, and I make it at least a couple of times a month. Fresh tilapia or other mild white fish, seared until crispy, then drizzled with a chunky citrus sauce, is *the* seafood to stuff into corn tortillas for tacos. This recipe comes from the Bellinghausen, a Mexico City restaurant established in 1915 and cherished by many families, including ours. Its classic hacienda style, complete with tiles and a working fountain, is so dignified that my sisters and I used to dress to the nines to eat there on Sundays. The menu never changes; it doesn't need to.

SAUCE

- ½ cup thinly sliced scallions (white and light green parts only)
- ½ cup chopped cilantro leaves
- ¼ cup freshly squeezed lime juice
- ¼ cup olive oil
- 2 tablespoons seeded (if desired) and chopped jalapeño or serrano chile, or to taste
- 1 tablespoon Maggi sauce (see page 211) or soy sauce
- Kosher or coarse sea salt

- 6 tilapia fillets (about 6 ounces each), or other mild white fish fillets, such as sea bass, grouper, red snapper, or rockfish, rinsed and patted dry
- ¼ teaspoon kosher or coarse sea salt, or to taste
- Pinch of freshly ground black pepper, or to taste
- All-purpose flour
- Vegetable oil
- 12 corn tortillas, store-bought or homemade (page 94), warmed

1. TO MAKE THE SAUCE: In a small bowl, combine the scallions, cilantro, lime juice, olive oil, jalapeño, and Maggi sauce, and stir to mix well. Set aside for at least 15 minutes. Season with salt if necessary to taste before serving.

2. Sprinkle the fish fillets with the salt and pepper. Spread flour on a large plate and coat each fillet thoroughly on both sides.

3. Heat ¼ inch of vegetable oil in a 12-inch skillet over medium-high heat until hot but not smoking. Add the fish, in batches to avoid crowding, and sear for about 3 minutes, until thoroughly browned on the bottom. Don't fiddle with the fillets; let them brown completely so they release easily from the pan. Turn and sear for about 3 minutes on the second side. The fish is ready when the thickest part is cooked through and it flakes easily with a fork. Put the fish on a paper-towel-lined baking sheet and keep warm in a low (250°F) oven.

4. Transfer the fish to a platter and pour the sauce on top. Or you can do as I do and flake the fish and serve it drizzled with the sauce, ready to make tacos. Serve with corn tortillas.

SWEET AND SALTY SALMON

✳ SERVES 6 ✳ PREPARATION TIME: 10 MINUTES, PLUS MARINATING TIME ✳ COOKING TIME: 15 TO 20 MINUTES ✳
MARINADE CAN BE MADE UP TO 24 HOURS AHEAD, COVERED, AND REFRIGERATED ✳

1 cup packed grated *piloncillo* (see page 262) or dark brown sugar

½ cup soy sauce

¼ cup freshly squeezed lime juice

2 tablespoons seeded (if desired) and minced jalapeño or serrano chile

2 tablespoons minced fresh ginger

1 tablespoon minced garlic

¼ teaspoon kosher or coarse sea salt, or to taste

¼ teaspoon freshly ground black pepper, or to taste

6 salmon fillets (about 6 ounces each), rinsed and patted dry

2 tablespoons coarsely chopped cilantro leaves for garnish

2 tablespoons thinly sliced scallions (white and light green parts only) for garnish

A sticky, sweet-sour glaze enrobing tender pieces of salmon makes this dish hard for even the fussiest eater to resist. This dish owes its particular flavor combination to the Spaniards and the trade route to the Americas they began in the 1600s. Those trips, which took as long as seven months, resulted in a fabulous exchange of ingredients. In came Eastern spices like soy sauce and ginger, along with porcelain, china, ivory, and silks, and out went Mexico's spices, cacao, vanilla, chiles, and avocados. Chiles marry so well with soy sauce and ginger that you find that flavor trio not only in Mexico but also in the Far East, where Mexican chiles were introduced.

1. In a medium saucepan, combine the *piloncillo*, soy sauce, lime juice, jalapeño, ginger, garlic, salt, and pepper and cook over medium heat, stirring, for a couple of minutes, just until the *piloncillo* has dissolved. Remove from the heat and let cool.

2. Place the salmon pieces in a baking dish large enough to hold them in a single layer and pour the marinade on top, turning to coat both sides. Cover and refrigerate for at least 30 minutes, or up to 4 hours, spooning the marinade over the fish one or two times.

3. Preheat the oven to 375°F. Remove the fish from the refrigerator at least 10 minutes before cooking.

4. Bake the fish for 15 to 18 minutes, or until it flakes easily with a fork. Place the salmon on individual plates or a serving platter, garnish with the cilantro and scallions, and serve.

✳ MEXICAN COOK'S TRICK: You will do the salmon a favor if you remember to spoon the marinade over it a couple of times while it sits in the refrigerator. Be sure to remove the fish from the refrigerator at least 10 minutes before it goes into the oven. You want it closer to room temperature than completely cold, so it will cook evenly.

SNAPPER WITH CREAMY ALMOND-CHIPOTLE PESTO

* SERVES 6 * PREPARATION TIME: 10 MINUTES, PLUS MARINATING TIME * COOKING TIME: 15 TO 20 MINUTES *
SAUCE CAN BE MADE UP TO 5 DAYS AHEAD, COVERED, AND REFRIGERATED *

Light and delicate, with the tang of cream, the subtle crunch of ground almonds, and the smokiness of chipotles in adobo, this red snapper baked in a creamy pesto is a great way to cook fish of any type. Make extra pesto—it is delicious served as a dip for fresh veggies or spread on crackers. Don't skip the toasted almonds that finish this recipe; you will find that final touch irresistible.

8 red snapper fillets (about 6 ounces each) or other firm, mild-flavored white fish fillets, such as sea bass, grouper, tilapia, or rockfish, rinsed and patted dry

2 tablespoons freshly squeezed lime juice

½ teaspoon kosher or coarse sea salt, or to taste

¼ teaspoon freshly ground black pepper, or to taste

PESTO

1 cup Mexican crema (see page 135), crème fraîche, or heavy cream

½ cup slivered almonds

1 tablespoon freshly grated Parmigiano-Reggiano, Pecorino Romano, or Cotija cheese

1 canned chipotle chile in adobo sauce (optional), plus 1–2 tablespoons adobo sauce, or to taste

½ teaspoon kosher or coarse sea salt

Unsalted butter

⅓ cup slivered almonds, toasted, for garnish

1. Place the fish fillets in a container large enough to hold them in a single layer. Sprinkle with the lime juice, salt, and pepper. Cover and marinate for at least 15 minutes, or up to 2 hours, in the refrigerator.

2. TO MAKE THE PESTO: Combine the cream, almonds, cheese, chile (if using), adobo sauce, and salt in a blender or food processor and puree. The sauce will be slightly grainy because of the almonds.

3. Preheat the oven to 375°F. Butter a large baking dish.

4. Arrange the fillets in a single layer in the baking dish. Spread 2 heaping tablespoons of the pesto over each fillet. Bake for 15 to 20 minutes, or until the fish flakes easily with a fork.

5. Garnish the fish with the toasted slivered almonds and serve.

CREAMY POBLANO MAHIMAHI

❋ SERVES 6 ❋ PREPARATION TIME: 10 MINUTES, PLUS MARINATING TIME ❋ COOKING TIME: 30 MINUTES ❋
SAUCE CAN BE MADE UP TO 3 DAYS AHEAD, COVERED, AND REFRIGERATED ❋

6 mahimahi fillets (about
6 ounces each), or other
firm, mild-flavored white
fish fillets, such as sea
bass, grouper, snook, tilapia, or rockfish, rinsed and
patted dry

2 tablespoons freshly
squeezed lime juice

2 garlic cloves, minced or
pressed

1 teaspoon kosher or coarse
sea salt, or to taste

¼ teaspoon freshly ground
black pepper, or to taste

1 cup Mexican crema (see
opposite page), crème
fraîche, or heavy cream

1 cup whole milk

2–3 poblano chiles (about 8
ounces), seeded and
coarsely chopped

½ teaspoon ground nutmeg

2 tablespoons unsalted butter,
plus more for the baking
dish

3 tablespoons all-purpose flour

1 cup shredded mozzarella
or Monterey Jack cheese
(optional)

2 tablespoons chopped
cilantro leaves for garnish
(optional)

Lime-marinated fish fillets are sauced with a luscious béchamel that is infused with a bit of heat and mesmerizing taste from poblano chiles. The result is an example of the centuries-old intermingling of French influences with traditional Mexican cooking. The pairing of poblanos and dairy is common in Mexican kitchens, and there is a reason why: They bring out the best in one another.

If you want to make this dish even more decadent, sprinkle the top with grated cheese and turn it into a gratin.

1. Place the fish fillets in a container large enough to hold them in a single layer. Sprinkle the lime juice, garlic, ½ teaspoon of the salt, and the pepper on top. Using your hands, rub the mixture all over the fillets. Cover and marinate for at least 15 minutes, or up to 2 hours, in the refrigerator.

2. Pour the cream and milk into a blender or food processor, add the poblanos, nutmeg, and the remaining ½ teaspoon salt, and puree until smooth.

3. Melt the butter in a medium saucepan over medium heat. Stir in the flour and cook, stirring constantly, for 2 to 3 minutes, or until the roux becomes almond brown and bubbles. Reduce the heat to medium-low and gradually add the chile puree, stirring constantly until completely blended and smooth. Simmer gently for 8 to 10 minutes, stirring occasionally; as it simmers, the sauce will thicken slightly around the edges of the saucepan. Remove from the heat.

4. Preheat the oven to 375°F. Butter a baking dish large enough to hold the fish in a single layer.

5. Lift the fish from the marinade with a slotted spatula and place it in the baking dish; discard the marinade. Spoon the

cream sauce generously over the fish. If desired, sprinkle the shredded cheese evenly over the top. Bake until the fish is opaque throughout and flakes easily with a fork, 15 to 20 minutes, depending on the thickness of the fillets.

6. Serve the fish, garnished with the chopped cilantro if desired.

* MEXICAN COOK'S TRICK: This sauce is thickened with a traditional French roux: A small amount of butter is cooked with a bit of flour until it becomes a sturdy thickener, then the milk is stirred in and cooked gently until thickened. As it cooks, it will bubble and its color will begin to darken; stop when it is almond colored. The more you cook it, the more nutty flavor you will add to the sauce. The darker you let the color go, the deeper flavor echo the sauce will have.

Mexican Crema is rich, tangy, slightly salty, and thick, although it is thinner than sour cream. In Mexico it goes by the name *crema fresca,* meaning "fresh cream," and outside big cities it is sold directly from the ranches where it is made. In the United States you can find it in Latin markets and, increasingly, in mainstream grocery stores.

If you can't find Mexican crema, you can substitute any other Latin-style cream, such as Salvadoran. You can also use its French cousin, crème fraîche, which while similar in consistency, is less tangy and salty. Depending on the recipe, you can also substitute sour cream or heavy cream. Generally speaking, for dishes where the cream will be cooked, I recommend heavy cream. For dishes where the cream will be drizzled or spooned on top, sour cream is better.

POULTRY

CHICKEN TINGA ...140

CHICKEN À LA TRASH (*POLLO A LA BASURA*) ...144

CHICKEN ENCHILADAS IN SALSA VERDE
    (*ENCHILADAS VERDES*) ...145

STICKY CHICKEN WITH APRICOTS, TAMARIND, AND CHIPOTLE ...146
    LATIN-STYLE TAMARIND CONCENTRATE OR SYRUP ...147

YELLOW MOLE WITH MASA DUMPLINGS
    (*MOLE AMARILLITO CON CHOCHOYOTES*) ...148
    MEXICAN MASA DUMPLINGS (*CHOCHOYOTES*) ...152

MEXICAN MEATBALLS WITH MINT AND CHIPOTLE
    (*ALBÓNDIGAS CON CHIPOTLE*) ...153

CRISPY CHICKEN MILANESA (*MILANESA DE POLLO*) ...156

SMOKY CHICKEN POTATO SALAD ...159

AZTEC CHICKEN CASSEROLE (*CAZUELA AZTECA*) ...160

MEXICAN THANKSGIVING TURKEY WITH CHORIZO, PECAN, APPLE,
    AND CORN BREAD STUFFING ...164
    CHORIZO, PECAN, APPLE, AND CORN BREAD STUFFING ...167

MY GRANDMOTHER, WHO WE CALLED LALI, came to Mexico from Austria in her early twenties, having survived years of war and the loss of most of her family. She taught my mom an important lesson: You can survive most hardships in life if you know how to cook—especially if you know how to cook chicken from scratch. And she meant from scratch. So my mom learned how to catch, kill, and pluck a chicken and then cook it a thousand different ways.

Lali was an elegant lady who ran her house with the precision of an Austrian watch—she was one of the hardest-working people I've ever known. She was always impeccably dressed in a suit and a freshly ironed shirt, low heels, stockings, and small but sparkly earrings. Eating a bowl of the simplest chicken soup in her home felt dignified.

She came from a long line of extraordinary cooks. Her sister, who had also found her way to Mexico through the Red Cross after surviving the concentration camps in Austria, started what became the most famous bakery in Acapulco from the 1950s through the '70s. Both sisters were steeped in European cooking traditions, but almost as soon as they set foot on Mexican soil, they began building bridges between their native cuisine and that of their adopted land with the greatest pride.

Lali taught me to bridge cultures as well: Just as she learned to adapt her European cooking in Mexico, I learned to tailor my Mexican cooking to the United States. She had an exquisite palate, but even more important than the marriage of seasoning and technique are her lessons that I have taken to heart—learning to cook chicken in a thousand different ways, just as my mom did. I hope this chapter will give you a batch of chicken recipes worthy of your own arsenal.

CHICKEN TINGA

❊ SERVES 6 ❊ PREPARATION TIME: 10 MINUTES ❊ COOKING TIME: 30 MINUTES ❊
CAN BE MADE UP TO 3 DAYS AHEAD, COVERED, AND REFRIGERATED ❊

8 ripe Roma (plum) tomatoes (about 2 pounds)

2–3 tomatillos (about 4 ounces), husks removed, rinsed

3 tablespoons vegetable oil

1 cup chopped white onion

2 garlic cloves, minced or pressed

½ teaspoon dried oregano, preferably Mexican

¼ teaspoon dried marjoram

¼ teaspoon dried thyme

1½ teaspoons kosher or coarse sea salt, or to taste

¼ teaspoon freshly ground black pepper

1 whole canned chipotle chile in adobo sauce (optional), plus 2 tablespoons adobo sauce, or to taste

5 cups shredded cooked chicken (see page 87) or rotisserie chicken

1½ cups broth from Mexican Chicken Broth (page 87) or canned chicken or vegetable broth

Shredded cooked chicken (rotisserie chicken works beautifully) is sauced with a combination of tomatoes, tomatillos, onion, garlic, chipotles in adobo sauce, and spices, all easy ingredients to keep on hand. I usually make a double batch and serve half of it one night with a side of Red Rice (page 224) and Refried Beans (page 220), or with Blissful Corn Torte (page 204) and a salad. Then I have the rest to repurpose over the next few days as a delicious filling for tasty tingadillas, tortas, or a topping for tostadas (see page 142).

1. Place the tomatoes and tomatillos in a medium saucepan, cover with water, bring to a simmer over medium-high heat, and cook for 8 to 10 minutes, or until the tomatoes and tomatillos are soft and mushy but not falling apart. With a slotted spoon, transfer to a blender or food processor. Cool slightly, then blend until smooth.

2. Heat the oil in a 12-inch skillet over medium heat. Add the onion and cook until soft and translucent, 4 to 5 minutes. Add the garlic and cook just until it is fragrant and lightly browned, about 1 minute. Carefully pour the tomato-tomatillo puree into the skillet; it will steam and bubble. Stir in the oregano, marjoram, thyme, salt, and pepper. Add the chipotle chile (if using) and adobo sauce, partially cover the skillet (the sauce will spatter), and simmer, stirring occasionally, until the sauce deepens in color, becomes a darker and earthier red, and is no longer soupy, 10 to 12 minutes; add more adobo sauce and chiles near the end if you want more heat.

3. Add the chicken and broth to the sauce and stir until well mixed. Cook, stirring occasionally, until the chicken has absorbed most of the sauce, 6 to 8 minutes more. Serve hot.

＊ MEXICAN COOK'S TRICK: Don't bother peeling or coring the tomatoes and tomatillos. Simply cook them whole in simmering water, then transfer them to the blender and cool slightly before pureeing.

Chipotles in Adobo Sauce Chipotles are jalapeño chiles that are picked fully ripe and red, so their grassy, fresh, and lively flavors are fully developed. They are left to dry on mats in the sun and smoked to infuse them with an intense aroma and flavor. They are then rehydrated and pickled in a rich adobo sauce made with vinegar, spices (including pureed dried chiles, like ancho), and sometimes tomatoes and brown sugar, or its Mexican equivalent, *piloncillo* (see page 262). They are spicy, sweet, smoky, and totally addictive.

There are many good brands available in the supermarket. My favorites are San Marcos and La Morena, because they aren't overly sweet. La Costeña and Herdez are right behind. Every brand tastes different, so be sure to taste a few to find your favorite. Adding a spoonful to quesadillas, sandwiches, salsas, soups, or stews will lend them an indescribable character.

Many Ways of Eating Chicken Tinga

TOSTADAS Crispy corn tortillas, called tostadas, are a sturdy base for a variety of toppings. Readily available in grocery stores, they can also be made easily at home (see page 66). Think of them as quick, crunchy Mexican pizzas, to be customized at will. Traditionally tostadas start with a layer of refried beans. A heartier topping like meat, chicken, seafood, or potatoes follows, then raw veggies like shredded lettuce and slices of tomato and avocado. Finally the whole thing is crowned with crumbled cheese, thick Mexican crema, and salsa. Chicken Tinga is one of the best tostada toppings I know of.

TINGADILLAS These are more filling and tastier than regular cheese quesadillas. Brush a soft flour tortilla with a bit of oil and lay it on a medium-hot *comal* or griddle, or in a heavy skillet (cast iron is perfect) or even a panini press. Spread some *tinga* on the tortilla and then add a handful of shredded meltable cheese such as Monterey Jack, Muenster, mild cheddar, or mozzarella. Top with another tortilla. When the bottom is golden brown, carefully flip the tingadilla and continue to cook it until the cheese oozes out and the second tortilla is golden and crisp. Cut into triangles and serve with a side of guacamole (page 38) and the salsa of your choice.

TORTAS Mexicans have been making French-style bread since the 1860s, when the emperor Maximilian ruled Mexico under the orders of Napoleon. Maximilian brought dozens of bakers, cheese makers, butchers, and pastry chefs with him from Austria and, as brief as his rule was (only three years), its mark on Mexico's cuisine has remained. Our most popular sandwiches, called tortas, are made with the Mexican version of French baguettes, called *bolillos* or *teleras*. They are similar in texture—crusty and crunchy—but smaller and chubbier. To make a Mexican torta, slather refried beans on one side of a split *bolillo*, *telera*, or chunk of baguette, top with a meaty filling like Chicken Tinga, a thick slice of cheese, hearty slices of avocado and tomato, and Pickled Jalapeños and Carrots (page 34). Tortas are perfect for wrapping and taking on the go.

CHICKEN À LA TRASH

∾ POLLO A LA BASURA ∾

✳ SERVES 6 ✳ PREPARATION TIME: 15 MINUTES ✳ COOKING TIME: 30 MINUTES ✳ CAN BE MADE
A COUPLE OF HOURS AHEAD, COVERED, AND REFRIGERATED ✳

1½ **pounds red potatoes, peeled and cut into ½- to ¾-inch cubes (about 4 cups)**

Kosher or coarse sea salt

¼ **cup hulled raw pumpkin seeds**

¼ **cup raw sunflower seeds**

6 **skinless, boneless chicken breast halves**

Freshly ground black pepper

¼ **cup vegetable oil**

2 **cups coarsely chopped white onions**

3 **garlic cloves, finely chopped**

1 **pound (3–4) poblano chiles, charred, sweated, peeled, stemmed, seeded, and cut into 1-x-½-inch strips (see page 27)**

⅔ **cup coarsely chopped pitted prunes**

⅓ **cup water**

The last time my sister Karen came to visit, she couldn't stop talking about *pollo a la basura*. Apparently Doña Tere, the main cook at the restaurant that Karen runs in Mexico City, had been making it as one of the weekly staff meals for months. It was such a hit that they finally added it to their menu.

The name alone hooked me, and the hook was set as she started describing the wild mix of ingredients. I don't mean to be pushy, but you *must* make this chicken. And don't bother serving it with anything on the side—it doesn't need it.

1. Cook the potatoes in a large saucepan of boiling salted water until tender, about 4 to 5 minutes; drain. Set aside.

2. Meanwhile, heat a small heavy skillet over medium-low heat. Add the pumpkin and sunflower seeds and cook, stirring often and taking care not to burn them, until you hear popping sounds from the pumpkin seeds and all the seeds begin to brown lightly, 4 to 5 minutes. Transfer to a small bowl.

3. Season the chicken with 1 teaspoon salt and pepper to taste. Heat the oil in a 12-inch skillet or casserole over medium-high heat until hot but not smoking. Add the chicken and brown on the first side, about 2 to 3 minutes. Flip the chicken to the other side and add the onions, making some room for them. Cook the onions, stirring often, until completely softened and beginning to brown, 6 to 8 minutes.

4. Add the garlic to the skillet and cook just until fragrant, about 1 minute. Add the poblanos and cook for another 2 to 3 minutes. Add the potatoes, give them a good gentle stir, and then add the prunes. Add ½ teaspoon salt and the water, cover, and cook for 12 to 15 minutes, stirring once or twice, until stewy. Taste for seasoning, adding more salt and pepper if needed.

5. When the chicken is ready, sprinkle the toasted seeds in the pan, gently toss, and serve.

CHICKEN ENCHILADAS IN SALSA VERDE

∾ ENCHILADAS VERDES ∾

* SERVES 6 * PREPARATION TIME: 10 MINUTES * COOKING TIME: 15 MINUTES * CAN BE PREPARED THROUGH STEP 4 A COUPLE OF HOURS AHEAD *

2 recipes Cooked Green Salsa (page 22)

Vegetable oil

12 corn tortillas, store-bought or homemade (page 94)

2 cups shredded cooked chicken (see page 87) or rotisserie chicken

½ cup Mexican crema (see page 135), crème fraîche, or sour cream

½ cup crumbled queso fresco, Cotija, farmer cheese, or mild feta

⅓ cup chopped white onion

* MEXICAN COOK'S TRICK: Enchiladas come two ways in Mexico. The most common are stuffed and rolled tortillas bathed in a salsa, but there is also a simpler version where the tortillas are drenched in a warm salsa, sprinkled with onion, cheese, and cream, and served as a side dish. To make these, skip the chicken and, instead of rolling them up, fold each salsa-dipped tortilla into a half-moon shape. Serve as a side to any grilled meat, seafood, or chicken. Prepared this way, they are the standard accompaniment to *Tampiqueña* (page 188).

Warm, tender corn tortillas stuffed with chicken and drizzled with a sprightly *salsa verde* and tangy Mexican crema are irresistible. I always make double or triple batches of *salsa verde* so I have extra to make enchiladas, one of the quickest and most satisfying meals around. Serve the enchiladas on their own or with a side of rice and beans or a simple green salad.

1. Preheat the oven to 375°F.

2. Heat the salsa in a medium saucepan over medium heat, then reduce the heat to the lowest possible setting and keep warm.

3. Heat ¼ inch of oil in a medium skillet over medium heat until hot but not smoking. The oil is ready if when you dip the edge of a corn tortilla into it, the oil bubbles happily around the edges without going wild. Using tongs, dip the tortillas into the oil one at a time for 10 to 15 seconds per side. The tortillas will first appear to soften, then begin to crisp. Drain the cooked tortillas on paper towels and cover them with aluminum foil or an inverted plate to keep warm. (Alternatively, you can lightly toast them on a well-heated *comal* or in a heavy skillet set over medium heat for 30 seconds per side.)

4. Using tongs, dip a tortilla into the salsa, then place on a plate, spoon 2 to 3 tablespoons chicken on top, and roll up. Place seam side down in a 9-x-13-inch baking dish. Repeat with the remaining tortillas. Cover the enchiladas with the remaining salsa and cover the baking dish tightly with foil.

5. Bake the enchiladas for 15 minutes, or until completely heated through. Drizzle on the cream, sprinkle with the cheese and onion, and serve.

STICKY CHICKEN WITH APRICOTS, TAMARIND, AND CHIPOTLE

✳ SERVES 6 ✳ PREPARATION TIME: 10 MINUTES ✳ COOKING TIME: 45 MINUTES ✳ CAN BE MADE UP TO 3 DAYS AHEAD, COVERED, AND REFRIGERATED ✳

The flavors in this dish are elusive: sweet, bright dried apricots combine with the tangy funk of tamarind and the rich smoke from chipotles in adobo sauce.

Flora Cohen, a wonderful cook of Syrian ancestry, showed me a version of this recipe when I lived in Mexico City. Flora taught cooking classes to clueless-in-the-kitchen brides-to-be to ensure that their husbands wouldn't starve. This recipe was our anchor in my early years of married life, and as our family has grown, I've watched all of my kids lick their plates clean. It's family food of the first order.

Whenever we are invited to a potluck, this is the dish our friends demand, which is lucky, as it can be made ahead, travels well, and reheats easily.

4 chicken thighs plus 4 chicken drumsticks, or one 3- to 4-pound chicken, cut into serving pieces

1½ teaspoons kosher or coarse sea salt, or to taste

½ teaspoon freshly ground black pepper, or to taste

½ cup vegetable oil

4 cups water or chicken broth

8 ounces (about ¾ cup) dried apricots, coarsely chopped

2 tablespoons apricot preserves

¾ cup Latin-style tamarind concentrate or syrup (recipe follows)

1 whole canned chipotle chile in adobo sauce (optional), plus 2 tablespoons adobo sauce

1. Sprinkle the chicken pieces with ¾ teaspoon of the salt and the pepper. Heat the oil in a 12-inch skillet or Dutch oven over medium-high heat until hot but not smoking. Add the chicken pieces skin side down in one layer, cooking them in batches if necessary, and brown for 4 to 5 minutes, or until the skin is crispy and browned. With tongs, flip the chicken pieces to the other side and brown for another 4 to 5 minutes.

2. Pour the water over the chicken and bring to a simmer. Add the apricots, apricot preserves, tamarind concentrate, chipotle chile (if using), adobo sauce, and the remaining ¾ teaspoon salt. Reduce the heat to medium and simmer steadily for 35 to 40 minutes, stirring occasionally, until the sauce thickens enough to coat the back of a wooden spoon.

3. Taste for salt and adobo sauce and adjust to your liking. Serve hot.

✳ MEXICAN COOK'S TRICK: Before sautéing chicken in oil, make sure that you pat chicken pieces completely dry. This will prevent you from being spattered when you add the chicken to the hot oil.

To get beautifully browned chicken, don't try to turn it too soon, or the skin will stick to the skillet. The skin needs to brown and crisp, which will release it from the pan before you flip it to the other side. Give it a good 4 to 5 minutes per side.

LATIN-STYLE TAMARIND CONCENTRATE OR SYRUP

✳ MAKES A GENEROUS 1 CUP ✳ PREPARATION TIME: 5 MINUTES ✳

Place all the ingredients in a bowl and mix until the tamarind and sugar are dissolved. It will keep, refrigerated, for up to 6 months.

3 tablespoons Indian or Middle Eastern tamarind concentrate or paste

½ cup sugar

½ cup boiling water

Tamarind Although tamarind did not originate in Mexico, it has been popular there since the Spaniards brought it from Africa in the 1500s. It has a unique earthy, sour flavor.

Tamarind is most often used as a concentrate to make one of the most popular *aguas frescas,* Mexico's delicious flavored waters, as well as in candies like the unusual and addictive tamarind candy spiced with ground chile, salt, and sugar that we eat like Americans eat cotton candy at the state fair. Over the last few decades, creative cooks have expanded its uses in margaritas (see Tamarind Margaritas, page 274) and in savory dishes like Sticky Chicken with Apricots, Tamarind, and Chipotle (opposite).

Tamarind can be found in Latin and Indian stores and, increasingly, in mainstream grocery stores. However, be warned that ready-made Latin tamarind concentrate, such as Delicia, is very different from Indian versions, such as Tamicon. The Indian kind is only tamarind pulp and is much thicker and paste-like, whereas the Latin version is a combination of tamarind concentrate, water, sugar, and sometimes lime juice. If you can find only Indian tamarind concentrate, you can turn it into a Latin one using the recipe above.

YELLOW MOLE WITH MASA DUMPLINGS

~ MOLE AMARILLITO CON CHOCHOYOTES ~

✳ SERVES 6 TO 8 ✳ PREPARATION TIME: 15 MINUTES ✳ COOKING TIME: 1 HOUR ✳ SAUCE CAN BE MADE UP TO 1 WEEK AHEAD, COVERED, AND REFRIGERATED; CHICKEN AND DUMPLINGS WILL KEEP REFRIGERATED FOR UP TO 3 DAYS ✳

MOLE SAUCE

- 2 ancho chiles, rinsed, stemmed, and seeded
- 2 guajillo chiles, rinsed, stemmed, and seeded
- 1 pound tomatillos (6–8), husks removed, rinsed
- 1 medium ripe tomato
- 4 garlic cloves
- 2 whole cloves
- 1 teaspoon ground cinnamon
- 1 teaspoon dried oregano, preferably Mexican
- 2 teaspoons kosher or coarse sea salt
- ¼ teaspoon freshly ground black pepper
- 3 tablespoons vegetable oil
- ¼ cup chopped white onion
- 5 cups broth from Mexican Chicken Broth (page 87) or canned chicken or vegetable broth
- 3 medium fresh *hoja santa* leaves or 5 dried (see Mexican Cook's Trick, page 150), or 2 cilantro sprigs (optional)

Mexican Masa Dumplings (page 152)

- 3 tablespoons vegetable oil
- 8 chicken breasts, thighs, or drumsticks, or a combination

Kosher or coarse sea salt and freshly ground black pepper

Cooking any one of Mexico's famously delicious moles makes me feel more like I'm in an alchemist's workshop than in a kitchen. This delicious *amarillito*, or "little yellow," mole is a classic. It is easy compared with how laborious some of Mexico's other moles can be—it can be made, as we Mexicans say, "with one hand on your hip." It is light and bright, but despite the fact that it's not actually yellow, the name has stuck.

The dish comes from Oaxaca, a state in southern Mexico known in the culinary world for its many versions of mole. The *chochoyotes,* or dimpled corn masa dumplings, enrich and thicken the sauce, and the dimple in the center of each one holds the sauce like a tasty, fluffy edible spoon.

Serve with a side of Simple Beans from the Pot (page 216).

1. TO MAKE THE SAUCE: Heat a *comal* or large skillet over medium heat until hot. Lay the chiles flat in the pan and toast them for 10 to 15 seconds per side until they become fragrant and pliable and their color darkens. Take care not to let them burn, or they will turn bitter. Remove from the heat.

2. In a medium saucepan, combine the toasted chiles with the tomatillos, tomato, and garlic. Add water to cover and bring to a boil, then reduce the heat to a medium simmer and cook for 10 minutes, or until the tomatillos and tomato are soft. Remove from the heat.

3. With a slotted spoon, transfer the chiles, tomatillos, tomato, and garlic to a blender or food processor and let cool slightly. Add the cloves, cinnamon, oregano, salt, and pepper and puree until smooth.

4. In a large pot, heat the oil over medium-high heat. Add the onion and sauté for 3 to 4 minutes, until soft and translucent. Add the tomatillo puree and cook until it thickens, about 10 minutes, stirring often.

(recipe continues)

Masa is the dough that anchors Mexican cuisine. It can be shaped into a thousand forms and enriched with tasty fats and seasonings to make tamales and dumplings. It's also used as the base of thick hot drinks sweetened with chocolate, nuts, or fruit, called *atoles*.

To make masa, field corn is dried, and the kernels are removed from the cobs, cooked, and soaked in hot water with slaked lime to soften the outer skins. Then the kernels are peeled, rinsed, and ground—an ancient technique called nixtamalization. After nixtamalization, the corn is much easier to grind and will form a smooth and malleable dough. The process also makes the corn much more nutritious and digestible, since it releases niacin and improves the balance of essential amino acids. Moreover, it helps the dough stay fresh longer, so that it doesn't sour.

Some people, especially out in the country, still make their own masa at home, but fortunately we can now buy good-quality nixtamalized corn flour in the grocery store to make our own masa with a stir of the spoon. Corn masa flour is not the same thing as cornmeal. Look for bags of instant corn masa flour, such as Maseca brand.

5. Add the chicken broth and *hoja santa* leaves, if using. Bring to a simmer over medium heat and cook for about 15 minutes. Remove from the heat.

6. Meanwhile, make the masa for the dumplings.

7. In a deep skillet or Dutch oven, heat the 3 tablespoons oil over medium-high heat until hot but not smoking. Sprinkle the chicken pieces with salt and pepper to taste. Working in batches, add the chicken to the pan skin side down and brown on each side for 4 to 5 minutes.

8. Return all the chicken to the pan, pour the mole sauce on top, and bring to a simmer. Reduce the heat to medium-low. Make the dumplings as directed on page 152. One by one, add them to the mole and cook for another 15 minutes, or until the dumplings are cooked through and the mole has thickened enough to coat the back of a wooden spoon. Serve.

✳ MEXICAN COOK'S TRICK: This recipe calls for the herb *hoja santa*; its name means "sacred leaf." The leaves are 3 to 8 inches long, green, and heart-shaped, with a distinctive smell and flavor that reminds me of anise seed. The leaves are found fresh or dried; the dried have a mellower flavor. For this dish, you can use a couple sprigs of cilantro instead, which, although quite different in flavor, complements the sauce nicely and, in fact, is used instead of *hoja santa* in some areas of Oaxaca.

Mexican Moles When people outside Mexico hear the word *mole* (from the Náhuatl word *molli*, meaning "sauce"), many immediately think of chicken bathed in a spicy chocolate sauce. That dish, *mole poblano*, is stupendous but time-consuming. There is a world of other moles out there, and a number of them are very simple to prepare. Moles are sauces that are flavored with a combination of fresh vegetables, such as onion, garlic, tomato, and tomatillo; herbs; and sometimes fruits, nuts, and seeds, and/or a thickener like masa, bread, or tortillas. Mole sauces are served on fish, seafood, and vegetables of all sorts, as well as chicken, turkey, or meat. Their base always includes at least one kind of chile.

All moles have one other thing in common: They should not be rushed. Their ingredients need time to make acquaintance with one another. And the sauces tend to get better with an overnight stay in the refrigerator, which makes pulling the whole dish together the next day a snap.

MEXICAN MASA DUMPLINGS

∿ CHOCHOYOTES ∿

❋ MAKES ABOUT 15 DUMPLINGS ❋ PREPARATION TIME: 10 MINUTES ❋ COOKING TIME: 12 TO 15 MINUTES ❋
MASA CAN BE MADE UP TO 1 HOUR AHEAD AND COVERED ❋

1 **cup instant corn masa flour, such as Maseca**

¾ **cup lukewarm water**

1½ **tablespoons lard or vegetable shortening**

¼ **teaspoon ground cinnamon**

1 **teaspoon kosher or coarse sea salt, or to taste**

½ **teaspoon sugar**

The combination of corn masa, salt, and spices harkens back to Aztec times. This recipe is a great one to make with kids, since forming the dumplings is just like rolling Play-Doh. Use them in other moles as well, or in any hot soup, just as you would noodles.

1. In a large bowl, mix the masa flour with the water, then knead for about 1 minute, until the dough is smooth and free of lumps. Add the lard, cinnamon, salt, and sugar and mix for another minute, until well incorporated and smooth.

2. Roll the dough into 1-inch balls, then, with your little finger, make a dimple in the middle of each dumpling.

3. Keep covered until ready to cook.

MEXICAN MEATBALLS WITH MINT AND CHIPOTLE

∿ ALBÓNDIGAS CON CHIPOTLE ∿

❋ SERVES 6 ❋ PREPARATION TIME: 10 MINUTES ❋ COOKING TIME: 40 MINUTES ❋ CAN BE MADE UP TO 2 DAYS AHEAD, COVERED, AND REFRIGERATED ❋

⅓ cup long- or extra-long-grain white rice (see page 223)

2 pounds ripe tomatoes or 5 cups canned tomato puree

¼ cup coarsely chopped white onion

1–2 chipotle chiles in adobo sauce (optional), plus 1–2 tablespoons adobo sauce

4 garlic cloves

7–8 fresh mint leaves, plus chopped mint for garnish

1½ pounds ground turkey or chicken

2 large eggs, lightly beaten

1 teaspoon kosher or coarse sea salt, or to taste

¼ teaspoon freshly ground black pepper, or to taste

2 tablespoons vegetable oil

1 cup broth from Mexican Chicken Broth (page 87) or canned chicken or vegetable broth

This recipe comes from Julio Torres, a former Mexican taquería cook with whom I work at the Mexican Cultural Institute in Washington, D.C. He makes a killer version of *albóndigas*, which we beg him to make for our staff lunches. The meatballs are fluffy and delicate, with the surprising note of mint paired with smoky chipotle tomato sauce. They are heavenly paired with Simple Beans from the Pot (page 216) and slices of avocado.

1. Cook the rice in boiling salted water for about 6 minutes, or until al dente. Drain and set aside.

2. If using whole tomatoes, place them in a medium saucepan, cover with water, and bring to a simmer over medium-high heat. Simmer for 8 to 10 minutes, or until the tomatoes are softened. Remove with a slotted spoon and place in a blender or food processor, along with ¼ cup of their cooking liquid. Or, if using the tomato puree, pour it into the blender. Add the onion, chipotle chiles (if using), adobo sauce, and 2 of the garlic cloves and puree.

3. Meanwhile, in a *molcajete*, mash the 2 remaining garlic cloves and the mint leaves until roughly pureed. Alternatively, mince together with a sharp knife.

4. In a large bowl, combine the turkey, eggs, rice, mint-garlic puree, ½ teaspoon of the salt, and the pepper. Mix thoroughly with your hands or a spatula.

5. Puree the tomato mixture until smooth. Heat the oil in a Dutch oven or other large pot over medium-high heat. Add the tomato puree and simmer for about 8 minutes, or until it thickens and changes color to a deeper red. Add the chicken broth and the remaining ½ teaspoon salt and reduce the heat to medium-low.

(recipe continues)

6. Set out a small bowl of water. Wet your hands and shape the turkey mixture into 1- to 2-inch meatballs, placing them gently into the simmering liquid as you go.

7. Cover the pot and simmer over medium-low heat for 20 minutes. If you want the sauce to thicken a bit more, which I always do, uncover the pot and let simmer for 10 more minutes. Serve garnished with chopped mint.

---

* MEXICAN COOK'S TRICK: The trick to making these meatballs is to add the rice while it is still slightly undercooked, so it will continue to cook and bind with the rest of the ingredients as the meatballs simmer. Otherwise the meatballs end up mushy rather than fluffy.

A Molcajete, standing on three short legs and often carved into the shape of an animal (most typically a pig), is Mexico's version of the mortar and pestle. The best ones are made of basalt volcanic rock, and they are really heavy—you may incur extra baggage charges if you carry yours home on a plane from Mexico! You can also find them in gourmet shops and Latin markets here in the United States and online.

Beauty and weight aside, a *molcajete* will infuse your kitchen with history, as you now have a tool that has been used for thousands of years. The porous volcanic rock helps the *molcajete* develop a memory of flavors, storing all the essences, oils, and aromas that have passed through it.

If you buy a new *molcajete*, you need to "cure" it by grinding away the rough edges of the bowl, which would otherwise leave grit in your food. There are a few ways to go about curing. Some people grind raw rice, others grind peeled garlic cloves, others use coarse sea or kosher salt; some do a combination. I play it safe and use them all. Work the ingredients over the entire interior surface of the bowl, then give it a quick soapy bath, rinse under cold running water, and start making your own history.

CRISPY CHICKEN MILANESA

∾ MILANESA DE POLLO ∾

* SERVES 6 * PREPARATION TIME: 20 MINUTES * COOKING TIME: 15 MINUTES * BREADED MILANESAS CAN BE LAYERED BETWEEN SHEETS OF PLASTIC WRAP OR PARCHMENT PAPER, COVERED, AND REFRIGERATED FOR UP TO 3 DAYS (OR FROZEN FOR UP TO 3 MONTHS) *

2 large eggs

2 tablespoons milk

1 cup Kellogg's Corn Flake crumbs or dried bread crumbs

½ cup finely crumbled queso fresco, Cotija, ricotta salata, or mild feta

½ teaspoon ground dried chile, such as piquín, or a Mexican mix, such as Tajín, or to taste

¼ teaspoon kosher or coarse sea salt, or to taste

6 boneless, skinless chicken breasts, pounded thin (see page 158)

Vegetable oil

Believe it or not, this Italian-sounding recipe is among Mexico's most popular dishes. The word *Milanesa* refers to beef, pork, veal, or chicken that has been pounded thin, breaded, and fried until deliciously crisp and golden brown. My addition of tangy crumbled cheese gives the breading an extra layer of flavor, and the pinch of ground chile takes the Milanesas a step beyond traditional versions. I could eat *Milanesa de pollo* every day for the rest of my life. My kids feel the same way: I usually prepare a double or triple batch at a time, store them uncooked in the freezer, and pull them out as needed during the week.

Try them with Chipotle Mashed Potatoes (page 212) and Pickled Chayote Salad (page 58).

1. In a large shallow bowl, whisk together the eggs and milk. Combine the corn flakes with the cheese, chile, and salt and spread on a plate.

2. Dip each chicken breast in the egg mixture, then coat it on both sides with the corn flake mixture, so the whole breast is covered. Set aside on a plate.

3. Heat ¼ inch of oil in a 12-inch skillet over medium heat until hot but not smoking, 2 to 3 minutes. Add as many chicken breasts as will fit in a single layer, without crowding the pan. If the edges of the *Milanesas* aren't bubbling in the oil, raise the heat to medium-high. Cook for 2 to 3 minutes on the first side, until golden brown and crisp, then gently flip and repeat on the other side. Remove the *Milanesas* from the pan and set them on a paper-towel-covered plate and keep warm. Repeat with the remaining chicken pieces, adding more oil if

needed. (If you are not serving them immediately, place the *Milanesas* in a baking dish, without the paper towels, and keep warm in a 250°F oven.) Serve hot.

* MEXICAN COOK'S TRICK: The trick to making a good *Milanesa* is to fry it at medium to medium-high heat in oil that has been given ample time to heat up. Let the chicken cook leisurely on the first side, without moving it, until it's crisp and golden on the bottom, then flip it to the other side. If you rush it and pump up the heat, you will end up with burned breading and raw meat. Conversely, if the heat is too low, the breading won't brown and may fall off. The heat is at the right temperature if the oil bubbles when you place the *Milanesas* in the pan and continues to bubble around their edges as they cook. You want medium-sized bubbles, though, not huge angry or barely noticeable ones.

Flattening Chicken Breasts is a satisfying task. One by one, place each chicken breast between two sheets of plastic wrap, parchment paper, or wax paper and pound them with the smooth side of a meat pounder or mallet. You can also use a small heavy skillet to pound them, or even roll them out with a rolling pin, putting pressure on them. You want the breasts to be between ¼ and ½ inch thick.

You can store the pounded chicken breasts in the refrigerator for up to 3 days or in the freezer for up to 3 months. Layer them between sheets of plastic wrap, parchment paper, or wax paper and seal in a plastic bag (be sure to press the air out before you close it).

SMOKY CHICKEN POTATO SALAD

❋ SERVES 6 ❋ PREPARATION TIME: 15 MINUTES ❋ COOKING TIME: 15 MINUTES ❋ CAN BE MADE UP TO 3 DAYS AHEAD, COVERED, AND REFRIGERATED ❋

This salad is a take on a dish my mom used to make. She used cooked chicken from Mexican *Caldo de Pollo* (page 87), but a rotisserie chicken works just as well. My spin on her recipe adds vinegar and chipotles in adobo sauce, which wake up the vegetables and add a smoky flavor.

Serve on hearty slices of toasted bread or use as a filling for sandwiches, tortas, or pitas. My husband loves it on top of shredded lettuce. And I get away with sneaking vegetables into the mix without setting off alarms from my youngest son.

½ cup mayonnaise

½ teaspoon Dijon mustard

1 tablespoon distilled white vinegar or white wine vinegar

1–2 canned chipotle chiles in adobo sauce, seeded if desired and chopped (optional), plus 2 tablespoons adobo sauce

Kosher or coarse sea salt and freshly ground black pepper

1 pound red potatoes, cut into ½- to ¾-inch cubes (about 2½ cups)

8 ounces carrots, peeled, halved lengthwise, and cut into ½-inch-thick slices (about 1½ cups)

1 cup fresh or frozen peas

6 cups shredded cooked chicken (see page 87) or rotisserie chicken

2 tablespoons chopped fresh chives (optional)

1. In a small bowl, combine the mayonnaise, mustard, vinegar, chipotle chiles (if using), adobo sauce, and salt and pepper to taste and mix well. Set aside.

2. Bring a medium saucepan of salted water to a boil. Add the potatoes and cook until tender but still firm, 4 to 5 minutes. Remove with a slotted spoon and place in a large bowl. Add the carrots to the simmering water and cook until tender but still firm, 2 to 3 minutes. Remove with a slotted spoon and place in the bowl with the potatoes. Repeat with the peas, cooking 1 to 2 minutes, and drain.

3. Toss the shredded chicken with the cooked vegetables. Gently mix in the chipotle mayonnaise. Sprinkle with the chives, if using. Serve immediately (I like it best when it's still warm), or let cool and refrigerate until ready to eat.

AZTEC CHICKEN CASSEROLE

∿ CAZUELA AZTECA ∿

✳ SERVES 8 ✳ PREPARATION TIME: 15 MINUTES ✳ COOKING TIME: 45 MINUTES ✳ CAN BE ASSEMBLED UP TO
24 HOURS AHEAD, COVERED, AND REFRIGERATED ✳

SAUCE

- **3 tablespoons vegetable oil**
- **½ cup chopped white onion**
- **2 garlic cloves, minced or pressed**
- **2 pounds ripe tomatoes, pureed, or one 28-ounce can tomato puree or crushed tomatoes**
- **½ teaspoon dried oregano, preferably Mexican**
- **1 bay leaf**
- **1 teaspoon kosher or coarse sea salt, or to taste**

- **3 cups fresh or thawed frozen corn**
- **Vegetable oil**
- **8 corn tortillas, store-bought or homemade (page 94)**
- **3 cups shredded cooked chicken (see page 87) or rotisserie chicken**
- **4 poblano chiles, charred, sweated, peeled, stemmed, seeded, and diced (see page 27)**
- **1 cup Mexican crema (see page 135), crème fraîche, or heavy cream**
- **1½ cups shredded mozzarella, Monterey Jack, or mild white cheddar cheese (about 6 ounces)**

This casserole is essentially a Mexican lasagna made with tortillas rather than pasta. In this version, I've layered crunchy corn and poblano peppers between the tortillas. Dishes like this are popular in Mexico and come with many sauce variations, from moles to green tomatillo or red tomato salsas, like the one used here.

Serve with a quick green salad to lighten it up, or if you want to make it heartier, ladle refried beans alongside.

If I am having a dinner party, I make individual servings by assembling mini casseroles in 5-inch round baking dishes or ramekins—which just happen to be the size of the corn tortillas.

1. TO MAKE THE SAUCE: Heat the oil in a medium saucepan over medium heat. Add the onion and cook, stirring, until soft and translucent, 5 to 6 minutes. Stir in the garlic and cook until fragrant, 30 seconds to 1 minute. Add the tomato puree, oregano, bay leaf, and salt and bring to a simmer, stirring occasionally. Simmer, stirring occasionally, for 8 to 10 minutes, or until the sauce thickens and deepens to a darker red. Remove from the heat and discard the bay leaf.

2. Preheat the oven to 375°F.

3. If using frozen corn, cook it in simmering water for 3 minutes to heat; drain completely and set aside.

4. Heat ¼ inch oil in a medium skillet over medium heat until hot but not smoking. The oil is ready if when you dip the edge of a tortilla into it, it bubbles happily around the edges without going wild. Using tongs, dip the tortillas one at a time in the oil for 10 to 15 seconds per side. The tortilla will first appear to soften and then it will begin to crisp. Drain the cooked tortillas on a paper-towel-lined plate. Alternatively, you can lightly toast the tortillas on a hot *comal* or skillet set over medium heat.

(recipe continues)

5. Spread one third of the tomato sauce in the bottom of a 9-x-13-inch baking dish. Layer 2 cups of the chicken, 2 cups of the corn, half of the poblano chiles, ⅓ cup of the cream, and one third of the cheese on top. Top with a layer of 4 tortillas. Repeat with another one third of the tomato sauce, the remaining chicken, corn, and poblanos, ⅓ cup of the cream, and another one third of the cheese. Top with the remaining 4 tortillas and then the remaining sauce, cream, and cheese. Cover the dish with foil.

6. Bake for 20 minutes, then uncover and bake for 15 to 20 more minutes, or until the cheese is bubbly and lightly browned. Serve hot.

* MEXICAN COOK'S TRICK: When making dishes that include corn tortillas that are bathed in sauce, such as enchiladas or this casserole, it's a good idea to follow the path of most Mexican cooks and first pass them through hot oil: They will become more resilient, will hold the sauce better, and won't crack as you roll, fold, or stack them. Cook the tortillas gently in hot oil until they just begin to crisp, 10 to 15 seconds per side, then drain on paper towels. Alternatively, you can lightly toast them on a hot *comal* or in a heavy skillet over medium heat.

Mexican Thanksgiving Chicken with Chorizo, Pecan, Apple, and Corn Bread Stuffing

MEXICAN THANKSGIVING TURKEY WITH CHORIZO, PECAN, APPLE, AND CORN BREAD STUFFING

❋ SERVES 10 TO 12 ❋ PREPARATION TIME: 20 MINUTES, PLUS MARINATING TIME ❋ COOKING TIME: AT LEAST 4 HOURS, PLUS RESTING TIME ❋ MARINADE CAN BE MADE UP TO A DAY AHEAD, COVERED, AND REFRIGERATED ❋

MARINADE

- 12 garlic cloves, unpeeled
- 6 tablespoons seasoned achiote paste, from a bar (preferably not from a jar; see page 166)
- 4 cups broth from Mexican Chicken Broth (page 87) or canned chicken or vegetable broth
- 4 cups bitter orange juice (see page 166) or a mixture of 1 cup each freshly squeezed orange juice, grapefruit juice, lime juice, and distilled white vinegar
- 1 tablespoon dried oregano, preferably Mexican
- 1 teaspoon ground cumin
- 1 teaspoon ground allspice
- 2 teaspoons kosher or coarse sea salt, or to taste
- 2 teaspoons freshly ground black pepper

I started making this Thanksgiving turkey a decade ago and tweaked the recipe obsessively each year. Then a couple of years ago, my friends told me to stop fiddling, declaring it perfect.

The turkey is marinated and cooked in a paste based on the flavors of the Yucatán Peninsula—charred onions and garlic, bright citrus, and pungent achiote, or annatto seed. It is roasted to crispy succulence, then bundled in mysteriously fragrant banana leaves (increasingly found in the frozen sections of international or Latin supermarkets) and/or aluminum foil for a final cooking that makes the meat so tender it practically falls off the bones.

You can also make this with chicken; see the photo on page 163.

1. TO MAKE THE MARINADE: Place the garlic on a baking sheet or in a broilerproof skillet. Broil, turning halfway through, until the papery skin of the garlic is burned and the cloves soften, about 6 to 9 minutes. Peel. In a blender or food processor, working in two batches, combine the garlic with the achiote paste, chicken broth, bitter orange juice, oregano, cumin, allspice, salt, and pepper and puree until smooth.

2. TO MARINATE THE TURKEY: Slide the turkey, breast side down, into a heavy-duty plastic bag large enough to hold the turkey. Pour the marinade into the bag and massage it into the bird, working it into the cavity and all the crevices. Place the bag in a roasting pan and refrigerate for at least 12 hours, or up to 48 hours, turning the bird a couple of times to redistribute the marinade.

3. Set an oven rack in the lowest position and preheat the oven to 450°F. Butter a baking dish.

4. Spread the onions and tomatoes in a large roasting pan. Set the turkey, breast side up, on top of the vegetables in the pan (reserve the marinade). Stuff the main cavity with as

much stuffing as it can hold. Place the rest of the stuffing in the baking dish; cover and refrigerate. Close the cavity by crossing the legs and tying with butcher's twine. Tuck the wing tips under the turkey. Pour the remaining marinade over the turkey.

TURKEY, STUFFING, AND GRAVY

16- to 18-pound turkey, patted
    dry

    A heavy-duty plastic bag
    large enough to hold the
    turkey

    Unsalted butter for the
    baking dish

4 red onions, sliced

8 ripe tomatoes (about 2
    pounds), coarsely chopped,
    or one 28-ounce can whole
    tomatoes, drained and
    coarsely chopped

    Chorizo, Pecan, Apple,
    and Corn Bread Stuffing
    (page 167)

2–3 banana leaves (optional)

3 tablespoons unsalted butter

3 tablespoons all-purpose
    flour

5. Roast the turkey for 30 minutes.

6. Cover the turkey with the banana leaves, if using. Cover the top of the pan with aluminum foil, sealing it as best as you can. The less steam that escapes, the better. Reduce the oven temperature to 350°F, place the turkey back in the oven, and roast for 3½ hours (or for at least 12 minutes per pound).

7. Remove the turkey from the oven and carefully remove the foil and leaves, being careful, as the steam is hot. The meat should be completely cooked through and nearly falling off the bone. Remove the turkey from the oven and let it rest, loosely covered with aluminum foil, while you make the gravy. Leave the oven on.

8. Meanwhile, strain the cooking juices into a medium saucepan, pressing on the solids with the back of the spoon to get as much liquid as possible; discard the solids. Set aside 1 cup of the liquid for the reserved stuffing. You will make gravy with the rest. Melt the butter in a saucepan over medium heat. Sprinkle the flour on top, mixing well with a wooden spoon, and cook for 3 to 4 minutes, letting it gently bubble, until the roux is golden brown. Add the rest of the liquid and simmer for 12 to 15 minutes, stirring occasionally, until it is a brick color and has thickened to the consistency of light cream.

9. While the sauce thickens, pour the reserved 1 cup liquid over the stuffing in the baking dish and bake for 20 minutes, or until it is hot throughout and the top is crisped.

10. Carve the turkey and serve with the stuffing.

Achiote Paste, or *recado rojo*, is one of the main seasonings of Mexico's Yucatán Peninsula. The word *recado* means "message," and indeed, every paste brings a particular "flavor message" to a dish. In Yucatán cooking, you will find four main pastes: black, or *chilmolé*, made from deeply charred ingredients; green, or pumpkin seed; brown, made from a mix of vinegar, spices, and garlic; and my favorite, the red achiote paste. It's made of charred garlic, bitter orange juice, fresh herbs, spices, and annatto seeds, the hard, brick-red, tiny "pebbles" that impart an appealing lightly metallic flavor. In Mexico they are considered poor man's saffron, since they have a similar pungent flavor and turn everything they touch, including fingers, a vivid yellow-orange.

Most Mexicans buy achiote paste that is already made, and luckily it is now widely available outside of Mexico, in the Latin aisles of markets or online. If you can, get a brand that comes from the Yucatán. Look for achiote paste that is sold in small bars (they are brick colored, about ½ inch thick and 2 to 3 inches long) and not the achiote that is sold in its pure annatto seed form or the wet paste that is sold in jars. Achiote keeps for months stored in the cupboard.

Bitter Orange Juice Bitter oranges are an atypical citrus fruit—ugly and often downright dirty looking—with a sharp flavor that can't be duplicated by ordinary orange juice. Their higher acidity makes them wonderful for marinating and pickling. Since they are hard to find even in Mexico, especially outside of the Yucatán, cooks have been turning to substitutions for decades. After dozens of tests in my kitchen, my magic formula is equal parts grapefruit, orange, and lime juices and distilled white vinegar.

CHORIZO, PECAN, APPLE, AND CORN BREAD STUFFING

✳ SERVES 10 TO 12 ✳ PREPARATION TIME: 20 MINUTES ✳ COOKING TIME: 15 MINUTES ✳ CAN BE MADE UP TO 2 DAYS AHEAD, COVERED, AND REFRIGERATED ✳

This stuffing is so good that there is never a single teaspoon left by the end of the meal.

1 pound Mexican chorizo (see page 219), casings removed, coarsely chopped

1½ white onions, chopped

4 garlic cloves, coarsely chopped

4 celery stalks, thinly sliced (about 1¼ cups)

2 Granny Smith apples, cored and chopped

1 cup coarsely chopped pecans

½ teaspoon dried thyme

½ teaspoon dried marjoram

½ teaspoon kosher or coarse sea salt

1½ pounds corn bread, cubed (about 8 cups)

1½ cups broth from Mexican Chicken Broth (page 87) or canned chicken or vegetable broth

1. Heat a 12-inch skillet over medium heat. Once it is hot, add the chorizo and cook, breaking it up with a wooden spoon or spatula, until browned and crisped, about 5 minutes.

2. Stir in the onions and sauté for 2 to 3 minutes, until softened. Stir in the garlic and cook until fragrant, less than 1 minute. Add the celery, apples, pecans, thyme, marjoram, and salt and cook for 5 to 6 more minutes, until the celery and apples have softened.

3. Scrape the mixture into a large bowl. Toss in the corn bread, pour over the chicken broth, and mix gently with a spatula or large wooden spoon until well combined.

HONEY-CHIPOTLE RIBS ...172

SHREDDED PORK IN ANCHO-ORANGE SAUCE (*CHILORIO*) ...175

PORK TENDERLOIN IN SWEET CITRUS SAUCE ...177

GUAJILLO-SOAKED CRUSTY BREAD STUFFED WITH POTATOES
AND CHORIZO (*PAMBAZOS*) ...179

STEAK TACOS WITH JAMAICA-JALAPEÑO SAUCE ...182

MEXICAN STEAK AND CHEESE IN PITA BREAD (*FAROLADAS*) ...185

ANCHO CHILE BURGERS WITH LIME AIOLI ...186
LIME AIOLI ...187

SPIRAL-CUT BEEF TENDERLOIN (*TAMPIQUEÑA*) ...188

PICADILLO EMPANADAS (*EMPANADAS DE PICADILLO*) ...190
PICADILLO (*PICADILLO DE CARNE*) ...192

BEEF BRISKET IN PASILLA AND TOMATILLO SAUCE (*CARNE ENCHILADA*) ...193

LAMB CHOPS IN GREEN PIPIÁN
(*PIPIÁN VERDE CON COSTILLITAS DE CORDERO*) ...195

IT'S RARE TO FIND A MEAL BASED ON A BIG CUT OF MEAT AT A MEXICAN TABLE. Meat is usually served in equal proportion to the side dishes, pampered with a rub, sauce, or spices, and wrapped up in soft corn tortillas. In those infrequent times when a meal does center around a large cut, such as the Spiral-Cut Beef Tenderloin or *tampiqueña*, the meat is very thinly sliced and served with abundant accompaniments, including saucy green enchiladas drizzled with Mexican crema, refried beans, avocado slices, sometimes a grilled piece of white cheese, charred poblano peppers, and always—always—corn tortillas.

This chapter illustrates just how varied the approaches to meat are in Mexico. Some dishes, like Beef Brisket in Pasilla and Tomatillo Sauce, which comes from the rustic kitchens of Michoacán in central Mexico, speak of different regions. Others, like Shredded Pork in Ancho-Orange Sauce, a signature Mexican cowboy food, arise from particular lifestyles. Still others are the product of cosmopolitan street life, where snacks like Guajillo-Soaked Crusty Bread Stuffed with Potatoes and Chorizo are devoured at midnight.

Modern-day family favorites make their appearance here as well, as in my take on America's barbecue, Honey-Chipotle Ribs, and my mother's Ancho Chile Burgers with Lime Aioli, which have been a birthday-party mainstay for decades. These two dishes remind us that just as Americans are transforming our foods and incorporating them into culture, we are making some traditional American dishes our very own.

HONEY-CHIPOTLE RIBS

⁕ SERVES 4 ⁕ PREPARATION TIME: 15 MINUTES, PLUS MARINATING TIME ⁕ COOKING TIME: 2 HOURS ⁕
SAUCE CAN BE MADE UP TO 1 WEEK AHEAD, COVERED, AND REFRIGERATED ⁕

This is hands-down my kids' favorite rib recipe. They begin lurking around the kitchen about an hour into the cooking, as soon as the fragrance takes over the house. I generally have to stop my youngest son from piling his entire plate full with just ribs, and there are always tears at that injustice. Pork ribs cook beautifully in the oven, and I prefer to cook them that way, since it's such a simple procedure.

You can substitute beef ribs for the pork ribs.

1 cup ketchup

⅔ cup honey

3 canned chipotle chiles in adobo sauce, seeded and minced, or to taste, plus ¼ cup adobo sauce

10 garlic cloves, minced or pressed

2 tablespoons olive oil

¼ cup Dijon mustard

¼ cup apple cider vinegar

2 tablespoons Worcestershire sauce

¼ cup Maggi sauce (see page 211) or soy sauce

2 tablespoons dried oregano, preferably Mexican

1 teaspoon freshly ground black pepper

3 pounds baby back ribs or spareribs

1. In a medium bowl, combine the ketchup, honey, chipotle chiles, adobo sauce, garlic, olive oil, mustard, vinegar, Worcestershire, Maggi sauce, oregano, and pepper. Mix well.

2. Line a large roasting pan with parchment paper or aluminum foil. Pour some sauce into the bottom of the pan, then add the ribs and pour the remaining sauce on top. Cover tightly with foil and marinate for at least 30 minutes, or up to 24 hours; if marinating for more than 30 minutes, refrigerate the ribs.

3. Preheat the oven to 350°F.

4. Roast the ribs, covered, for 1½ hours.

5. Remove the pan from the oven and carefully remove the aluminum foil, taking care not to get burned by the steam. Spoon the thickened sauce from the bottom of the pan on top of the ribs and roast, uncovered, for 30 minutes more, or until they are beautifully browned and sticky. Remove from the oven and let rest for 10 minutes.

6. Slice the ribs into 2- to 3-bone pieces and serve.

SHREDDED PORK IN ANCHO-ORANGE SAUCE

∾ CHILORIO ∾

❋ SERVES 8 ❋ PREPARATION TIME: 25 MINUTES ❋ COOKING TIME: 1 HOUR AND 20 MINUTES ❋ CAN BE MADE UP
TO 5 DAYS AHEAD, COVERED, AND REFRIGERATED ❋

3 **pounds boneless pork butt
(shoulder) or loin, preferably with some fat, cut
into 2-inch chunks**

1¼ **cups freshly squeezed
orange juice**

1¼ **cups water**

1¼ **teaspoons kosher or coarse
sea salt, or more to taste**

4 **ancho chiles (2 ounces),
rinsed, stemmed, and
seeded**

½ **cup coarsely chopped white
onion**

4 **garlic cloves**

½ **cup chopped fresh Italian
parsley**

1 **teaspoon dried oregano,
preferably Mexican**

¼ **teaspoon ground cumin**

¼ **teaspoon freshly ground
black pepper, or to taste**

⅔ **cup apple cider vinegar**

3 **tablespoons vegetable oil**

16 **flour tortillas, warmed**

Chilorio, pork cooked in orange juice until it's falling-apart tender and then finished in an ancho chile sauce, is a specialty of the northern state of Sinaloa. It is probably the region's most popular dish: Home cooks make it weekly, it's on the menu of nearly every restaurant, and it's sold ready-made in markets. It's so popular, it has even crossed borders sold in cans (it is, of course, infinitely tastier when made at home).

Chilorio can be refashioned in many ways and, like many stewed meats, is even better after reheating. Serve it northern-Mexican style, with flour tortillas. The stuffed tortillas are called *burritas*, which are different from the U.S. burritos in that they are made with nothing other than the meat inside; anything else is on the side. I always accompany it with Chunky Guacamole (page 38).

1. Place the pork in a heavy 12-inch skillet or Dutch oven. Add the orange juice, water, and 1 teaspoon of the salt and bring to a boil over high heat. Reduce the heat to medium and simmer for 40 to 45 minutes, or until most of the liquid has cooked away and the meat is lightly browned and has rendered most of its fat. Set aside to cool.

2. Meanwhile, place the chiles in a bowl, cover with hot water, and soak for 10 to 15 minutes, until softened.

3. Place the chiles, along with 1½ cups of their soaking liquid, in a blender or food processor, along with the onion, garlic, parsley, oregano, cumin, the remaining ¼ teaspoon salt, the pepper, and vinegar and puree until completely smooth.

4. When it is cool enough to handle, shred the pork with your hands or two forks and place it and any juices in a large bowl.

(recipe continues)

5. In the pot in which the meat was cooked, heat the oil over medium heat. Pour in the chile puree, bring to a simmer, and simmer for 8 to 10 minutes, stirring often, until thickened and darkened. Toss in the shredded meat and juices and cook until the meat has absorbed most of the chile sauce, 20 to 25 minutes. Taste for salt.

6. Serve the meat rolled up in the warm flour tortillas or with the tortillas on the side.

* MEXICAN COOK'S TRICK: Although *chilorio* is traditionally made with pork, you can also make it with chicken breasts, legs, and/or thighs. Be sure to use chicken with skin and bones for the most flavor.

Corn Versus Flour Tortillas One of my favorite Mexican sayings is "The table is empty without corn tortillas." We mop sauces off plates with them; use them as the base for tacos, quesadillas, tostadas, and enchiladas; and fry them to turn them into crispy scoops.

Flour tortillas are not as ubiquitous in Mexico as corn tortillas. Though they appear throughout the country in such dishes as quesadillas and burritos, they are most common in the northern part—and across the border in the United States. Whereas corn tortillas are sturdy and earthy in flavor and fat free, flour tortillas have a mellow sweetness, since they are made with all-purpose flour and quite a bit of fat, be it lard or vegetable shortening. Mexicans rarely fry or crisp flour tortillas, and they are not used in dishes like enchiladas or chilaquiles, because they are not sturdy or resilient enough to hold the sauce.

PORK TENDERLOIN IN SWEET CITRUS SAUCE

❋ SERVES 8 TO 10 ❋ PREPARATION TIME: 10 MINUTES ❋ COOKING TIME: 1 HOUR AND 35 MINUTES ❋ MARINADE CAN BE MADE UP TO 24 HOURS AHEAD, COVERED, AND REFRIGERATED ❋

MARINADE

1 cup freshly squeezed orange juice

¼ cup freshly squeezed lime juice

¼ cup apple cider vinegar

1 cup packed grated *piloncillo* (see page 262) or dark brown sugar

5 garlic cloves, minced or pressed

5 bay leaves

3 banana leaves (optional; see page 178)

3 tablespoons olive oil

1½ teaspoons kosher or coarse sea salt, or to taste

½ teaspoon freshly ground black pepper, or to taste

4 pounds pork tenderloins (2–3)

In this recipe, pork tenderloin is quickly browned, soaked in a citrus and *piloncillo* (or brown sugar) marinade, wrapped in fragrant banana leaves (or foil), and roasted in a jungle-like steam bath. The grassy, tropical flavors of the leaves infuse the pork, and then, while the meat rests, the marinade is simmered down to a rich, tangy sauce.

Trust me, this is a dish you'll want to try. Enjoy it with a side of Chipotle Mashed Potatoes (page 212) or Blissful Corn Torte (page 204) and Everyday Green Salad (page 44). If you have any leftovers, you'll win the prize for the tastiest filling for a torta (sandwich).

1. TO MAKE THE MARINADE: Mix together the orange and lime juices, vinegar, *piloncillo*, garlic, and bay leaves in a bowl.

2. Preheat the oven to 350°F.

3. If using the banana leaves, layer them in a large baking dish: Place the first one lengthwise so it covers the whole dish, leaving the ends hanging over the dish on both ends. Place the second leaf crosswise so it covers half or so of the dish and the third one crosswise over the other half of the dish, with the sides hanging over the dish on both ends.

4. Heat the oil in a 12-inch heavy skillet or Dutch oven over high heat. Sprinkle the salt and pepper over the pork tenderloins. Once the oil is hot, place the tenderloins in the skillet and brown for about 2 minutes on each side, using a pair of tongs to turn them. Remove from the skillet and place in the middle of the baking dish. Pour the marinade over the top, then lift the meat to make sure the marinade coats the bottom as well. Cover the meat with the banana leaves, if you have them; if not, cover tightly with aluminum foil.

(recipe continues)

5. Place the pork in the oven and cook for 1 hour and 20 minutes, or until the marinade has thickened and the pork slices easily. Remove it from the oven and carefully open the banana leaves or foil. Transfer the meat to a cutting board and allow to rest, loosely covered with one of the banana leaves or foil while you reduce the sauce.

6. Pour the marinade into a medium saucepan. Discard the bay leaves, bring the marinade to a simmer over medium-high heat, and simmer for 10 to 15 minutes, or until it coats the back of a spoon.

7. Slice the meat into ½-inch-thick slices and serve with the sauce drizzled over the top. Pass the extra sauce in a bowl at the table.

Banana Leaves are one of the most sensuous of Mexican ingredients. Though not edible on their own, they are used as a wrapper to cook many things, including tamales, meats, fish, and poultry, and they lend an intense jungle fragrance to everything they touch. Cooking in banana leaves concentrates the flavors of the wrapped ingredients and helps keep them moist. The leaves are pliable yet very strong and resistant to intense heat, smoke, or steam—and they freeze well.

Banana leaves are a beautiful deep green. You buy them folded, and they can be up to ten feet long. You can find them in plastic bags in the freezer section of Latin and ethnic markets and some supermarkets. They will keep in your freezer, well sealed, for at least a year.

GUAJILLO-SOAKED CRUSTY BREAD STUFFED WITH POTATOES AND CHORIZO

∾ PAMBAZOS ∾

❋ SERVES 8 TO 10 ❋ PREPARATION TIME: 25 MINUTES ❋ COOKING TIME: 35 MINUTES ❋ FILLING AND SALSA CAN BE MADE UP TO 4 DAYS AHEAD, COVERED, AND REFRIGERATED ❋

Imagine the most outrageous and gloriously messy sandwich— the very essence of Mexican street food: Crusty rolls are soaked in a guajillo chile sauce and sizzled on a griddle until they crisp. Then they are slathered with refried beans, stuffed with a mixture of potato and chorizo, topped with dressed shredded lettuce, and drizzled with Mexican crema and crumbled fresh cheese. Too much? No, never, ever enough.

FILLING

- 2 **pounds red potatoes (about 4 medium), peeled and cubed**
- 1 **pound raw Mexican-style chorizo, Latin-style chorizo, or spicy Italian sausage, casings removed, chopped**
- 1 **cup coarsely chopped white onion**

  Kosher or coarse sea salt and freshly ground black pepper

SAUCE

- 8 **guajillo chiles, rinsed, stemmed, and seeded**
- ¼ **cup coarsely chopped white onion**
- 1 **garlic clove**
- 1 **teaspoon kosher or coarse sea salt**

1. TO MAKE THE FILLING: Put the potatoes in a medium saucepan, cover with salted water, bring to a boil, and cook until tender, about 8 to 10 minutes. Drain.

2. Meanwhile, heat a large skillet over medium-high heat. Add the chorizo and cook for about 5 minutes, breaking it up into small pieces with a wooden spoon. When it begins to brown, add the onion and cook for 2 to 3 minutes, until the onion has softened and the chorizo is cooked through and browned.

3. Add the potatoes and roughly crush them with a fork or potato masher until mashed but still somewhat chunky. Season to taste with salt and pepper. Set aside.

4. TO MAKE THE SAUCE: Heat a *comal* or large skillet over medium heat until hot. Lay the chiles flat in the pan and toast them for 10 to 15 seconds per side, until they become fragrant and pliable and their color darkens.

5. Transfer the chiles to a medium saucepan and add the onion and garlic. Cover with water, bring to a boil over medium-high heat, and simmer for about 15 minutes, or until the chiles have rehydrated and softened.

6. Transfer the chiles, onion, and garlic to a blender, along with ¼ cup of the cooking liquid and the salt; puree until smooth. Strain the sauce through a colander or strainer into a bowl and set aside.

(recipe continues)

1 **head romaine lettuce, separated into leaves, rinsed,
dried, and thinly sliced
crosswise**

5 **tablespoons olive oil**

2 **tablespoons distilled white
vinegar**

 **Kosher or coarse sea salt
and freshly ground black
pepper**

 Pinch of sugar

 Vegetable oil

8–10 **sturdy buns, such as hard
rolls, *bolillos*, *teleras*,
Portuguese buns, or 3-
to 4-inch-long pieces
baguette**

1 **cup refried beans, homemade (page 220) or store-
bought**

1 **cup Mexican crema (see
page 135), crème fraîche,
or sour cream**

1 **cup crumbled queso fresco,
Cotija, farmer cheese, or
mild feta (about 4 ounces)**

7. Place the lettuce in a large bowl. Add the oil, vinegar, a
sprinkle of salt and pepper, and the sugar and toss until well
combined.

8. TO ASSEMBLE THE PAMBAZOS: Brush a 12-inch *comal*,
skillet, or griddle liberally with oil and set over medium heat.
Working in batches, dip each roll or piece of bread into the
guajillo sauce, turning until completely covered; don't cut
them open. Add to the hot pan and fry, turning once, until
lightly browned on both sides and hot. Remove to individual
plates and split each one in half. Spread the bottoms with
a layer of refried beans, then cover with a generous amount
of the potato-chorizo filling. Top with the dressed lettuce, a
drizzle of cream, and a sprinkle of crumbled cheese, then
cover with the other halves of the rolls (or bread). Serve with
lots of napkins.

❋ MEXICAN COOK'S TRICK: The traditional *pambazo* is made with *pan
basso*, a bread that's been made since Mexico was a Spanish colony.
It is toothier than the typical Mexican *bolillo* or *telera* (the Mexican-
style baguette). *Pan bassos* can be hard to find, but *pambazos* are just
as wonderful when made with any bread that can stand up to being
soaked, crisped, and stuffed.

STEAK TACOS WITH JAMAICA-JALAPEÑO SAUCE

✳ MAKES 12 TACOS; SERVES 6 ✳ PREPARATION TIME: 5 MINUTES, PLUS MARINATING TIME ✳
COOKING TIME: 40 MINUTES ✳

MARINADE

- **2 cups Jamaica Flower Concentrate (page 270)**
- **2 bay leaves**
- **3 whole cloves**
- **¾ teaspoon kosher or coarse sea salt, or to taste**
- **¼ teaspoon freshly ground black pepper, or to taste**

- **1 1½-pound flank steak**
- **1 jalapeño or serrano chile, halved and seeded, or to taste**
- **Vegetable oil**
- **Kosher or coarse sea salt and freshly ground black pepper**
- **12 corn tortillas, store-bought or homemade (page 94), warmed**
- **1 ripe Hass avocado, halved, pitted, meat scooped out, and sliced**
- **½ cup crumbled queso fresco, Cotija, farmer cheese, or mild feta**

Flank steak, known in Mexico as *arrachera*, is packed with flavor and stands up to the strongest of marinades. Although it is typical to tenderize tough cuts of meat in acidic marinades made with wine, vinegar, or citrus, in my kitchen experiments, I've found that a *Jamaica* flower concentrate works just as well, infusing the meat with a delicious, flowery flavor. I punch it up with cloves, bay leaves, and jalapeño chiles.

As the meat cooks, the sugars in the marinade create a beautifully charred crust. The slices of steak are irresistible when slipped into fresh tortillas and finished with avocado and tangy queso fresco.

1. TO MAKE THE MARINADE: Place the *Jamaica* concentrate, bay leaves, cloves, salt, and pepper in a medium saucepan, bring to a boil over medium-high heat, and then simmer until reduced by half, about 15 minutes. Remove from the heat and let cool.

2. Place the flank steak in a baking dish big enough so that it can lie flat. Pour the cooled marinade over the steak, cover, and refrigerate for at least 2 hours, or up to 48 hours.

3. When ready to cook, remove the meat from the refrigerator. Pour the marinade into a medium saucepan and bring to a simmer over medium-high heat. Add the jalapeño, reduce the heat, and simmer until the sauce is thick enough to coat the back of a spoon, about 15 minutes. Pour into a heatproof bowl and set aside (the sauce will thicken considerably as it cools).

(recipe continues)

Jamaica (Hibiscus) Flowers Mexicans love the tangy, vibrant flavor of the dried hibiscus flowers called *Jamaica*. Not just any hibiscus, these are the flowers of *Hibiscus sabdariffa*, also known as Jamaican red sorrel. Hibiscus flowers are reminiscent of rose hips (think Red Zinger tea) and are packed with just as much vitamin C. In Mexico pregnant women drink *Jamaica* to help reduce water retention and soothe digestion.

The deep red, nearly purple flowers are quite tough and are essentially flavorless until they are soaked or simmered to release their tart flavor into the soaking or simmering liquid, which turns a beautiful vivid red. They are also sometimes fried.

In Mexico *Jamaica* traditionally shows up in teas or in intense concentrates that are turned into ice pops, sorbets, or *aguas frescas*, "fruit waters" (see page 268). Modern cooks are becoming more adventurous with *Jamaica*, coming up with all kinds of delectable ways to use it. See, for example, Jamaica Vinaigrette (page 48) and Steak Tacos with Jamaica-Jalapeño Sauce (opposite).

4. Brush a grill pan or 12-inch heavy skillet with oil and set over medium-high heat until hot. Sprinkle the meat with salt and pepper to taste and grill for 5 minutes per side for medium-rare. Alternatively, preheat the broiler, place the meat on a baking sheet, and broil for 5 to 6 minutes per side for medium-rare. Transfer to a cutting board and let rest for 5 to 10 minutes, loosely covered with foil.

5. Thinly slice the steak across the grain. For each taco, place a couple slices of meat in the center of a warmed corn tortilla, add a slice of avocado and some queso fresco, and drizzle with the sauce.

------

* MEXICAN COOK'S TRICK: I like flank steak that is on the thinner side, with some fat, so that as the meat cooks, the fat melts into the meat and helps it brown. The thinness also makes the meat cook more quickly and better absorb the marinade.

MEXICAN STEAK AND CHEESE IN PITA BREAD

∾ FAROLADAS ∾

✳ SERVES 4 ✳ PREPARATION TIME: 5 MINUTES ✳ COOKING TIME: 15 MINUTES ✳

12 ounces skirt steak

Kosher or coarse sea salt and freshly ground black pepper

2 tablespoons vegetable oil

4 pita breads

2 cups shredded Monterey Jack, mild cheddar, Muenster, or mozzarella cheese (about 8 ounces)

Reminiscent of a Philly cheesesteak sandwich, but stuffed into a pita (which has been at home in Mexico for the past couple of centuries) and grilled to oozing decadence, *farolada* is a genius creation from El Farolito Taquería in Mexico City.

The skirt steak cooks in only 5 minutes, so you can have a sumptuous meal ready in about 15 minutes. Serve with slices of ripe avocado and Charred Tomato Salsa (page 18), which bring out the smoky, rustic taste of the seared meat.

1. Cut the steak into 4 pieces and sprinkle with salt and pepper to taste.

2. Heat the oil in a large skillet or grill pan over medium-high heat until hot but not smoking. Add the steak and cook for about 2 minutes per side, or until browned. Remove from the heat and let rest for at least 5 minutes.

3. Thinly slice the meat across the grain, then cut into small bite-sized pieces. Set aside.

4. Heat a *comal*, griddle, or large skillet over medium heat. Heat the pita breads for about 1 minute per side, so that they are easy to open. Cut them in half to make pockets.

5. Stuff each pocket with some of the shredded cheese, meat, and then a bit more cheese. Be generous, and don't worry if some of the meat or cheese falls out of the pockets. Place the pitas on the hot *comal* and cook until they are lightly browned and crisp and the cheese begins to ooze out. Then do what I do: Let that oozing cheese get crispy and brown too. Serve immediately.

✳ MEXICAN COOK'S TRICK: At El Farolito, cooks use Mexican-style double Manchego, a high-fat, ultracreamy cheese. Here Monterey Jack comes close, but you can use any cheese that melts well.

ANCHO CHILE BURGERS WITH LIME AIOLI

❋ SERVES 8 TO 10 ❋ PREPARATION TIME: 20 MINUTES ❋ COOKING TIME: 10 TO 12 MINUTES ❋ MEAT MIXTURE CAN BE SEASONED UP TO 24 HOURS AHEAD OF TIME, COVERED, AND REFRIGERATED ❋

4 **ancho chiles (2 ounces), rinsed, stemmed, and seeded**

1 **cup coarsely chopped white onion**

3 **garlic cloves**

1½ **pounds ground beef**

1½ **pounds ground veal**

2 **large eggs, lightly beaten**

1½ **teaspoons kosher or coarse sea salt, or to taste**

½ **teaspoon freshly ground black pepper, or to taste**

Vegetable oil

8–10 **slices Monterey Jack, mild cheddar, Muenster, or mozzarella cheese (optional)**

8–10 **hamburger buns**

Lime Aioli (recipe follows)

People outside Mexico often don't realize how much Mexicans love American food. Hamburgers and hot dogs are a street-food staple in the tiniest of towns as well as in the big-city plazas. Just as some Mexican foods took on a new spin after they landed in the United States, American dishes often take on a life of their own once they've arrived south of the border.

Smoky, juicy, and robust, these ancho chile burgers have been in my family for almost forty years. The ancho chile seasoning paste doesn't overwhelm the beefy taste, but instead makes the flavors stand up tall. The lime aioli provides just the right finishing touch.

1. Place the chiles in a small bowl and cover with boiling water. Let soak for 10 to 15 minutes, until softened.

2. Lift the chiles from the water with a slotted spoon and place them in a blender, along with ¼ cup of the soaking liquid, the onion, and garlic; puree until smooth.

3. In a large bowl, combine the ground beef and veal. Add the chile mixture, eggs, salt, and pepper. Mix with a fork or spatula until well combined. Shape the meat into 8 to 10 patties.

4. Brush a grill grate or a 12-inch skillet with oil and heat over medium heat until very hot. Add the patties (cooking in batches if using the skillet), and cook for 4 to 6 minutes per side, depending on how well cooked you like them: I like mine medium, about 5 minutes per side. If using cheese, top each patty with a slice of the cheese after you flip them to the second side. When they are cooked, slip the patties into the buns and serve with the aioli.

❋ MEXICAN COOK'S TRICK: You can use any kind of ground meat you like. The veal lends a gentle quality to the patties both in flavor and texture. I sometimes make the patties with equal amounts of pork, veal, and beef, as does my mom.

LIME AIOLI

✳ MAKES A GENEROUS 1 CUP ✳ PREPARATION TIME: 5 MINUTES ✳ CAN BE MADE UP TO 2 DAYS AHEAD, COVERED, AND REFRIGERATED ✳

You'll find all kinds of uses for this aioli: as a spread on other sandwiches, in tuna salad, or on top of halves of hard-boiled egg.

1 cup mayonnaise

1 teaspoon grated lime zest

2 tablespoons freshly squeezed lime juice

3 garlic cloves, minced or pressed

1 teaspoon kosher or coarse sea salt, or to taste

¼ teaspoon freshly ground black pepper, or to taste

Combine all the ingredients in a small bowl. Serve or refrigerate.

SPIRAL-CUT BEEF TENDERLOIN

∾ TAMPIQUEÑA ∾

❋ SERVES 6 ❋ PREPARATION TIME: 10 MINUTES ❋ COOKING TIME: 12 MINUTES ❋

1 **2-pound center-cut beef tenderloin roast, cut into
6 equal pieces**

**2 tablespoons freshly
squeezed lime juice**

**2 garlic cloves, minced or
pressed**

**Kosher or coarse sea salt
and freshly ground black
pepper**

Vegetable oil

This spectacular beef tenderloin dish was created by the restaurateur José Ines Loredo, who opened the Tampico Club in Mexico City. Now you can eat it nearly everywhere in Mexico.

The recipe is quite simple: Sprinkle lime juice, garlic, salt, and pepper onto thin slices of meat that you cut by unfurling a chunk of tenderloin with a sharp knife so it resembles a fruit roll-up. The *tampiqueña* is then cooked. Don't be intimidated, as it is quite fun to do, and the results are delicious, not to mention fast. You can have dinner on the table in 20 minutes.

Tampiqueña is traditionally served as part of a combo-style platter with Refried Beans (page 220), Creamy Poblano Rajas (page 209), a couple of *Enchiladas Verdes* (page 145), avocado, and sometimes a slice of grilled sturdy white cheese.

1. Stand 1 piece of beef on edge and, with a sharp knife, make a cut about ¼ inch deep into the top of the meat, then cut around the circumference of the piece to make a ¼-inch-thick strip of beef. Continue cutting in the same way, stopping to turn the meat when you need to, until you have a long ¼-inch-thick strip of meat; the length will vary depending on the thickness of the tenderloin. When you stop to turn the beef, you will get a slight zigzag pattern in the meat, which is what you want. If the piece of tenderloin was thick and you end up with a very long strip, you may want to cut it into 2 pieces. Continue with the rest of the pieces.

2. Sprinkle the strips of meat on both sides with the lime juice, garlic, and salt and pepper to taste.

3. Lightly brush a *comal*, large griddle, grill pan, grill grate, or 12-inch skillet with oil, and heat over medium-high heat until very hot but not smoking. Add the meat, in batches if necessary, and cook for about 2 minutes per side, or to your liking. It should take a total of 3 minutes for medium-rare, 6 minutes for well-done. Serve.

PICADILLO EMPANADAS

∾ EMPANADAS DE PICADILLO ∾

❋ MAKES 12 TO 14 MEDIUM EMPANADAS ❋ PREPARATION TIME: 20 MINUTES, PLUS RESTING TIME ❋ COOKING TIME: 20 TO 25 MINUTES ❋ DOUGH CAN BE MADE UP TO 24 HOURS AHEAD, COVERED, AND REFRIGERATED; UNCOOKED EMPANADAS CAN BE COVERED AND REFRIGERATED FOR UP TO 4 DAYS OR FROZEN FOR UP TO 6 MONTHS ❋

½ **pound (2 sticks) unsalted butter, at room temperature, plus more for the baking sheets**

8 **ounces cream cheese, at room temperature**

2⅓ **cups all-purpose flour, plus more for dusting**

½ **teaspoon kosher or coarse sea salt**

Picadillo (recipe follows)

1 **large egg, lightly beaten**

½ **cup sesame seeds**

❋ MEXICAN COOK'S TRICK: Once you've assembled the empanadas, you can place them on baking sheets and freeze. Once they are frozen, store them in plastic bags in the freezer, then take them out as you need them. Thaw for 10 minutes at room temperature before baking.

The nuns from the Mexican convent of Our Lady of the Immaculate Conception get the credit for these empanadas. When they arrived in Mexico City from Spain around the 1540s, they began combining Spanish and Mexican ingredients in their kitchens with great passion. Their cooking instincts were led in part by a sweet tooth, which may explain the exotic flavors in these savory pastries. The balance of spices and olives paired with the delicate sweetness of the dough make it hard not to eat one after the other.

1. In a large bowl, beat the butter and cream cheese with an electric mixer at medium speed until creamy, 4 to 5 minutes. Add the flour and salt and mix for 1 minute more. Turn the dough out onto a lightly floured surface and knead until smooth and elastic, about 1 minute. Form the dough into a ball, wrap in plastic wrap, and refrigerate for at least 15 minutes, or up to 24 hours.

2. When you are ready to make the empanadas, preheat the oven to 375°F with racks in the upper and lower thirds. Butter two baking sheets.

3. Sprinkle flour over the countertop. Divide the dough in half and roll out half the dough ¼ inch thick. Using a cookie cutter or a glass, cut out rounds 4 to 5 inches in diameter. Repeat with scraps and the remaining dough.

4. Spoon about 1½ tablespoons of the picadillo into the center of each dough round. Brush the edges of each round with the beaten egg, fold it in half to make a half-moon, and seal the edges with the tines of a fork, taking care not to tear the dough.

5. Put the empanadas on the baking sheets and lightly brush the top of each with the egg and sprinkle with sesame seeds.

6. Bake the empanadas until golden brown, 20 to 25 minutes. Serve hot or at room temperature.

PICADILLO

∾ PICADILLO DE CARNE ∾

✳ MAKES ABOUT 4 CUPS ✳ PREPARATION TIME: 10 MINUTES ✳ COOKING TIME: 40 MINUTES ✳ CAN BE MADE UP
TO 2 DAYS AHEAD, COVERED, AND REFRIGERATED ✳

One of my favorite traditional fillings, picadillo is used in empanadas and quesadillas, as well as tacos, tortas, and stuffed chiles. There are many versions, but this one is at the top of my list. Raisins, almonds, and green Manzanilla olives elevate the simply seasoned minced meat into something special.

You can also serve picadillo alongside beans or rice.

3 tablespoons olive oil

¼ cup chopped white onion

1 garlic clove, finely chopped

1 pound ground pork or a combination of ground pork, beef, and veal

¾ teaspoon kosher or coarse sea salt, or to taste

1½ pounds ripe tomatoes, chopped and pureed, or one 28-ounce can crushed tomatoes or tomato puree

2 cups broth from Mexican Chicken Broth (page 87), canned chicken or vegetable broth, or water

½ teaspoon ground cinnamon

Pinch of ground cumin

Pinch of ground cloves

¼ cup slivered almonds, lightly toasted

¼ cup raisins

¼ cup pitted and coarsely chopped Manzanilla olives

1. Heat the oil in a large skillet over medium-high heat. Add the onion and cook until soft and translucent, 3 to 4 minutes. Add the garlic and cook until fragrant, about 1 minute. Add the meat and salt and cook for 8 to 10 minutes, stirring occasionally, until the meat is lightly browned.

2. Pour in the tomato puree and bring to a simmer, then reduce the heat and simmer, stirring often, until the puree deepens in color and thickens, 5 to 6 minutes. Add the broth, cinnamon, cumin, and cloves, stir well, and cook for 15 minutes more.

3. Stir in the almonds, raisins, and olives and cook for another 5 minutes. The filling should still be moist, since it will dry out a little as it cools. Taste for seasoning and adjust if needed. Let cool.

BEEF BRISKET IN PASILLA AND TOMATILLO SAUCE

∿ CARNE ENCHILADA ∿

❋ SERVES 6 TO 8 ❋ PREPARATION TIME: 15 MINUTES, PLUS SOAKING TIME ❋ COOKING TIME: 3 HOURS ❋
CAN BE MADE UP TO 2 DAYS AHEAD, COVERED, AND REFRIGERATED ❋

1 **4-pound beef brisket, trimmed of excess fat and cut into 2-inch chunks**

10 **garlic cloves**

10 **black peppercorns**

2 **teaspoons kosher or coarse sea salt, or to taste**

8–9 **pasilla or New Mexico chiles (about 3 ounces), rinsed, stemmed, and seeded**

1½ **pounds tomatillos, husks removed, rinsed**

2 **cups boiling water**

¼ **cup vegetable oil**

2 **cups coarsely chopped white onions, plus (optional) chopped onion for garnish**

1 **tablespoon grated *piloncillo* (see page 262) or dark brown sugar, or more to taste**

Cilantro leaves for garnish (optional)

6–8 **warmed corn or flour tortillas (optional)**

The intriguing flavors of this dish come from a simple combination of two deeply Mexican ingredients: earthy, slightly bitter pasilla chiles and bright, tangy tomatillos. The combination is characteristic of the state of Michoacán in central Mexico, where I first tasted the dish, prepared by an amazing cook named Berenice Flores.

Make the dish for a party or in place of your regular brisket for the Jewish High Holidays. Serve with Baby Potatoes with Lime and Parsley (page 210) or rice and warmed tortillas.

1. Place the beef chunks, garlic, peppercorns, and 1½ teaspoons of the salt in a large pot or casserole. Cover with water and bring to a boil over high heat, skimming any foam from the surface. Reduce the heat to medium-low, partially cover, and simmer for about 2½ hours, or until the meat is very tender but isn't falling apart. Remove from the heat and set aside.

2. Meanwhile, heat a *comal* or skillet over medium heat until hot. Lay the chiles flat in the pan and toast them for 10 to 15 seconds per side, until they become fragrant and pliable and their color darkens; don't let them burn. Place the chiles in a large bowl.

3. Char the tomatillos (see page 19) on a baking sheet under the broiler or on a hot *comal* or grill pan or in a large heavy skillet over medium heat for about 10 minutes, turning once, until their skin is blistered and their flesh is completely soft. Add them to the bowl with the chiles. Cover with the boiling water and soak for at least 30 minutes, or up to 3 hours. Drain.

4. Working in batches if necessary, pour the chile-tomatillo mixture into a blender or food processor and puree until smooth. Set aside.

(recipe continues)

5. Scoop out 3 cups of the beef cooking liquid from the pot and set aside. Drain the meat thoroughly in a colander.

6. Heat the oil in a large pot or Dutch oven over medium-high heat until hot but not smoking. Add the meat and let it sear and brown for 4 to 5 minutes, stirring. Reduce the heat to medium, add the onions, and cook, stirring, for 4 to 5 minutes, until softened. Add the chile puree, the 3 cups reserved cooking liquid, the remaining ½ teaspoon salt, the *piloncillo,* and bring to a simmer. Simmer over medium heat, stirring occasionally, until the sauce thickens and deepens in color, about 20 minutes; it should be thick enough to coat the back of a wooden spoon. Taste for salt and *piloncillo*, and add more if necessary.

7. Transfer to a serving platter, garnish with chopped onion and cilantro, if desired, and serve with warmed tortillas, if desired.

Pasilla Chiles, the dried form of the chilaca chile, are the most common chiles in the Mexican state of Michoacán. In some towns, you'll see patios covered with mats where hundreds, even thousands, of chilacas are dried in the sun to be turned into pasillas.

When the chiles are fresh, they are long, shiny, and light green in color, quite similar to the Anaheim chile. When dried, they retain their shape but turn dark brown, almost black, with soft, wrinkled skin. In some areas they are called black chiles, or *chiles negros*.

Pasillas have a mildly spicy, earthy flavor, with a strong sour accent. Like other chiles, pasillas are used for table sauces, soups, stews, rubs, marinades, and moles. If you have a hard time finding them, you can use New Mexico dried chiles instead, but know that they are less intense and less sour.

LAMB CHOPS IN GREEN PIPIÁN

～ PIPIÁN VERDE CON COSTILLITAS DE CORDERO ～

✳ SERVES 6 ✳ PREPARATION TIME: 15 MINUTES PLUS MARINATING TIME ✳ COOKING TIME: 45 MINUTES ✳
PIPIÁN SAUCE CAN BE MADE UP TO 4 DAYS AHEAD, COVERED, AND REFRIGERATED ✳

LAMB CHOPS

- 3 garlic cloves, minced or pressed
- 2 tablespoons finely chopped fresh rosemary or 2 teaspoons dried
- 2 tablespoons olive oil
  Freshly ground black pepper
- 12 single loin or double rib lamb chops (4–5 pounds total)
  Kosher or coarse sea salt

PIPIÁN VERDE

- 1 pound tomatillos, husks removed, rinsed
- 3 garlic cloves
- 1–2 jalapeño or serrano chiles
- 1⅓ cups hulled raw pumpkin seeds, lightly toasted (see page 46)
- ⅓ cup coarsely chopped white onion
- 1⅓ cups loosely packed cilantro leaves and top part of stems
  Kosher or coarse sea salt
- 3 tablespoons vegetable oil
- 3 cups broth from Mexican Chicken Broth (page 87) or canned chicken or vegetable broth

Velvety green, with a subtle and delicate flavor, *pipián verde* is a luxurious, hefty sauce made from ground pumpkin seeds intermingled with the tart, bright flavor of tomatillos. As with moles, there are as many variations as there are cooks. This version, which is the simplest of all that I've tried, is also the most magnificent. It can top nearly anything, but it's majestic paired with crusty grilled lamb chops. That said, I have been told a few times that this *pipián verde* is so good I should consider serving it as a soup.

1. TO MARINATE THE CHOPS: Combine the garlic, rosemary, olive oil, and pepper to taste in a small bowl. Place the lamb chops in a baking dish or zip-lock bag and thoroughly coat with the marinade. Cover and refrigerate up to 24 hours.

2. TO MAKE THE PIPIÁN: Place the tomatillos, garlic, and chiles in a medium saucepan, cover with water, and bring to a simmer over medium-high heat. Cook until the tomatillos have changed color from bright to dull green and are soft but not breaking apart, about 10 minutes. Remove from the heat.

3. In a blender or food processor, process the pumpkin seeds until finely ground. Add the tomatillos, garlic, chiles, 1 cup of the tomatillo cooking liquid, the onion, cilantro, and 2 teaspoons salt. Puree until smooth.

4. Heat the oil in a large pot or Dutch oven over medium heat. When the oil is hot, pour in the puree and broth and stir well. Bring to a simmer and simmer, partially covered, for 30 to 35 minutes, stirring often, until the sauce has thickened enough to coat the back of a wooden spoon and has "broken," with little pools of oil on top. Remove from the heat. (At this point, the *pipián* can be cooled, covered, and stored in the refrigerator to use another day.)

(recipe continues)

5. Preheat a grill or broiler to high heat.

6. Sprinkle the lamb chops on both sides with salt to taste. Grill or broil until nicely browned on the outside and cooked to your liking inside, about 3 minutes per side for medium-rare, 6 minutes per side for well-done. Remove from the heat, cover, and let rest for 5 minutes.

7. Serve the chops with a couple of generous spoonfuls of warmed *pipián verde* on top of each one, and pass more at the table.

....

✴ MEXICAN COOK'S TRICK: You can cook the lamb on a grill, in a grill pan, or on a griddle or under the broiler: Just be certain to have it blazing hot before you put the chops on so that you get a good char.

SIDES

CRAZY STREET CORN (*ELOTES CALLEJEROS*) ...202

BLISSFUL CORN TORTE ...204

GREEN BEANS WITH ORANGE AND PISTACHIOS ...207

CREAMY POBLANO RAJAS (*RAJAS CON CREMA*) ...209

BABY POTATOES WITH LIME AND PARSLEY ...210

CHIPOTLE MASHED POTATOES ...212

CITRUS SWEET POTATOES WITH CHILE DE ÁRBOL ...213

SAUTÉED ZUCCHINI WITH POBLANO PEPPERS (*COLACHE DE CALABACITAS*) ...215

SIMPLE BEANS FROM THE POT (*FRIJOLES DE OLLA*) ...216

CHARRO BEANS (*FRIJOLES CHARROS*) ...218

REFRIED BEANS (*FRIJOLES REFRITOS*) ...220

MY FAVORITE GREEN RICE (*ARROZ VERDE*) ...221

RED RICE (*ARROZ ROJO*) ...224

GUAJILLO AND GARLIC PASTA ...227

MEXICAN-STYLE PASTA (*FIDEO SECO*) ...228

MY OLDEST SON WON'T EAT ANY FRUIT, BUT HE WILL EAT VEGETABLES. My middle son always wants plain rice and food that is cooked the exact same way every single time. My youngest one is extremely adventurous, but it's impossible to predict what adventure he's willing to take. My husband will eat just about anything, cooked in just about any way, but the more options he sees on the table, the happier he is.

Enter my savior: side dishes. They help me negotiate everyone's preferences without making me feel like a short-order cook. They can turn a meal into a real event, and I have a hard time preparing fewer than two for dinner, especially since I like to have extras around for lunches.

What's more, because most side dishes do well made ahead and reheated, many can be repurposed. Take beans, for example. They can go from Simple Beans from the Pot to a mate for Mexican Meatballs with Mint and Chipotle (page 153) or they can be pureed for dishes like Hearty Pinto Bean Soup (page 70).

The sides in this chapter are delicious enough to squeeze that main dish right off the plate. My Favorite Green Rice is the star at my table at least once every single week, and it is just as happy stuffed into vegetables, made into impromptu fried rice, or reheated with sunny-side-up eggs on top. Blissful Corn Torte, which nearly steals the show from most main dishes, becomes lunch when paired with a simple green salad and a piece of cheese, and there is nothing better for breakfast than a wedge accompanied by *Café de Olla* (page 279).

CRAZY STREET CORN

∾ ELOTES CALLEJEROS ∾

✳ SERVES 6 ✳ PREPARATION TIME: 10 MINUTES ✳ COOKING TIME: 10 MINUTES ✳ CORN CAN BE GRILLED
OR BOILED AN HOUR AHEAD AND KEPT WARM, COVERED ✳

6 **ears corn, husked and
rinsed**

1 **tablespoon vegetable oil if
grilling**

Softened unsalted butter

Mayonnaise

1 **cup thoroughly crumbled
queso fresco, Cotija,
farmer cheese, or mild feta**

Kosher or coarse sea salt

**Dried ground chile, such as
piquín, or a Mexican mix,
such as Tajín**

3 **limes, halved**

Messy goodness on a stick: Crunchy, juicy, sweet corn slathered in butter and mayo, coated in crumbled queso fresco, sprinkled with chile powder and salt, and drizzled with lime juice is one of the ubiquitous street foods of Mexico. I stalk corn vendors when I am there, and my kids follow in my footsteps. Though my boys usually have radically different preferences, this is one dish they are all crazy for. When you serve it, just lay out all the garnishes and lots of napkins and let everyone have a go.

1. To grill the corn, prepare a medium fire in an outdoor grill or heat a grill pan over medium heat. Lightly brush the corn with the oil. Add the corn to the grill or pan and cook, turning every 3 minutes, until tender and slightly charred, 9 to 12 minutes. Alternatively, you can cook the corn in a big pot of boiling water until tender, 4 to 8 minutes, depending on the freshness of the corn. Remove the corn from the heat, or drain it, and pile on a platter, along with corn holders or thick wooden skewers.

2. Serve with the garnishes so everyone can fix their corn the way they want. The traditional way is to spread on a layer of butter, then a layer of mayonnaise. Next, thoroughly cover the corn with the crumbled cheese, either by rolling the corn on a plate of the cheese or sprinkling it on. Finish with a shower of salt and ground chile, then a squeeze or two of lime juice.

✳ MEXICAN COOK'S TRICK: Grilling the corn draws out the sugars and caramelizes them, creating a rustic sweetness that is magical with the garnishes.

BLISSFUL CORN TORTE

✳ SERVES 12 ✳ PREPARATION TIME: 15 MINUTES ✳ COOKING TIME: 40 TO 45 MINUTES ✳ CAN BE MADE UP TO 3 DAYS AHEAD, COVERED, AND REFRIGERATED ✳

½ pound (2 sticks) unsalted butter, at room temperature, plus more for the baking dish

¾ cup granulated sugar

8 large eggs, separated, at room temperature

¾ cup rice flour (see Mexican Cook's Trick, page 206)

1 tablespoon baking powder

½ cup heavy cream

4 cups fresh or thawed frozen corn kernels

1 cup whole milk

1 teaspoon kosher or coarse sea salt

Confectioners' sugar for sprinkling (optional)

Is this a bread? A pudding? A soufflé? Falling somewhere between corn soufflé and corn bread, this torte is made with a buttery batter of rice flour studded with the crunch of roughly pureed corn kernels. It's too good to be simply a side dish. I sometimes serve it topped with Creamy Poblano Rajas (page 209) as is usual in Mexico. I always secretly hope for leftovers, so I can enjoy a square with confectioners' sugar and fresh berries for breakfast.

1. Place a rack in the middle of the oven and preheat the oven to 350°F. Butter a 9-x-13-inch baking dish.

2. With an electric mixer, beat the butter in a large bowl on high speed until creamy. Add the granulated sugar and beat until thoroughly mixed and fluffy. Reduce the speed to low and add the egg yolks one by one, beating until they are well incorporated.

3. In a small bowl, combine the rice flour and baking powder. Add a bit of the dry ingredients and then a bit of the heavy cream alternately to the butter mixture, continuing until you've added them all, beating until well mixed.

4. In a blender or food processor, pulse the corn kernels with the milk until roughly pureed. Add to the butter mixture and beat until well combined, scraping down the sides of the bowl with a spatula as needed. If using a stand mixer, pour the butter-corn mixture into a large bowl.

5. In another large bowl beat the egg whites and salt with clean beaters until stiff peaks form. Gently fold one fifth of the beaten egg whites into the butter-corn mixture until blended. Gently fold in the remaining egg whites, taking care not to deflate them. It's OK if the batter looks streaky.

(recipe continues)

6. Pour the batter into the baking dish. Bake for 40 to 45 minutes, or until the torte is springy to the touch and lightly browned. Cool slightly.

7. The torte can be served warm, at room temperature, or cold. Serve cut into squares. Sprinkle confectioners' sugar on top if you like (I always do).

* MEXICAN COOK'S TRICK: Rice flour, made from finely milled raw rice, is used throughout Mexico to make all kinds of vegetable tortes such as this one. You can combine it with all-purpose flour, using a half-and-half ratio. Rice flour has a lovely texture that is airy yet gently grainy. What's more, it is wheat- and gluten-free, for people who have intolerances to either or both. You can find it at health food stores and large supermarkets.

GREEN BEANS WITH ORANGE AND PISTACHIOS

✳ SERVES 4 ✳ PREPARATION TIME: 10 MINUTES ✳ COOKING TIME: 20 MINUTES ✳ CAN BE MADE A COUPLE OF HOURS AHEAD, LEFT IN THE PAN, AND THEN REHEATED ✳

Snapped green beans are gently cooked with onion and garlic, then simmered in orange juice and a bit of apple cider vinegar until it thickens and turns into a plate-licking syrup, then finished with toasted pistachios. I bet you will end up adding more pistachios next time just to avoid the fight for the last ones on the platter.

1 tablespoon olive oil

¼ cup chopped white onion

2 garlic cloves, finely chopped

1 pound green beans, ends trimmed and cut diagonally into 1-inch pieces

Heaping ½ teaspoon kosher or coarse sea salt, or to taste

Freshly ground black pepper

½ cup freshly squeezed orange juice

1 tablespoon apple cider vinegar

3 tablespoons pistachios, toasted, plus more if desired

1. Heat the oil in a large skillet over medium heat. Add the onion and cook for 2 to 3 minutes, until soft and translucent. Stir in the garlic and cook until fragrant, about 1 minute. Toss in the green beans, sprinkle with the salt and pepper to taste, and cook until the beans begin to soften, 5 to 6 minutes.

2. Pour in the orange juice and vinegar and cook, stirring occasionally, for another 6 to 8 minutes, or until the beans are thoroughly cooked and the sauce is slightly thickened.

3. Transfer the beans to a serving platter, sprinkle with the toasted pistachios, toss, and serve.

✳ MEXICAN COOK'S TRICK: To toast pistachios or any other kind of nut, you need gentle constant heat, or the nuts will brown too quickly and not have the chance to toast through to the center. Set a *comal* or heavy skillet over medium-low heat and watchfully toast the nuts, stirring frequently, until they are lightly browned and fragrant; do not allow them to burn. Transfer to a plate to cool.

CREAMY POBLANO RAJAS

～ RAJAS CON CREMA ～

* SERVES 8 * PREPARATION TIME: 5 MINUTES * COOKING TIME: 25 MINUTES * CAN BE MADE UP TO 2 DAYS AHEAD, COVERED, AND REFRIGERATED *

3 tablespoons unsalted butter

1½ cups slivered white onions

1 pound poblano chiles, charred, sweated, peeled, stemmed, seeded, and sliced into 1-x-½-inch strips (see page 27)

1 teaspoon kosher or coarse sea salt, or to taste

¼ teaspoon freshly ground black pepper, or to taste

1 cup Mexican crema (see page 135), crème fraîche, or heavy cream

½ cup crumbled queso fresco, Cotija, farmer cheese, feta, or ricotta salata

The word *rajas* refers to strips of chiles, and some of the most popular are made with poblano chiles, which are charred, sweated, and peeled. Some cooks finish them by adding cooked onions, others add tomatoes or even corn. My preferred version is admittedly decadent. I gently cook onions in butter until all their sweetness has been coaxed out, then mix them into the poblanos along with cream and salty cheese. Serve as a topping for Blissful Corn Torte (page 204) or as a side to grilled meats or seafood, or spoon into warm corn tortillas for some of the tastiest tacos you will ever have.

1. Heat the butter in a large skillet over medium-low heat until melted and foamy. Add the onions and cook, stirring occasionally, until soft, translucent, and starting to gently brown around the edges, about 15 minutes.

2. Increase the heat to medium-high and add the poblano chile strips. Sprinkle with the salt and pepper and cook for 2 to 3 minutes, until the chiles have lightly browned. Reduce the heat to medium, add the cream and cheese, and cook, tossing gently, until the sauce thickens, 5 to 6 minutes. Serve hot.

BABY POTATOES WITH LIME AND PARSLEY

✳ SERVES 4 ✳ PREPARATION TIME: 5 MINUTES ✳ COOKING TIME: 25 MINUTES ✳ POTATOES CAN BE BOILED A DAY AHEAD, COVERED, AND REFRIGERATED ✳

1 **pound baby red potatoes**

2 **tablespoons olive oil**

2 **tablespoons Maggi sauce (see page 211) or soy sauce**

1 **tablespoon Worcestershire sauce**

2 **tablespoons freshly squeezed lime juice**

¼ **teaspoon kosher or coarse sea salt, or to taste**

Pinch of freshly ground black pepper, or to taste

2 **tablespoons chopped fresh Italian parsley**

This is one of my favorite ways to eat potatoes, simmered until just tender and then finished off in a skillet. You wind up with a dry crispy coating and a smooth creaminess inside. Lightly seasoned with a dash of salty Maggi or soy sauce and a squeeze of lime, they fly off the serving platter.

1. Bring a medium saucepan of salted water to a boil over medium-high heat. Add the potatoes, reduce the heat slightly, and cook at a medium simmer for 12 minutes, or until the potatoes are just cooked through and the tip of a knife can pierce them easily; they shouldn't be falling apart. Drain thoroughly.

2. Heat the oil in a 12-inch skillet over medium heat until hot but not smoking. Add the potatoes and cook for 5 to 6 minutes, stirring occasionally. Sprinkle with the Maggi, Worcestershire, lime juice, salt, and pepper and toss as the potatoes continue to brown on all sides, 6 to 8 more minutes.

3. Sprinkle with the parsley, give it another stir, and serve.

✳ MEXICAN COOK'S TRICK: Don't let the potatoes overcook in the water, or the skins will split and the insides will become mushy.

Maggi Sauce Open the cupboard in any Mexican kitchen, and you will find a bottle of Maggi seasoning sauce front and center. Though Swiss in origin, it is completely entrenched in our cuisine. An almost-black liquid-vegetable extract, Maggi tastes like a combination of soy sauce and beef bouillon. It provides umami, the fifth taste people talk about so much.

Mexican cooks use Maggi to flavor everything from marinades to salsas to vinaigrettes, and it is a crucial ingredient in many famous drinks, including *Michelada,* Mexican-style beer (page 277).

You can find Maggi in Latin stores as well as the international aisles of supermarkets. If you need a substitute, try a Japanese soy sauce like Kikkoman.

CHIPOTLE MASHED POTATOES

✳ SERVES 6 ✳ PREPARATION TIME: 5 MINUTES ✳ COOKING TIME: 20 MINUTES ✳ CAN BE MADE UP TO 24 HOURS AHEAD, COVERED, AND REFRIGERATED ✳

Mashing potatoes with their skins on gives them a rustic texture. I take that effect one step further by mashing them with scallions cooked in butter and chipotle in adobo sauce. I finish them with a splash of milk to bring it all together and ramp up the fluff factor. We eat these potatoes at least once a week, with Crispy Chicken Milanesa (page 156).

3 pounds red potatoes, quartered

4 tablespoons (½ stick) unsalted butter

¼ cup thinly sliced scallions (white and light green parts only)

1 canned chipotle chile in adobo sauce, seeded if you like, and chopped, plus 1 tablespoon adobo sauce, or to taste

½ cup whole milk

Kosher or coarse sea salt and freshly ground black pepper

1. Bring a large pot of generously salted water to a rolling boil over high heat. Add the potatoes, reduce the heat slightly, and cook at a medium simmer for 12 to 15 minutes, until they can be easily pierced with the tip of a knife. Drain and set aside.

2. Melt the butter in a large heavy skillet over medium heat. When it begins to foam, add the scallions and cook, stirring occasionally, until they soften, 2 to 3 minutes. Add the chipotle chile, adobo sauce, potatoes, and milk and mash the potatoes roughly with a potato masher or a wooden spoon. Sprinkle with salt and pepper to taste and cook for a couple more minutes.

3. Add more chopped chipotle chile and/or adobo sauce, if desired, and serve hot.

✳ MEXICAN COOK'S TRICK: Leftover mashed potatoes make great tacos. Just warm some corn tortillas, spread them with a couple tablespoons of the potatoes, add some melty cheese, roll up, and toast on a hot *comal*, or deep-fry them. Serve with big dollops of Mexican crema and the salsa of your choice.

CITRUS SWEET POTATOES WITH CHILE DE ÁRBOL

❀ SERVES 6 ❀ PREPARATION TIME: 15 MINUTES ❀ COOKING TIME: 1 HOUR ❀

3 pounds sweet potatoes, peeled

4 tablespoons (½ stick) unsalted butter, plus more for the baking dish

¾ cup packed grated *piloncillo* (see page 262) or dark brown sugar

½ cup freshly squeezed orange juice

2 tablespoons freshly squeezed lime juice

2 chiles de árbol, rinsed, stemmed, seeded, toasted, and chopped (see Mexican Cook's Trick), or more to taste

¼ teaspoon kosher or coarse sea salt, or to taste

Sweet potatoes have been eaten in Mexico since pre-Hispanic times. These tender baked sweets are cloaked in a lip-smacking mixture of orange, lime, and butter, with the additional snap of chiles de árbol. Their smoky flavor is just what the sweet syrup needs. I made this dish for our first Thanksgiving dinner in Washington, D.C., and have been preparing it every year since. Boiling the sweet potatoes before baking them gives them a soft, creamy texture that can't be duplicated by simply roasting them.

1. Place the sweet potatoes in a large pot, cover with water, and bring to a boil over medium-high heat. Reduce the heat to low, cover, and simmer for 25 to 35 minutes, or until the tip of a knife can easily pierce a potato. Drain and let cool.

2. Meanwhile, place the butter, *piloncillo*, and orange and lime juices in a small saucepan and heat over medium-low heat until the butter melts. Bring to a simmer and simmer for 4 to 5 minutes, or until the mixture thickens into a light syrup. Remove from the heat.

3. Preheat the oven to 425°F. Butter a 9-x-13-inch baking dish.

4. Slice the potatoes into ½- to ¾-inch rounds. Layer the sweet potato slices in rows in the baking dish. Pour the syrup evenly over them and sprinkle on the chiles and salt. Bake for 10 minutes. Spoon some of the syrup over the top of the sweet potatoes. Bake until the potatoes have a nicely glazed crust, 10 to 12 minutes more. Serve hot.

(recipe continues)

✺ MEXICAN COOK'S TRICK: Once toasted and chopped, chiles de árbol can be used as a topping for many dishes, including pizza. To make them ahead, remove the stems, then make a slit down one side and remove the seeds. Toast them on a *comal* or skillet over medium-low heat for 20 to 30 seconds on each side. They will become fragrant, their inner skin will become opaque, and their outer skin will be toasty dark brown in color; be careful not to let them burn. Remove from the heat, and chop. Remember to wash your hands with soap and water afterward. The chiles can be stored in an airtight container at room temperature for up to 2 months.

Chiles de Árbol The elegant-looking chile de árbol is a deep red-orange, 1½ to 2 inches long, and thin, with a shiny finish and thick smooth skin. It is hot and incredibly flavorful.

Its name translates as "chile from the tree," which makes no sense to me, as it grows on a bushy plant like any other chile. It's known by many other names, including *bravo* ("aggressive"), *pico de paloma* ("dove's beak"), *cola de rata* ("rat's tail"), *rojo* ("red"), and *sanjuanero* ("from San Juan"). Don't let the heat scare you away, as this chile has depth beyond the heat.

SAUTÉED ZUCCHINI WITH POBLANO PEPPERS

∿ COLACHE DE CALABACITAS ∿

✷ SERVES 4 TO 6 ✷ PREPARATION TIME: 10 MINUTES ✷ COOKING TIME: 10 MINUTES ✷ POBLANOS CAN BE PREPPED UP
TO 2 DAYS AHEAD, COVERED, AND REFRIGERATED ✷

2 **tablespoons unsalted butter**

1 **tablespoon vegetable oil**

½ **cup chopped white onion**

1 **garlic clove, minced or
   pressed**

1 **poblano chile (about 5
   ounces), charred, sweated,
   peeled, stemmed, seeded,
   and cut into ½-inch-wide
   strips (see page 27)**

5 **cups diced green zucchini
   (1½ pounds)**

½ **teaspoon kosher or coarse
   sea salt, or to taste**

Pinch of sugar, or to taste

**Freshly ground black pep-
per**

**Queso fresco, Cotija, farmer
cheese, or mild feta,
crumbled (optional)**

This recipe comes from an old cookbook I found in a general store in the small city of Los Mochis, in the northern Mexican state of Sinaloa. The book was so worn that I couldn't tell the publication date or the name of the person who compiled it. What I can tell is that it is a book of delicious recipes gathered from local families and that it is at least a century old. The word *colache*, from *colachi*, in the language of the Yaqui tribe that has lived in Northern Mexico for ages, refers to dishes made with diced cooked zucchini. Many versions have queso fresco sprinkled on top.

1. Heat the butter and oil in a large skillet over medium heat until the butter is melted and bubbly. Add the onion and cook until soft and translucent, 3 to 4 minutes. Add the garlic and cook for another minute, taking care not to let it brown. Toss in the poblano chile and cook for 1 to 2 minutes, stirring frequently.

2. Raise the heat to medium-high and add the zucchini. Sprinkle with the salt, sugar, and pepper to taste and cook until the zucchini is tender but still firm, about 4 minutes. Sprinkle with the cheese, if using, and serve.

✷ MEXICAN COOK'S TRICK: You can use any kind of zucchini you have handy, but I prefer the green variety with speckles of cream called *Calabacita Bola*, also known as courgette or round zucchini, or the *Calabacita Italiana*, also known as *Tatuma*. They both have a more delicate and sweet flavor than other zucchini.

SIMPLE BEANS FROM THE POT

∾ FRIJOLES DE OLLA ∾

✳ MAKES 5 GENEROUS CUPS COOKED BEANS AND 2 CUPS COOKING LIQUID ✳ PREPARATION TIME: 3 MINUTES ✳
COOKING TIME: ABOUT 1½ HOURS ✳ CAN BE MADE UP TO 4 DAYS AHEAD, COVERED, AND REFRIGERATED ✳

1 **pound (about 2½ cups) dried black or pinto beans**

½ **large white onion**

1 **tablespoon kosher or coarse sea salt, or to taste**

2 **cilantro sprigs or 3–4 fresh epazote leaves (optional; see page 107)**

Home-cooked beans are helpful, well-behaved, adaptable, and easy to make. Yes, they take some time to cook, but they need only as much babysitting as a ten-year-old—you just need to sneak a peek every now and then. Whether in Mexico or not, you will always find a pot of beans cooking in any Mexican home, filling the kitchen with a warm, earthy aroma and comforting steaminess, an ambiance I hanker for when I am hungry or homesick.

With a side of warm corn tortillas and pickled chiles or salsa, you really don't need anything else. Of course, if you have some ripe avocado and fresh crumbled cheese too, you will have a feast.

1. Rinse the beans in cold water, pick them over, and drain. Place them in a large pot or casserole and cover with at least 3 inches of water. Add the onion and bring to a rolling boil over high heat. Reduce the heat to medium-low and cook at a happy simmer, partially covered, until the beans are cooked through and soft, 1¼ to 1½ hours, depending on their age.

2. Add the salt and cilantro, if using, and cook for 15 minutes more, or until the beans are so soft that they come apart if you hold one between your fingers, and the broth has thickened to a soupy consistency. If the beans are not quite there and the broth is drying out, add more water.

3. Remove the onion and herbs with a slotted spoon before serving the beans.

✳ MEXICAN COOK'S TRICK: Make a delicious bean puree by combining 5 cups cooked beans with 1 cup of their liquid (or 5 cups rinsed canned beans plus a cup of water or chicken broth) and salt to taste in a blender or food processor and pureeing until entirely smooth. Use in Hearty Pinto Bean Soup (page 70) or for Scrambled Egg Packets (page 98).

Cooking Beans There are many myths about cooking dried beans. Let's take soaking. Soaking beans reduces the cooking time by about one quarter, but beans don't need to be soaked overnight—or even at all. And if you soak them too long (more than 12 hours), they may begin to ferment.

To cook beans, rinse them in a colander and sort through them to remove any broken beans or pebbles. Put them in a pot, cover them generously with water, and add ½ white onion (just slice the onion in half and peel away the outer layer, but leave the root end intact to ease scooping out later). If you love the flavor of garlic, drop in a couple of cloves.

Whatever you do, don't add salt at the beginning of cooking, because it can toughen the beans. Add the salt once the beans are already cooked and soft, at least an hour into the cooking. This is also when I add flavor-enhancing herbs like cilantro or epazote.

If the beans aren't fully cooked and the pot is running out of water, add hot water, not cold, as cold will slow the cooking and toughen the beans.

Canned beans can be used interchangeably with home-cooked beans in a pinch. If you use canned, drain and rinse the beans well before using. That said, homemade beans are a thousand times tastier.

CHARRO BEANS

∿ FRIJOLES CHARROS ∿

✳ SERVES 4 TO 6 ✳ PREPARATION TIME: 15 MINUTES ✳ COOKING TIME: 20 MINUTES ✳ CAN BE MADE UP TO
2 DAYS AHEAD, COVERED, AND REFRIGERATED ✳

6 ounces bacon, chopped

8 ounces Mexican chorizo,
casings removed, chopped

½ cup chopped white onion

1–2 jalapeño or serrano chiles,
halved, seeded if desired,
and finely chopped

8 ounces ripe tomatoes, cored
and chopped

5 cups Simple Beans from the
Pot (page 216), plus 1 cup
cooking liquid, or 5 cups
canned beans, rinsed and
drained, plus 1 cup water

Kosher or coarse sea salt
(optional)

There are at least as many ways to cook beans as there are days in a year. Some are plain, like Simple Beans from the Pot (page 216), and others, like this one, explode with flavor and can fuel a battalion on the run. Spicy chorizo, smoky bacon, and the bright, fresh flavors of onion, jalapeño, and tomato take these beans for a ride, and they'll make you feel like a macho *charro* ("cowboy").

If you think this dish sounds outrageous, consider that other common versions add cured meats, *chicharrones* (fried pork rinds), ham, and cheese, on top of the bacon and chorizo.

Serve these beans with a side of warm corn tortillas, some quesadillas, or a crunchy baguette, and slices of a ripe avocado if you have one handy. They are also a great accompaniment for grilled meats.

1. Cook the bacon in a large skillet over medium-high heat until it is lightly browned and starting to crisp, 3 to 4 minutes. Add the chorizo and cook, using a wooden spoon or spatula to break it into smaller pieces, until it starts to brown and crisp, about 4 to 5 minutes.

2. Add the onion and jalapeño(s), mix well, and cook until they soften, 2 to 3 minutes. Add the tomatoes and continue cooking, stirring occasionally, until they are thoroughly softened, 4 to 5 more minutes.

3. Add the beans and their liquid, stir well, and reduce the heat to medium. Cook until the beans are moist but no longer soupy, 8 to 10 more minutes. Taste and add salt if needed. Serve hot.

✳ MEXICAN COOK'S TRICK: Use your favorite Mexican chorizo (see sidebar, opposite) or any fresh uncooked Latin-style chorizo, or even Italian sausage, spicy or not. You can also use turkey or chicken bacon and chorizo if you want to avoid pork; however, you may need to add a tablespoon or two of vegetable oil as the beans cook, since these meats are significantly lower in fat.

Mexican Chorizo Bold and rich, Mexican chorizo is a fresh sausage with a deep, burnt-red color. Dried chiles and a mix of spices make the pork flake as it browns, and vinegar gives it a welcome hint of acidity. Mexican chorizo is sold raw and needs to be cooked before eating.

Spanish chorizo, on the other hand, has been smoked and cured. Seasoned with garlic and paprika, the sausage is ready to slice and eat, like salami. It cannot be substituted for Mexican chorizo.

Given a choice, I always opt for Mexican chorizo over other Latin varieties. Surprisingly, one of the best substitutes for Mexican chorizo is spicy Italian sausage.

REFRIED BEANS

⌒ FRIJOLES REFRITOS ⌒

✳ MAKES ABOUT 4 CUPS; SERVES 6 TO 8 ✳ PREPARATION TIME: 5 MINUTES ✳ COOKING TIME: 20 MINUTES ✳
CAN BE MADE UP TO 4 DAYS AHEAD, COVERED, AND REFRIGERATED ✳

¼ cup vegetable oil

½ cup chopped white onion

5 cups Simple Beans from the Pot (page 216), made with black or pinto beans, plus 1 cup of their cooking liquid (for the streamlined version, see below)

1 tablespoon kosher or coarse sea salt, or to taste

Feeding a pack of growing monsters seven days a week can be a challenge, so I follow the tradition of the people in the Yucatán Peninsula and "repurpose" beans: I make a double batch on Monday and use them throughout the week, ending with refried beans, the delicious caboose of Mexican cuisine, at the end of the week.

Use *refritos* as a companion to any main dish or as a topping for tostadas, stuff them into enchiladas or spread on tortas, or serve as a main course with rice. The trick to great refried beans is to cook them down at a leisurely pace and to give them time to get so thick they can almost stand and walk out of the pan onto your plate.

1. Heat the oil in a large skillet over medium heat until hot but not smoking. Add the onion and cook until softened and beginning to brown around the edges, 4 to 5 minutes.

2. For the traditional method, add the beans 1 cup at a time and some of the liquid and mash with a potato masher. Alternatively, for a streamlined version, which is smoother, add the bean puree (see Mexican Cook's Trick) all at once. Cook, stirring frequently, until the beans have become a smooth, very thick puree, 15 to 20 minutes. Season with the salt before serving.

✳ MEXICAN COOK'S TRICK: Refried beans are traditionally cooked in lard. Like many cooks, I have switched to oil with success.

You can make them the traditional way by mashing them with the onion and oil, or the more streamlined way, using pureed cooked beans. (Use 5 cups canned beans, rinsed and drained, plus 1 cup water [puree the beans with the liquid].) I opt for the second method, as it's just as tasty and much easier.

MY FAVORITE GREEN RICE

∽ ARROZ VERDE ∽

✹ SERVES 6 TO 8 ✹ PREPARATION TIME: 10 MINUTES ✹ COOKING TIME: 25 MINUTES, PLUS RESTING TIME ✹ CAN BE MADE UP TO 2 DAYS AHEAD, COVERED, AND REFRIGERATED ✹

Flavored with poblano chile, cilantro, and onion, this dish will change any notion you may have that rice is a boring side dish. The chiles contribute color, texture, and perfume; this is not spicy. Rich and lush, green rice is the perfect companion to almost any main dish, but don't hesitate to serve it in the center of the plate with a side of black beans, a sprinkle of cheese, and a simple tossed green salad. It's my kind of quick lunch when no one else is home. It is by far my all-time favorite rice. If you have leftovers, reheat and top with sunny-side-up eggs.

2 cups long- or extra-long-grain white rice (see page 223) or jasmine rice

2 poblano chiles (about 11 ounces), seeded and cut into chunks

½ cup water, plus 2 tablespoons more if needed

⅔ cup cilantro leaves

2 garlic cloves

1½ teaspoons kosher or coarse sea salt, or to taste

2½–3 cups broth from Mexican Chicken Broth (page 87) or canned chicken or vegetable broth

3 tablespoons vegetable oil

⅓ cup coarsely chopped white onion

1 tablespoon freshly squeezed lime juice, or more to taste

½ cup crumbled queso fresco, Cotija, farmer cheese, or mild feta (optional)

1. Soak the rice in a bowl of hot water to cover for about 5 minutes. Drain in a sieve and rinse under cold water until the water runs clear; drain well.

2. In a blender or food processor, puree the chiles with the ½ cup water, cilantro, garlic, and salt until smooth. Pass the puree through a fine sieve into a large liquid measuring cup; note the amount and set aside. Pour enough of the chicken broth into another liquid measuring cup to make 4 cups liquid total—you want to keep the two liquids separate, since you will add the puree first.

3. Heat the oil in a medium saucepan over medium-high heat until hot but not smoking. Add the rice and cook, stirring often, until the color changes to a milky white, 3 to 4 minutes. Add the onion and sauté until slightly softened, 1 to 2 minutes.

(recipe continues)

4. Pour in the poblano puree and cook until it darkens, thickens, and has mostly been absorbed by the rice, 2 to 3 minutes. Stir in the chicken broth and lime juice, bring to a rolling boil, cover, and reduce the heat to the lowest possible setting. Cook until most of the liquid has been absorbed but there is still some moisture in the pan, about 15 minutes. The rice should be cooked and tender; if it is not but all the liquid has been absorbed, add 2 tablespoons water, cover again, and cook for a couple more minutes. Let the rice rest, covered, for at least 5 minutes.

5. Fluff the rice with a fork and serve with the crumbled cheese on top, if using.

✳ MEXICAN COOK'S TRICK: There are as many versions of *arroz verde* as there are green ingredients in Mexican kitchens. Some versions use other chiles, like jalapeño or serrano, and fresh green things like cilantro, chives, parsley, or even spinach. Feel free to give any combination a try. Just stick to the general formula of 1 part rice to 2 parts liquid.

Cooking Rice the Mexican Way When I moved to Texas, a Mexican neighbor, tired of hearing about my batches of gloppy rice, took pity on me and taught me her family tricks.

* For true Mexican-style rice, use long- or extra-long-grain white rice (found in Latin markets) or jasmine rice. The grains of these varieties remain separate as they cook and aren't sticky, like the shorter-grained rices used for sushi, for example.
* Soak the rice in hot water for 5 minutes, then drain it, rinse it with cold water, and let it drain in a colander. If you don't have time to soak it, just give it a good rinse in a strainer.
* The general ratio for liquid is 2 parts liquid to 1 part rice. The cooking liquid can be anything from a flavorful puree to chicken broth to water, or a combination.

ESSENTIAL STEPS

1. SAUTÉ THE RICE IN OIL. For Mexican-style rice, the grains are cooked in hot oil before any liquid is added, adding another layer of flavor. Cook, stirring frequently, for 4 to 5 minutes, or until the color changes to deep milky white and the grains make a heavy sound as you stir, as if you were playing with wet sand in a bucket.
2. ADD THE LIQUID. After you pour in the cooking liquid, let it come to a rolling boil, then cover the pan and reduce the heat to as low as possible.
3. FINISH THE COOKING. The rice is ready when it is soft, tender, and cooked through. This ideally happens just when most of the liquid has been absorbed but there is still some moisture in the pan. If all the liquid has been absorbed but the rice is not yet cooked through, simply add 2 tablespoons water, cover again, and let cook for a couple more minutes. It's nice to have a saucepan with a transparent lid so you can see what is going on inside without losing steam when you lift the lid.
4. LET THE RICE REST. Once the rice is ready, remove from the heat and let sit, covered, for 5 minutes before you fluff it with a fork and serve. Rice reheats beautifully and can be made up to 2 days ahead, covered, and refrigerated; reheat in a covered saucepan over low heat with 2 tablespoons water.

RED RICE

∾ ARROZ ROJO ∾

✳ SERVES 6 TO 8 ✳ PREPARATION TIME: 10 MINUTES ✳ COOKING TIME: 25 MINUTES, PLUS RESTING TIME ✳
CAN BE MADE UP TO 2 DAYS AHEAD, COVERED, AND REFRIGERATED ✳

2 cups long- or extra-long-grain white rice (see page 223) or jasmine rice

1 pound ripe tomatoes, quartered, or one 14½-ounce can tomatoes

⅓ cup coarsely chopped white onion

2 garlic cloves

1 teaspoon kosher or coarse sea salt, or to taste

About 3 cups broth from Mexican Chicken Broth (page 87) or canned chicken or vegetable broth

3 tablespoons vegetable oil

2 fresh Italian parsley sprigs

¾ cup peeled and diced carrots (optional)

½ cup fresh or frozen green peas (optional)

½ cup fresh or frozen corn kernels (optional)

1–2 jalapeño or serrano chiles, left whole (optional)

2 tablespoons water, if needed

This version of Mexico's classic red rice comes from the kitchen of the Chepe train that winds its way through the Copper Canyon in northern Mexico. Amazed as I was to see a fully working kitchen rocking along old wooden tracks and a dining room with meals served by waiters on formally set tables, I was even more incredulous when I forked chef Jesus Lay's excellent rice into my mouth.

Red rice gets its zest from being cooked in a seasoned tomato puree. Diced fresh carrots, corn, and peas are steamed in the rice until they are tender but still crunchy. Any vegetable will work, and Mexican cooks tend to sneak in a couple of whole jalapeño or serrano chiles too. If you are having Mexicans over, watch out: Those chiles are the treasures we all hunt for.

1. Soak the rice in a bowl of hot water to cover for about 5 minutes. Drain in a sieve and rinse under cold running water until the water runs clear; drain well.

2. In a blender or food processor, puree the tomatoes with the onion, garlic, and salt until smooth. Pass the puree through a strainer into a large liquid measuring cup; note the amount and reserve. Pour enough chicken broth into another liquid measuring cup to make 4 cups liquid total—you want to keep the two liquids separate, since you will add the puree first.

3. Heat the oil in a medium saucepan over medium-high heat until hot but not smoking. Add the rice and cook, stirring often, until the rice becomes milky white, 3 to 4 minutes. Pour in the tomato puree, mix gently, and cook until the puree darkens, thickens, and has mostly been absorbed by the rice, about 3 minutes.

(recipe continues)

4. Stir in the chicken broth and add the parsley, carrots, peas, corn, and chiles, if using. Bring to a rolling boil, cover, and reduce the heat to the lowest setting. Cook for about 15 minutes, or until most of the liquid has been absorbed but there is still some moisture in the pan. The rice should be cooked and tender; if it is not but all the liquid has been absorbed, add the 2 tablespoons water, cover again, and cook for 2 more minutes. Remove from the heat and let the rice rest, covered, for at least 5 minutes.

5. Fluff the rice with a fork and serve.

....

✳ MEXICAN COOK'S TRICK: Mexican cooks often soak rice in hot water to get rid of excess starch, any dirt, and the talc that is sometimes used as a milling aid, as well as to soften and relax the rice. Removing the excess starch helps keep the grains separate, so the cooked rice is fluffier and less sticky.

GUAJILLO AND GARLIC PASTA

✳ SERVES 6 ✳ PREPARATION TIME: 10 MINUTES ✳ COOKING TIME: 15 MINUTES ✳

1 pound thin spaghetti or vermicelli

½ cup olive oil

5 garlic cloves, finely chopped

5 guajillo chiles, rinsed, seeded, and finely chopped

1 tablespoon finely chopped fresh rosemary or 1 teaspoon dried

1 tablespoon finely chopped fresh oregano or 1 teaspoon dried, preferably Mexican

1½ teaspoons finely chopped fresh thyme or ½ teaspoon dried

1½ teaspoons finely chopped fresh marjoram or ½ teaspoon dried

Kosher or coarse sea salt and freshly ground black pepper

½ cup grated Cotija, Parmigiano-Reggiano, Pecorino Romano, or ricotta salata

2 tablespoons coarsely chopped fresh Italian parsley (optional)

Pasta and guajillo chiles are always on hand in my pantry. When I add minced garlic and herbs, I have a satisfying dish in minutes. Think of this as the classic Italian *aglio e olio* ("garlic and oil") gone out salsa dancing.

1. Bring a large pot of salted water to a rolling boil. Add the pasta, let it come to a boil again, and boil, uncovered, until the pasta is al dente, 6 to 7 minutes. Scoop out 1 cup of the pasta cooking water and set aside. Drain the pasta.

2. Heat the olive oil in a 12-inch skillet over medium heat. Add the garlic and cook just until fragrant, 20 seconds, stirring constantly. Add the chiles and cook, stirring, for another 20 seconds, or until lightly browned. Don't let them burn. Stir in the rosemary, oregano, thyme, and marjoram and cook for another 20 to 30 seconds.

3. Add the pasta to the skillet and toss well. Pour in the reserved pasta water, toss, and cook for another couple minutes. Remove from the heat and season with salt and pepper to taste.

4. Serve, garnished with the cheese and the parsley, if using.

✳ MEXICAN COOK'S TRICK: You can use fresh or dried herbs—whatever you have handy—but if you use fresh herbs, you will have a more fragrant dish. As for substitutions, my rule of thumb is to add only a third of the amount called for if using dried.

MEXICAN-STYLE PASTA

∼ FIDEO SECO ∼

❋ SERVES 4 ❋ PREPARATION TIME: 10 MINUTES ❋ COOKING TIME: 30 MINUTES ❋ CAN BE MADE UP TO
2 DAYS AHEAD, COVERED, AND REFRIGERATED ❋

Yes, Mexicans do eat pasta—our own special versions. This one is the most popular of them all. The dried pasta is briefly fried, giving it a nutty flavor, then cooked in a tomato sauce spiced with chile until it is tender, not al dente. Finally, it's dressed with Mexican crema, some punchy crumbles of fresh cheese, and slices of smooth avocado. No matter how satisfied you are, you'll still reach for an extra helping.

1½ pounds ripe tomatoes

1 garlic clove

½ cup coarsely chopped white onion

¾ teaspoon kosher or coarse sea salt, or to taste

¼ teaspoon freshly ground black pepper

3 tablespoons vegetable oil

8 ounces spaghetti, angel hair, or fettuccine, broken into smaller pieces

2 cups broth from Mexican Chicken Broth (page 87) or canned chicken or vegetable broth

2 bay leaves

1 canned chipotle chile in adobo sauce, seeded if desired, plus 1–2 tablespoons adobo sauce (optional)

½ cup Mexican crema (see page 135), crème fraîche, or sour cream

½ cup crumbled queso fresco, Cotija, farmer cheese, or mild feta

1 ripe Hass avocado, halved, pitted, meat scooped out, and sliced

1. Place the tomatoes and garlic in a medium saucepan, cover with water, and bring to a simmer over medium-high heat. Simmer until the tomatoes are thoroughly softened and the skins have started to split, about 10 minutes.

2. Transfer the tomatoes and garlic, along with ½ cup of the cooking liquid, to a blender or food processor and let cool slightly. Add the onion, salt, and pepper and puree until smooth.

3. Heat the oil in a large pot or casserole over medium heat. Add the pasta pieces and sauté for 1 to 2 minutes, stirring constantly, until they are nicely browned and smell toasty; take care not to burn them. Stir in the tomato puree; it will sizzle and splatter. Cook, stirring often, until the puree thickens and darkens, 5 to 6 minutes.

4. Add the chicken broth, bay leaves, and chipotle chile and the optional adobo sauce, and cook, stirring occasionally, until the pasta is tender and the tomato sauce has thickened further, 10 to 12 minutes. Discard the bay leaves.

5. Serve with the cream, cheese, and avocado garnishes on top.

DESSERTS

TRIPLE ORANGE MEXICAN WEDDING COOKIES
    (POLVORONES DE NARANJA) ...234
PIGGY COOKIES (COCHINITOS, MARRANITOS,
    PUERQUITOS) ...236
SCRIBBLE COOKIES (GARABATOS) ...239
APRICOT-LIME-GLAZED MINI POUND CAKES (GARIBALDIS) ...242
CAJETA CREPES WITH TOASTED PECANS ...245
SWEET PLANTAIN FRITTERS (TORREJAS DE PLÁTANO MACHO) ...249
ALISA'S MARBLED POUND CAKE (PANQUE MARMOLEADO) ...251
TRES LECHES CAKE (PASTEL TRES LECHES) ...254
GUAVA CHEESECAKE ...256
IMPOSSIBLE CHOCOFLAN (CHOCOFLAN IMPOSIBLE) ...259
BERRIES WITH LIME SYRUP ...262
TOMATILLO AND LIME JAM (MERMELADA DE TOMATE CON LIMÓN) ...263

NO MATTER THE TIME OF DAY, NO MATTER THE DAY OF THE WEEK, there is always something sweet in a Mexican home. Since sweets are always around, people rarely have more than one helping.

But when I moved to the United States and my husband and I started having kids, I began to notice differences in the two cultures' approach to sweets. At my oldest son's first official play date here at our house when he was about four, the frown on the face of his friend's mom when she picked up her son said it all. Seeing the chocolate smeared around his mouth, she asked if he had dessert. Yes. When? How much? I had wrapped up some cookies for him to take home since he loved them so much. She wasn't happy. These days, however, my friends anticipate my treats with pleasure, and when they come to my house, they know what they are in for.

I've included many of my favorite sweets in this chapter. There are Mexican Wedding Cookies, which have little to do with weddings, but after seeing the festive triple-orange infusion I give mine, you may feel like throwing a party, be it a wedding or not. The recipe for traditional Piggy Cookies has been one of the most requested by Mexicans living abroad, since these soft cookies capture so much of the charm of small-town *panaderías*, or "little bakeries." *Garabatos*, or Scribble Cookies, are one of the first things I run for as soon as I hit Mexico City, and my kids and I enjoy making them at home.

Come to our house on a weekend, and you'll sit down to Sweet Plantain Fritters, which could easily beat out French toast in a brunch Olympics, or Cajeta Crepes with Toasted Pecans, where French technique and Mexican ingredients find common ground. And for a showstopper, you won't believe how impossibly easy it is to make the Impossible Chocoflan. All the treats in this chapter are good at any time of the day, for dessert or whenever you want them. We all need something sweet.

TRIPLE ORANGE MEXICAN WEDDING COOKIES

∿ POLVORONES DE NARANJA ∿

✳ MAKES 26 TO 30 COOKIES, DEPENDING ON SIZE ✳ PREPARATION TIME: 15 MINUTES, PLUS CHILLING TIME ✳ COOKING TIME: 20 MINUTES ✳ DOUGH CAN BE MADE UP TO 24 HOURS AHEAD; COOKIES CAN BE STORED IN AN AIRTIGHT CONTAINER FOR UP TO 5 DAYS ✳

½ pound (2 sticks) cold unsalted butter, cut into small pieces, plus more for the cookie sheets

1 cup confectioners' sugar, plus more for dusting

1 large egg

1 large egg yolk

1 tablespoon packed grated orange zest

¼ cup freshly squeezed orange juice

2 tablespoons Grand Marnier or other orange flavored liqueur

3½ cups all-purpose flour, plus more for dusting

½ teaspoon baking soda

I was born and raised in Mexico City, where I attended many wedding celebrations, and my husband and I were married in a very Mexican way—but I had never heard of Mexican wedding cookies until I moved to the United States and started getting nonstop requests from American friends for a recipe. It took me a while to realize that the cookies that are so well liked north of the border were what I knew as *polvorones*. I grew up eating them, and they are dearly loved south of the border too, where they are an everyday cookie found in just about any bakery shop.

The name *polvorón* comes from the Spanish word *polvo*, which translates as "dust" or "powder." The cookies, firm on the outside, break into the finest of crumbs the moment they are in your mouth, and it takes just a couple of seconds for them to melt deliciously and disappear.

You can flavor *polvorones* with nuts, vanilla, chocolate, or cinnamon. In this recipe, I give them an orange overload: a gentle bite from the zest, sweetness from the juice, and sophistication from Grand Marnier.

If you are taking the cookies to a party, cut colored tissue paper into 3- to 4-inch squares and wrap the cookies like candies, as is done in Mexico for special occasions.

1. In a food processor, pulse the butter with the confectioners' sugar until combined. Add the egg, yolk, orange zest, juice, and Grand Marnier and pulse, until thoroughly mixed. The dough will look rather loose: That's OK.

2. Add the flour and baking soda and pulse until the mixture starts to come together into small chunks. Scrape down the sides of the bowl with a spatula if necessary, and pulse again. Turn the dough out, gather it into a ball, and wrap it in plastic wrap. Refrigerate for at least 30 minutes or up to 24 hours.

3. Preheat the oven to 350°F, with racks in the upper and lower thirds. Line two cookie sheets with parchment paper or butter them and dust them with flour.

4. Roll the dough into 1- to 1½-inch balls and place on the cookie sheets, spacing them 1 inch apart. Give each one a light pat on the top to flatten it slightly.

5. Bake until the cookies are cooked through, their bottoms are golden brown, and their tops are light golden brown, about 18 to 20 minutes. Remove the cookies from the oven and transfer them to a cooling rack to cool completely. Sift a generous load of confectioners' sugar over the cooled cookies.

*   MEXICAN COOK'S TRICK: When rolling the dough into balls, don't overwork it, or the butter may heat to the point of melting, making the dough greasy and resulting in cookies that toughen and burn along the edges. The dough is overworked if it starts to feel oily in your hands and sticks to your fingers. If this happens, place it in a bowl in the refrigerator for 15 minutes or so, until it cools and firms up.

PIGGY COOKIES

∿ COCHINITOS, MARRANITOS, PUERQUITOS ∿

✳ MAKES 24 TO 28 COOKIES ✳ PREPARATION TIME: 20 MINUTES, PLUS CHILLING TIME ✳ COOKING TIME: 30 MINUTES ✳
DOUGH CAN BE REFRIGERATED FOR UP TO 2 DAYS; COOKIES CAN BE STORED IN AN AIRTIGHT
CONTAINER FOR UP TO 4 DAYS ✳

1¾ cups (10 ounces) firmly packed grated *piloncillo* (see page 262) or dark brown sugar

¾ cup water

1 Ceylon cinnamon stick (*canela*; see page 238)

½ pound (2 sticks) unsalted butter, cut into small pieces, at room temperature, plus more for the cookie sheets

2 tablespoons honey

4¼ cups all-purpose flour, plus more for dusting

1 teaspoon baking powder

1 teaspoon baking soda

½ teaspoon kosher or coarse sea salt

2 large eggs, lightly beaten, at room temperature, plus 1 large egg, lightly beaten, for glaze

Confectioners' sugar for dusting (optional)

These cookies go by the many endearing names for pigs in Spanish: *cerdito, cochinito, marranito,* or *puerquito.* This is the recipe that is the most requested on my blog by Mexicans living abroad. The piggies' honeyed nuttiness comes from the *piloncillo,* raw brown sugar, that flavors the sticky dough. It's so irresistible that I have to hide it from my boys.

Although they are made like cookies, cut like cookies, shaped like cookies, and baked like cookies, piggies are more like a delightful marriage between a traditional *bizcocho* or *pan dulce* ("sweet roll") and a cookie. The moment you take them from the oven, they are at their softest and fluffiest—closer to a sweet roll. If you cover them as soon as they cool, they will remain soft and fluffy for a while, but as the days go by, they will harden and have the snap of a traditional cookie. If you want them to harden faster, don't cover them.

You can find pig-shaped cookie cutters online, or use any shape you like—but then, you need to change their name.

1. In a medium saucepan, combine the *piloncillo,* water, and cinnamon and bring to a simmer over medium heat. Lower the heat to medium-low and simmer for about 15 minutes, or until the *piloncillo* has dissolved and the liquid thickens to a light syrup. Turn off the heat and remove the cinnamon stick. Add the butter and honey and stir until they melt.

2. In a large bowl, whisk together the flour, baking powder, baking soda, and salt. Make a well in the center and pour in the *piloncillo* mixture. Mix with a rubber spatula until well combined. Add 2 of the eggs and stir until thoroughly mixed. The dough will be very sticky and gooey.

3. Place two long pieces of plastic wrap, one running horizontally and one vertically, in a medium bowl, letting the ends overhang the edges of the bowl. With a rubber spatula, scrape the dough onto the plastic wrap, then bring the edges of the wrap over the dough and secure tightly

(leave the dough in the bowl). Refrigerate for at least 2 hours, or up to 2 days.

4. Preheat the oven to 375°F, with racks in the upper and lower thirds. Butter two cookie sheets.

5. Sprinkle flour on a work surface and a rolling pin. Cut the dough in half. Working with one piece at a time, roll out the dough about ¼ inch thick. Using a 3-inch piggy cookie cutter, press straight down on the dough to cut out cookies, moving the cutter slightly on the work surface to make it easier to lift up the cookies. Gather the scraps into a ball and roll out again. Transfer the cookies to the prepared cookie sheets, spacing them about 1 inch apart. If the dough becomes too sticky, roll it into a ball, wrap it again in plastic wrap, and place it in the freezer for 5 to 10 minutes before rolling again.

6. Gently brush the cookie tops with the remaining egg. Bake in batches for 7 to 9 minutes, or until the cookies are puffed and golden on top. Remove from the oven and transfer to a cooling rack to cool completely. Sift confectioners' sugar on top of the cooled cookies, if desired.

✳ MEXICAN COOK'S TRICK: After you mix this dough, it will be gooey, sticky, and quite runny; do not worry. When you wrap it and refrigerate it, it will harden and become manageable, rollable, and cookie-cutter friendly.

True Cinnamon In Mexican kitchens, you will usually find one type of cinnamon: Ceylon, also known as real or true cinnamon and called *canela* in Spanish. Ceylon cinnamon originated in Sri Lanka, formerly Ceylon—hence the name. The other variety, cassia, is grown in China, Vietnam, and Indonesia, and it is the predominant cinnamon sold in the U.S. market. Though there are currently no labeling laws in the United States requiring producers to identify the type, Ceylon is becoming more and more available, and it's worth tracking down.

Ceylon cinnamon is subtler and sweeter, with a warmer, more intriguing flavor and aroma. Equally important, it is softer and much kinder to the blades of your blender or food processor. Ceylon cinnamon crumbles easily because it has many thin, papery layers (it resembles a light brown cigar). Cassia is hard and woody and almost impossible to break or crumble. It also has a flatter, more one-dimensional, harsher flavor than Ceylon cinnamon.

SCRIBBLE COOKIES

∾ GARABATOS ∾

* MAKES 16 TO 18 COOKIES * PREPARATION TIME: 10 MINUTES, PLUS CHILLING TIME *
COOKING TIME: 15 TO 20 MINUTES * DOUGH CAN BE MADE UP TO 24 HOURS AHEAD; COOKIES CAN BE STORED
IN AN AIRTIGHT CONTAINER FOR UP TO 5 DAYS *

DOUGH

10 ounces (2½ sticks) unsalted butter, at room temperature, plus butter for the cookie sheets

½ cup sugar

2 large eggs, at room temperature

4 cups all-purpose flour, plus more for dusting

Pinch of kosher or coarse sea salt

FILLING

1 cup heavy cream

8 ounces bittersweet chocolate, chopped

3 tablespoons sugar

Garabatos means "scribbles" in Spanish, and the original cookie comes from D'Elvis, a bakery shop in Mexico City. It's owned by the Bleiers, a couple of Bulgarian origin. Mrs. Bleier has been making them since the 1950s in the front part of her house, which became the bakery. The cookies are so famous and sought after that the owners' son started a chain of coffee shops called Garabatos, where the main attraction is these cookies: thick chocolate ganache sandwiched between round butter cookies with chocolate dribbled on top. The boys and I have a blast drizzling those scribbles.

As delicious as the cookies are when freshly made, they are even more so after being refrigerated. The cookie and the chocolate harden a little, making their melt-in-the-mouth quality even more sublime.

1. TO MAKE THE DOUGH: In a large bowl, beat the butter with an electric mixer at medium speed until creamy, 3 to 4 minutes. Add the sugar and beat until fluffy, another 3 minutes. Add the eggs one by one, beating well after each addition; scrape down the sides of the bowl as needed. Reduce the mixer speed to low and add the flour ½ cup at a time, then add the salt, beating until thoroughly mixed.

2. Turn the dough out, gather into a ball, and wrap it in plastic wrap. Refrigerate for at least 30 minutes, or up to 24 hours.

3. Preheat the oven to 350°F, with racks in the upper and lower thirds. Butter two cookie sheets.

4. Lightly dust your work surface and a rolling pin with flour. Roll out the dough about ¼ inch thick. Cut out the cookies with a 3-inch round cookie cutter or a glass and place them ½ inch apart on the cookie sheets.

(recipe continues)

5. Bake for 15 to 20 minutes, or until the cookies are just golden. Remove the cookies from the oven and transfer to a cooling rack to cool completely.

6. TO MAKE THE FILLING: In a medium saucepan, combine the cream and chopped chocolate and stir constantly over low heat until the chocolate is completely melted. Add the sugar and stir to dissolve. Remove from the heat and let the filling cool slightly until thickened.

7. Turn half of the cookies flat side up and spread a heaping tablespoon of the chocolate on each one; reserve the remaining chocolate to make the scribbles on top. Let the chocolate settle on the bottom cookies for at least 5 minutes. Top with the remaining cookies, flat side down, sandwiching them together lightly.

8. Scrape the remaining chocolate into a pastry bag fitted with a small plain tip, scrape it into a small plastic bag and snip off a bottom corner, or use a fork to drizzle the chocolate. (You can also spoon it into a squeeze bottle.) Drizzle the chocolate on top of the cookies, making your own scribble designs. Let the cookies stand until the filling is set, then store in an airtight container at room temperature or in the refrigerator (see the headnote).

* MEXICAN COOK'S TRICK: Be sure to let both the cookies and the filling cool before putting them together. If the filling is hot, it will be too runny. If the cookies are still warm, they will melt the filling.

APRICOT-LIME-GLAZED MINI POUND CAKES

∾ GARIBALDIS ∾

❋ MAKES ABOUT 60 MINI-MUFFIN-SIZED OR 30 CUPCAKE-SIZED CAKES ❋ PREPARATION TIME: 25 MINUTES ❋
COOKING TIME: 30 TO 45 MINUTES ❋ CAN BE KEPT, COVERED, AT ROOM TEMPERATURE FOR UP TO 5 DAYS ❋

Giuseppe Garibaldi was a famous Italian who inspired and helped many Latin American countries fight for their independence in the nineteenth century, and one of Mexico's favorite *bizcocho* or *pan dulce* ("sweet rolls") is the Garibaldi, created in a bakery founded by Italian immigrants. The shop, El Globo, was established in Mexico City in 1884. Now it's owned by a big food company, but luckily, the recipe for these soft and tender mini pound cakes has not been changed. With a sweet-tart lime glaze and a crunch from the nonpareils (called *chochitos* or *grageas* in Spanish) sprinkled all over them, the little cakes couldn't look or taste more celebratory.

CAKES

- 4 sticks (1 pound) unsalted butter, cut into small pieces, at room temperature, plus more for the pans
- 1¼ cups sugar
- 5 large eggs, at room temperature
- 4 cups all-purpose flour, plus more for dusting
- 1 tablespoon baking powder
- Pinch of kosher or coarse sea salt
- ¾ cup heavy cream

GLAZE

- 1 cup apricot preserves
- 3 tablespoons freshly squeezed lime juice

- 1 cup white nonpareils or other sprinkles of your choice

1. Preheat the oven to 375°F, with racks in the upper and lower thirds. Butter 24 mini-muffin cups or 12 standard muffin cups and lightly dust with flour; set aside.

2. TO MAKE THE CAKES: In a large bowl, beat the butter with an electric mixer at medium-high speed until creamy, about 5 minutes. Add the sugar and continue to beat with the mixer at medium speed until light and fluffy, about 3 more minutes. Add the eggs one by one, beating until well blended; stop to scrape down the sides of the bowl as needed.

3. In a medium bowl, whisk together the flour, baking powder, and salt. Gradually add the flour mixture to the butter mixture, alternating with the heavy cream and mixing with the mixer at low speed until well combined.

4. Spoon the batter into the muffin tins, filling them no more than three-quarters full (set the remaining batter aside). Bake for about 10 minutes for mini-muffin-sized cakes, or 12 to 15 minutes for standard cupcake-sized cakes, or until a toothpick inserted into the center of a cake comes out

clean. Remove the cakes from the oven and, when cool enough to handle, remove them from the tins and place them on a cooling rack to cool completely. Repeat to make more batches, buttering and flouring the cooled muffin tins.

5. TO MAKE THE GLAZE: In a medium saucepan, combine the apricot preserves and lime juice and heat over medium heat, stirring occasionally, until the preserves have melted. Pour into a small bowl.

6. Place the nonpareils in another small bowl.

7. Holding a cake by its bottom, dip as much of it as you can into the apricot glaze, then gently but swiftly roll the glazed area in the nonpareils. (If you roll too slowly or press too hard, the nonpareils will become covered with glaze and be hard to work with.) Repeat with the remaining cakes, placing the finished cakes on a platter.

8. Let the cakes cool, then cover. They taste even better the next day, when the glaze will have soaked in and the nonpareils softened a bit.

✶ MEXICAN COOK'S TRICK: Dunk as much of each cake as possible into the glaze while it is still warm, so it will be absorbed and spread more easily, making the sprinkles stick.

CAJETA CREPES WITH TOASTED PECANS

❋ MAKES TEN TO TWELVE 9-INCH CREPES; SERVES 5 TO 6 ❋ PREPARATION TIME: 10 MINUTES, PLUS RESTING TIME ❋
COOKING TIME: 20 MINUTES ❋ BATTER CAN BE MADE UP TO 12 HOURS AHEAD; CREPES CAN BE MADE
AHEAD AND REFRIGERATED FOR UP TO 4 DAYS OR FROZEN FOR UP TO 4 MONTHS (SEE MEXICAN COOK'S TRICK) ❋

Delicate crepes soaked in a warm milky caramel sauce and topped with toasted pecans are one of the fanciest and most classic of Mexican desserts, and the ultimate symbol of the country's everlasting love affair with French cuisine. For a grown-up take, you can add a splash of rum to the sauce. Don't be intimidated, crepes are easy to make. A friend used to say that preparing them is like raising kids: You wish you had had the practice of the third when you had your first.

Cajeta, and its Argentinean counterpart, the milder dulce de leche, are both readily available in the United States. On rainy days, the kids and I slice apples in quarters and top them with the leftover *cajeta* from the jar.

CREPES

- 1 cup all-purpose flour
- 2 large eggs
- 1 large egg yolk
- 1 cup whole milk
- 2 tablespoons sugar
-   Pinch of kosher or coarse sea salt
- ⅓ cup (5⅓ tablespoons) un-salted butter, melted, plus more for the pan
- ½ cup water

SAUCE

- 2 cups *cajeta* (see page 246) or dulce de leche
- 1½ cups whole milk
- 1 tablespoon rum (optional)

- ½ cup coarsely chopped pe-cans, lightly toasted, for garnish
-   Vanilla ice cream (optional)

1. TO MAKE THE CREPES: Place the flour, eggs, egg yolk, milk, sugar, salt, and melted butter in a blender or food processor and blend until smooth. Add the water and blend again until smooth. Alternatively, you can mix the ingredients by hand. Pour the batter into a container, cover, and refrigerate for at least 30 minutes, or up to 12 hours. (This rest makes the crepes fluffier.)

2. When ready to make the crepes, stir the batter with a whisk or fork until well combined and smooth.

3. Set a crepe pan over medium-high heat. Once it is hot, butter the surface: The butter should foam. Tilt the pan, ladle a scant ¼ cup batter over the lower side, and quickly tilt and turn the pan to spread the batter over the entire surface of the pan. Cook for 20 to 25 seconds, until the edges are beginning to dry and the bottom is lightly browned. With a small spatula or fork, lift up one edge of the crepe and quickly turn it over with your fingers. Cook the second side for 10 to 15 seconds, or until lightly browned. Remove the crepe

Mexican Cajeta Latin America's famously sticky and delicious *cajeta* and dulce de leche are both milk-based caramel sauces, but they are very different. For generations, Mexico's *cajeta* has been made by simmering down goat's milk with sugar in copper pots until it reaches a glorious caramel color and is thick enough to stand a spoon in. Today, however, people also prepare it with cow's milk or a combination of both. Argentina's dulce de leche, which has always been made with cow's milk, has a milder taste. Given a choice, as a loyal Mexican, I go for goat's-milk *cajeta*, and I always choose *cajeta* of any kind over dulce de leche, since *cajeta* is more distinctively flavored.

When I was a kid, *cajeta* was sold in small round wooden boxes, tied up with brightly colored ribbons. We used to get dozens of those little boxes in the markets for our birthday parties, and we would lick them dry. The word *caja*, or "box," is where many think the name originates. You can still find these charming boxes in a town called Celaya in the state of Guanajuato in north-central Mexico.

Today *cajeta* is readily available in the United States in Latin markets, and the store-bought product is just as good as homemade—if you know which brands to buy. Look for Las Sevillanas or Coronado.

Spread *cajeta* on sliced fruit like bananas or apples (think caramel apples) or crepes (see page 245), sandwich it between Maria cookies (see page 257), or use it to flavor desserts like flans, cakes, ice cream, milkshakes, and even gelatin. *Cajeta* is the ingredient that takes Impossible Chocoflan (page 259) over the top. Don't forget the ultimate, though: directly from the spoon in the middle of the afternoon.

from the pan and place on a plate. Repeat with the rest of the batter, stacking the crepes on top of one another, with the darker side down. (That side will become the outside of the crepe when you fill or fold them.) After making 3 or 4 crepes, you may need to butter the pan again.

4. TO MAKE THE SAUCE: Bring the *cajeta* and milk to a gentle simmer in a medium saucepan over medium heat, stirring, and simmer for 2 minutes, or until the *cajeta* is thoroughly dissolved. Remove from the heat and stir in the rum, if using.

5. TO ASSEMBLE THE CREPES: Place one crepe on a plate and spread 2 tablespoons of the *cajeta* sauce over the surface. Fold the crepe in half, add a couple more tablespoons of sauce, and spread it around. Fold the crepe again to make a triangle shape and pour a few more tablespoons sauce on top. Repeat with the remaining crepes and sauce.

6. Serve 2 crepes per person, garnished with the toasted pecans and a scoop of vanilla ice cream on the side, if desired.

＊ MEXICAN COOK'S TRICK: To make the crepes ahead, stack the cooked crepes as above, placing a piece of plastic wrap between every 3 to 4 crepes. (That way, they will be easy to separate when you are ready to use them.) Once they have cooled, wrap the stack in plastic wrap and place in a sealed plastic bag and refrigerate or freeze. To reheat, remove as many as you need and heat one at a time in a skillet over medium heat for 15 to 20 seconds.

SWEET PLANTAIN FRITTERS

∽ TORREJAS DE PLÁTANO MACHO ∽

* MAKES ABOUT 12 FRITTERS; SERVES 6 * PREPARATION TIME: 10 MINUTES * COOKING TIME: 15 MINUTES *
BATTER CAN BE MADE UP TO 12 HOURS AHEAD, COVERED, AND REFRIGERATED *

4 cups peeled and sliced ripe
   plantains (about 3; see
   page 250)

3 large eggs, at room temperature

1 cup sugar

1²/₃ cups all-purpose flour

1 tablespoon baking powder

Pinch of kosher or coarse
   sea salt

Vegetable oil

Honey, maple syrup, or additional sugar

Torrejas are a deluxe Mexican version of French toast, served covered in syrup, honey, or sugar. The most unusual version comes from the state of Campeche in southeast Mexico. Instead of bread or a pancake batter, they are made with ripe plantains and are utterly delicious.

Fluffy, with a crispy crust and soft bite, the fritters can be eaten for dessert or as a luxurious breakfast with Spiced Sweet Mexican Coffee (page 279) or, if you are feeling decadent, with hot chocolate.

1. Place the plantains and eggs in a blender or food processor and puree until smooth. Add the sugar and process again until smooth. Pour the mixture into a large bowl and add the flour, baking powder, and salt, mixing with a rubber spatula until thoroughly combined. The batter will look fluffy, with streaks from the plantains.

2. Heat ¾ inch of oil in a 12-inch skillet over medium heat until very hot but not smoking, 5 to 6 minutes. With a ladle or large spoon, carefully drop a scant ⅓ cup batter for each fritter into the hot oil, taking care to not overcrowd the skillet. Fry the fritters, without moving them, until the bottoms turn golden brown and form a nice crust, about 2 minutes. Turn and continue to fry until the second side is golden brown and crispy, 1½ to 2 minutes more. When the fritters are ready, lift them from the oil with a slotted spoon or skimmer and place on a paper-towel-lined platter. Repeat with the remaining batter.

(recipe continues)

3. Serve the fritters hot or at room temperature with honey, maple syrup, or sugar.

* MEXICAN COOK'S TRICK: As you add the batter to the hot oil, you may need to adjust the heat to keep the oil around the edges of the fritters at a happy, steady simmer. Start with medium heat and then turn it up to medium-high if need be. Depending on your stovetop, you may need to lower it to medium again. If you need to add more oil to keep it at ¾-inch deep, be sure to give the new oil a couple minutes to heat up again before you add more fritters.

Plantains are now available virtually everywhere in the United States. In most areas of Mexico they are called *plátanos machos* ("macho bananas") because they look like jumbo bananas, though they are not. While they are from the same family as bananas, culinarily they are much more like a vegetable. They must be cooked, since they are unpleasant raw.

They are at their starchiest when their skin is green. Unlike bananas, when they turn yellow and start to show black freckles, they are only beginning to mature and develop their sugar content. They are ripe and at their sweetest when almost entirely black and very soft.

They will ripen fastest in the warmest area of the kitchen or in a paper bag at room temperature, where they take about 3 days to go from yellow to black. When they are fully ripened, they will keep in the refrigerator for about 3 days.

Plantains can be steamed, grilled, baked, or fried. They are also used to thicken and add flavor to some sauces, moles, and stews.

ALISA'S MARBLED POUND CAKE

∽ PANQUE MARMOLEADO ∽

❋ SERVES 10 ❋ PREPARATION TIME: 15 MINUTES ❋ COOKING TIME: 1 HOUR ❋ CAN BE STORED, COVERED, AT ROOM TEMPERATURE FOR UP TO 2 DAYS ❋

½ **pound (2 sticks) unsalted butter, at room temperature, plus more for the pan**

1½ **cups all-purpose flour, plus more for the pan**

1¼ **cups granulated sugar**

1 **teaspoon vanilla extract**

1 **teaspoon baking powder**

¼ **teaspoon kosher or coarse sea salt**

4 **large eggs**

½ **cup sour cream**

¼ **cup hot water**

¼ **cup unsweetened cocoa powder**

Confectioners' sugar for dusting (optional)

My sister Alisa Romano is a masterful professional baker with a restaurant in Miami, where she prepares the best home-style treats. She has perfected this traditional recipe for marbled pound cake, a vanilla cake with a dense, dark chocolaty center. I pack it into my sons' lunch boxes for school, and they have been offered many bribes to share it. I like to slice off a thick piece and cut it into bite-sized squares, saving the pieces that have the most chocolate for last.

When I serve it to guests, I like to spoon some Berries with Lime Syrup (page 262) on the side of each slice.

1. Preheat the oven to 350°F, with a rack in the middle. Butter a 9-x-5-inch loaf pan. Line the bottom with parchment paper and butter the paper. Dust the pan lightly with flour; set aside.

2. In a large bowl, beat the butter with an electric mixer on medium-high speed until creamy, about 3 minutes. Add the sugar and continue beating until well combined and fluffy, another 2 minutes. Add the vanilla and continue beating until well incorporated, another minute.

3. Sift the flour, baking powder, and salt into a bowl. Break the eggs into another bowl. Add half of the eggs and half of the sifted flour mixture to the butter mixture, beating on medium-low speed until well combined and scraping down the sides of the bowl with a rubber spatula as needed. Repeat with the remaining eggs and flour. Add the sour cream and continue beating until the batter is smooth.

4. In a small bowl, combine the hot water with the cocoa powder. Pour half the cake batter into another bowl and fold in the cocoa-water mixture with a rubber spatula until thoroughly mixed.

(recipe continues)

5. Spread the vanilla batter in the loaf pan. Pour the chocolate batter on top, in a straight line down the center. With a knife or spoon, make a whirling design from one side of the pan to the other.

6. Bake the cake for about 1 hour, or until a toothpick inserted into the center comes out clean. Transfer to a rack to cool.

7. Invert the cooled cake onto a rack, remove the parchment paper, and invert again onto a plate. Dust the top of the cake with confectioners' sugar, if desired (I always do), before slicing and serving.

❋ MEXICAN COOK'S TRICK: You've probably noticed that when you add cocoa powder to a batter, the cocoa dust flies everywhere. So, depending on the recipe, I combine it with the dry ingredients or with hot water. This way the dust settles, and the water brings out and intensifies the cocoa's full flavor.

TRES LECHES CAKE

∾ PASTEL TRES LECHES ∾

✳ SERVES 10 TO 12 ✳ PREPARATION TIME: 25 MINUTES, PLUS CHILLING TIME ✳ COOKING TIME: 25 MINUTES ✳
CAN BE ASSEMBLED UP TO 3 DAYS AHEAD ✳

Unsalted butter

CAKE

9 **large eggs, separated, at room temperature**

1 **cup granulated sugar**

1 **tablespoon vanilla extract**

2 **cups all-purpose flour**

1 **teaspoon baking powder**

SAUCE

1 **14-ounce can sweetened condensed milk**

1 **12-ounce can evaporated milk**

1 **cup whole milk**

1 **tablespoon vanilla extract**

WHIPPED CREAM

2 **cups heavy cream**

¼ **cup confectioners' sugar**

8 **ounces strawberries or other berries (optional)**

Think of this as a Latin version of Italy's tiramisu. A sponge cake is soaked in a creamy vanilla sauce made from three milks (condensed, evaporated, and whole—the *tres leches*) and refrigerated. This dessert lets you go as far as your imagination can fly. Want to go down to the tropics? Switch the evaporated milk for coconut milk. Feeling like chocolate? Mix in 4 ounces of melted chocolate. Like a hint of alcohol? Add a couple of table-spoons of rum. Finish it all off with a fluffy layer of whipped cream.

1. TO MAKE THE CAKE: Preheat the oven to 350°F, with a rack in the middle. Butter a 9-x-13-inch baking pan and line the bottom with a piece of parchment paper.

2. In a large bowl, beat the egg whites with an electric mixer on medium-high speed for 4 to 5 minutes, or until they hold soft peaks. Reduce the speed to medium and slowly add the sugar, beating until the whites hold stiff, shiny peaks; set aside. Wash the beaters.

3. Pour the egg yolks into another large bowl and beat on medium-high speed until fluffy and pale yellow, about 5 minutes. Add the vanilla and continue beating for another minute.

4. Gently and slowly fold the egg yolk mixture into the egg white mixture, taking care not to deflate the whites. In a bowl, combine the flour with the baking powder and fold into the egg mixture ¼ cup at a time, scraping the bottom and sides of the bowl with the spatula to mix well. The batter will look a bit streaky.

5. Pour the batter into the prepared pan. Bake the cake until a toothpick inserted in the center comes out clean, 22 to 25 minutes. The top of the cake should be lightly browned and feel spongy to the touch. Place the pan on a wire rack to cool.

6. Invert the cake onto a rack and remove the pan and parchment paper. Cover the cake with an upside-down platter large enough to hold the cake and the sauce and invert again so the cake is right side up. Using a fork, poke holes all over the top of the cake, so it will absorb the sauce.

7. TO MAKE THE SAUCE: In a large bowl, combine the three milks and vanilla and stir to blend well. Pour the sauce over the cake. Don't worry if it looks like there is too much sauce—the spongy cake will absorb it all. Cover and refrigerate for at least 2 hours.

8. When you are ready to finish the cake, make the whipped cream: In a large bowl, whip the cream with an electric mixer on medium speed until it holds soft peaks, 5 to 6 minutes. Reduce the speed to low and add the confectioners' sugar, then increase the speed to medium-high and beat until stiff peaks form. Spread the whipped cream over the top and sides of the cake.

9. To serve, slice the cake and spoon fresh berries, if using, on top of each serving or on the side.

* MEXICAN COOK'S TRICK: After the soaked cake has been refrigerated for a couple of hours, you can add the whipped cream and return the cake to the refrigerator for up to 3 days, or you can add the whipped cream right before serving.

Harvesting Vanilla The vanilla plant is a temperamental species of orchid, and there is a delicate art to harvesting the pods. Vanilla grown outside of Mexico must be pollinated by hand, since the only insect that will pollinate it is the stingless *Melipona* bee, which lives only in Mexico. Once the orchid has formed a pod, it's treated like a moody pregnant woman. Traditional growers, called *vainilleros*, are always male. They make sure the plants have utter comfort, receive the right amount of light and shade, and are protected from cold. They pick the pods when they're still green so they won't crack and lose the essential oils that give them their flavor and aroma. Even today in traditional orchards, women are not allowed to harvest the pods, because it's believed that vanilla beans demand the faithful ministrations of male admirers and are jealous of other women.

Once the pods have been harvested, they are immersed in hot water or put in a hot oven to stop them from maturing further. Then they are carefully placed on mats to bask in the sun during the day. At night, they are placed in drawers to sweat. This process is repeated every day for twenty to twenty-eight days. This long, drawn-out process leads to deeply aromatic flavor.

GUAVA CHEESECAKE

✳ SERVES 10 TO 12 ✳ PREPARATION TIME: 30 MINUTES, PLUS CHILLING TIME ✳ COOKING TIME: 45 MINUTES ✳
CAN BE COVERED AND REFRIGERATED FOR UP TO 4 DAYS ✳

CRUST

6 tablespoons (¾ stick) unsalted butter, melted, plus
more for the pan

1½ cups finely ground Maria
cookies (see sidebar, op-
posite), vanilla wafers, or
graham crackers

1 teaspoon sugar

GUAVA SPREAD

12 ounces guava or quince
paste (see sidebar,
opposite)

5 tablespoons water

CREAM CHEESE FILLING

1 pound cream cheese, at
room temperature

⅓ cup sugar

1 teaspoon vanilla extract

3 large eggs, at room temperature

¼ cup heavy cream

SOUR CREAM TOPPING

1½ cups sour cream

¼ cup sugar

I devoured a version of this dessert, a take on the popular combination of soft Mexican Manchego cheese with slices of guava or another fruit paste, at the charming and sunny coffee shop in the Sweets Museum in the city of Morelia, in Michoacán, in western Mexico. I was so mesmerized by it I came back home determined to re-create it with my students.

The cheesecake boasts four very different layers that come together seamlessly: a crisp, sturdy cookie crust; a layer of bright guava paste; a thick layer of cream cheese filling; and lastly a slick of tangy sour cream.

1. Place an oven rack in the lower third of the oven and preheat the oven to 350°F. Butter a 9- to 10-inch springform pan and set aside.

2. TO MAKE THE CRUST: In a medium bowl, combine the ground cookies, sugar, and melted butter until thoroughly mixed. Turn the cookie mixture into the springform pan. With your fingers, pat it evenly over the bottom of the pan, gently pushing it up the sides to make a crust ½ to 1 inch high. Refrigerate while you make the filling.

3. TO MAKE THE GUAVA SPREAD: Place the guava paste and water in a blender or food processor and process until smooth; set aside.

4. TO MAKE THE FILLING: In a large bowl, beat the cream cheese with an electric mixer at medium speed until smooth and light, 3 to 4 minutes. Add the sugar and vanilla and continue beating until well mixed, scraping down the sides of the bowl as needed. Add the eggs one at a time, beating until thoroughly combined after each addition, again scraping down the bowl as needed. Add the cream and continue beating until the mixture is well blended and smooth; set aside.

(recipe continues)

Guava Paste Imagine your favorite fruit jam thick enough to be shaped into a brick and sliced. That is a fruit *ate*, or "paste." In Mexico the most famous *ates* are made with guava, quince, mango, pear, and *tejocote*, a crabapple-like fruit. The tradition comes to Mexico from Spain, which in turn, got it from the Arabs.

Fruit pastes are made by simmering fruit pulp with sugar over low heat until it is very thick and then spreading it out in a layer to dry. Typically *ates* are served in slices, either on their own or accompanied by slices of cheese, to be nibbled on for dessert.

Candies are made with fruit pastes, some rolled out so thin they look like fruit roll-ups and finished with a sprinkle of sugar. You can also use *ates* in pies or empanadas and to top cookies. Look for *ates* in Latin stores and in the Latin section of supermarkets.

Maria Cookies How did an English tea biscuit conquer Mexico? Marie biscuits (called Maria cookies in Spain) were created in an English bakery in the later part of the nineteenth century to celebrate the wedding of Marie, Duchess of Russia, to Alfred, Duke of Edinburgh. The cookies became popular all over Europe but put down their deepest roots in Spain, which eventually exported them to Mexico, where it has been the best-selling cookie for more than a century.

Now made by many competing companies, *galletas María*, with a signature ornate border, are eaten right out of the package with coffee or Mexico's famous hot chocolate, and they are used to make sandwich-like treats with *cajeta* (see page 246) for kids. They are also perfect for pie or tart crusts, as in Guava Cheesecake (opposite). If you can't find Maria cookies, substitute graham crackers.

5. With a rubber spatula, gently spread the guava mixture evenly in the prepared crust. Gently turn the cream cheese filling onto the guava layer and spread evenly.

6. Bake for 35 minutes, or until the filling is set and the top is lightly browned. Remove from the oven and let cool for at least 10 minutes before you add the topping. Leave the oven on.

7. MEANWHILE, MAKE THE TOPPING: Mix the sour cream and sugar together in a medium bowl until well blended.

8. Spoon the topping over the cheese filling, return to the oven, and bake for 10 more minutes, until the topping looks set. Remove from the oven and let the cheesecake cool for about 10 minutes. Then cover and refrigerate for at least 4 hours, or preferably, overnight.

9. To serve, run the tip of a wet knife around the sides of the pan to release the cheesecake. Remove the sides of the pan, then slice and serve the cake.

❋ MEXICAN COOK'S TRICK: There are many ways to crumble the cookies or graham crackers for the crust. The easiest is to place them in a blender or food processor, breaking them in pieces as you do so, and then pulse until fine. A more old-fashioned way is to place the cookies in a plastic bag and crush them with a rolling pin or the bottom of a heavy skillet. You can decide how even and fine you want the crumbs. I like them finely ground.

IMPOSSIBLE CHOCOFLAN

~ CHOCOFLAN IMPOSIBLE ~

* MAKES 12 INDIVIDUAL FLANS * PREPARATION TIME: 20 MINUTES, PLUS CHILLING TIME *
COOKING TIME: 50 TO 55 MINUTES * CAN BE COVERED AND REFRIGERATED FOR UP TO 4 DAYS *

Unsalted butter

1 cup *cajeta* (see page 246) or dulce de leche

CAKE

8 tablespoons (1 stick) unsalted butter, at room temperature

¾ cup sugar

1 large egg, at room temperature

¾ cup all-purpose flour

⅓ cup unsweetened cocoa powder

½ teaspoon baking powder

½ teaspoon baking soda

Pinch of kosher or coarse sea salt

¾ cup buttermilk

FLAN

1 14-ounce can sweetened condensed milk

1 12-ounce can evaporated milk

4 large eggs

1 teaspoon vanilla extract

½ cup coarsely chopped pecans, lightly toasted

This traditional Mexican dessert earned its name from the trick that happens in the oven while it's baking. A flan mixture and cake batter are layered in ramekins. They look like a total mess, but in the oven, they switch places, and the chocolaty cake ends up on top. Impossible? No, magic! It tastes magical too: a rich chocolate cake layered with creamy flan and liquid *cajeta*. Fortunately, they're small enough that you won't be expected to share.

These individual chocoflans are perfect for an elegant dinner party or an afternoon snack.

....

1. Preheat the oven to 350°F, with a rack in the middle. Butter twelve 4-ounce ramekins.

2. Drizzle a generous 1 tablespoon of the *cajeta* over the bottom of each mold. Set aside.

3. TO MAKE THE CAKE: In a large bowl, beat the butter with an electric mixer at medium speed until creamy, about 3 minutes. Add the sugar and continue beating until fluffy, about 2 more minutes. Add the egg and beat until well blended.

4. Sift together the flour, cocoa, baking powder, baking soda, and salt into a medium bowl. With the mixer on low, beat half the flour mixture and then half the buttermilk into the butter mixture, scraping down the sides of the bowl as needed. Repeat with the remaining flour mixture and buttermilk, beating until thoroughly mixed and fluffy. Set aside.

5. TO MAKE THE FLAN: Combine the condensed milk, evaporated milk, eggs, and vanilla in a blender and blend until smooth. Alternatively, whip together vigorously in a large bowl with a wire whisk.

(recipe continues)

6. Spoon 2 heaping tablespoons of the cake batter into each ramekin, filling them two-thirds full. Gently pour the flan mixture on top of the cake batter, filling the ramekins to just below the rim. The contents of the ramekins will look messy, with bits of the cake batter floating in the flan mixture. Don't worry, that is the way it should look.

7. Place the ramekins in a large baking pan or dish at least 1½ inches deep. Pour enough hot water into the pan to reach halfway up the sides of the ramekins. Cover the pan with aluminum foil and seal tightly.

8. Carefully place the pan in the oven and bake for 50 to 55 minutes, or until the surface of the cakes feels firm and a toothpick inserted into the center comes out clean. Carefully open the aluminum foil to check—the steam from the pan will be very hot. Remove the baking pan from the oven and remove the aluminum foil.

9. When the ramekins are cool enough to handle, remove them from the water bath (I use sturdy tongs) and let cool completely on a wire rack. Cover each ramekin with plastic wrap and refrigerate for at least 2 hours before serving.

10. When ready to serve, remove the chocoflans from the refrigerator and remove the plastic wrap. The flans won't look their most beautiful before you unmold them, but don't worry! Run the tip of a knife around the edges of a ramekin, place an inverted plate on top, and flip. Give the flan a few seconds to drop onto the plate, or hold the mold and plate with both hands as you give it a nice shake. Remove the ramekin and drizzle any *cajeta* remaining in the mold on top of the flan. Repeat with the remaining chocoflans, garnish with the chopped pecans, and serve.

BERRIES WITH LIME SYRUP

✳ SERVES 8 ✳ PREPARATION TIME: 10 MINUTES, PLUS MACERATING TIME ✳ CAN BE MADE UP TO
12 HOURS AHEAD, COVERED, AND REFRIGERATED ✳

Drizzle berries with a quick and easy lime and *piloncillo* syrup, shower them with fresh lime zest, and let them luxuriate for a bit, and you have a bowlful of berries ready to attend a gala.

1 **pound strawberries, stemmed and cut into halves or quarters, depending on size**

8 **ounces blueberries**

4 **ounces blackberries**

4 **ounces raspberries**

Grated zest of 1 lime

¼ **cup freshly squeezed lime juice**

3 **tablespoons grated *piloncillo* or dark brown sugar, or to taste**

1. Place the berries in a large bowl, along with the lime zest.

2. In a small bowl, mix the lime juice with the *piloncillo*, stirring until well dissolved. Pour the syrup over the berries and toss to combine. Cover and refrigerate for at least 30 minutes before serving.

✳ MEXICAN COOK'S TRICK: You can use frozen berries in this recipe as well. Freezing your own berries is very easy to do. Just rinse, drain, and pat dry (if using strawberries, remove the stems and caps). Then place them in a single layer on a baking sheet and pop them into the freezer for an hour to overnight, so they freeze separately and won't stick to one another when you transfer them to a bag. Transfer to a freezer bag, seal tightly, and place them back in the freezer. They will keep for up to a year.

Piloncillo (also called *panela* or *panocha*) is cane sugar in its most unrefined form: crushed, juiced, boiled down, and poured into molds called *pilones*—hence the name. Once the *piloncillo* juice hardens, it turns into solid blocks, which are wrapped and stored.

Because *piloncillo* is so hard, you need to either grate or finely chop it with a sharp knife. If you can't find *piloncillo*, you can substitute dark brown sugar, but the flavor will be less complex. *Piloncillo* has a deep flavor with a hint of caramel and coffee. It reminds me of Mexican countryside food: real and made from scratch.

Look for *piloncillo* in Latin markets or in the Latin aisle of the supermarket. It is worth the hunt. The rich, dark, intricate flavor of this unrefined sugar will give even your morning coffee a boost.

TOMATILLO AND LIME JAM

∾ MERMELADA DE TOMATE CON LIMÓN ∾

✳ MAKES ABOUT 1¼ CUPS ✳ PREPARATION TIME: 5 MINUTES ✳ COOKING TIME: 30 TO 35 MINUTES ✳
KEEPS, TIGHTLY COVERED AND REFRIGERATED, FOR UP TO 3 MONTHS ✳

**1 pound tomatillos, husks
removed, rinsed, and
coarsely chopped**

1½ cups sugar

1 cup water

**Zest of 1 lime, removed
with a vegetable peeler
and cut into ½-inch pieces**

**¼ cup freshly squeezed lime
juice**

**Pinch of kosher or coarse
sea salt**

The first time I tried tomatillo jam was with the famed Mexico City chef Enrique Olvera, who has an exquisite palate and is inspiringly adventurous in the kitchen. He combined the tomatillos with vinegar and sugar; I use freshly squeezed lime juice and zest instead of vinegar for a citrusy spark. The jam's tart, fruity kick is delicious with morning toast, on a cheese platter as a spread for crackers, as a filling for a tart, or on top of cookies or pound cake.

1. Place the tomatillos, sugar, water, lime zest, juice, and salt in a medium saucepan and bring to a simmer over medium-high heat. Cook, stirring occasionally, for 15 minutes.

2. Reduce the heat to medium and continue cooking until the mixture has thickened but is still slightly runny, about 15 minutes more. Turn off the heat and let cool.

3. Pour the jam into a glass jar, seal tightly, and refrigerate.

✳ MEXICAN COOK'S TRICK: The jam will thicken considerably as it cools, so be sure to stop cooking it before it is too thick—don't let the melted sugar get any color.

DRINKS

JAMAICA WATER (*AGUA FRESCA DE JAMAICA*) ...268

JAMAICA FLOWER CONCENTRATE (*CONCENTRADO DE JAMAICA*) ...270

LIME AND MINT WATER (*AGUA FRESCA DE LIMÓN CON MENTA*) ...271

ORANGE AND ANCHO CHILE CHASER (*SANGRITA*) ...272

CREAMY PEANUT AND VANILLA APÉRITIF (*TORITOS*) ...273

TAMARIND MARGARITA ...274

SALTY, SWEET, AND SPICY CHILE POWDER ...275

SPINNING TOP (*TROMPO ZACATECANO*) ...276

BEER MEXICAN-STYLE (*MICHELADA*) ...277

BANANA AND CAJETA MILKSHAKE ...278

SPICED SWEET MEXICAN COFFEE (*CAFÉ DE OLLA*) ...279

WALK INTO ANY MEXICAN MARKET, AND YOU WILL BUMP INTO GIANT GLASS BARRELS filled with the colorful and vibrant flavored waters called *aguas frescas*. They are one of the pillars of Mexico's rich beverage tradition, a heritage of the Arab influences brought by our Spanish conquerors.

I can't remember a time when I've eaten in a Mexican home without finding a pitcher of flavored water of some sort on the table. *Aguas* are made from scratch every day with all sorts of flavorings, including lime, mint, tart red *Jamaica* flowers, tamarind, watermelon, pineapple, cactus, and mango, or whatever is fresh and in season.

Beyond *aguas*, the world of Mexican drinks is as exotic and multilayered as our food. They've been influenced by the waves of immigrants and cultural exchanges that have become an essential part of the Mexican lifestyle. Whether accompanying a fancy sit-down dinner or with a quick taco at a food stand, a Mexican drink can turn the heat up or down, cool your tongue, or take you to spicy new heights, depending on how it pairs with what you're eating.

Try a sweet, silky, icy Creamy Peanut and Vanilla Apéritif with anything that has citrus or heat. A Spiced Sweet Mexican Coffee jump-starts the day, and I can't think of a more interesting way to whet the appetite than with a Tamarind Margarita, the glass rimmed with a spicy, sweet, salty mix. For a party, whip up a batch of homemade *Sangrita* to chase all the superb varieties of tequila now available. And since Mexican hospitality is legendary, it's not enough for us to simply offer you a cold beer—we have to dress it up by adding a twist of lime, a rim of salt, and perhaps a hint of savory spice or heat, so that even something as simple as a lager becomes a *Michelada*, a uniquely Mexican experience. Many of the drinks I'm sharing with you in this section will lift your spirits, as well as help you welcome friends, put them at ease, and give them an authentic taste of Mexico.

JAMAICA WATER

∾ AGUA FRESCA DE JAMAICA ∾

❋ SERVES 4 TO 6 ❋ PREPARATION TIME: 5 MINUTES ❋ CAN BE MADE UP TO 2 DAYS AHEAD, COVERED, AND REFRIGERATED (STIR BEFORE SERVING) ❋

2 cups Jamaica Flower Concentrate (page 270)

6 cups water

Ice cubes

1 orange, tangerine, or grape-fruit, peeled and cut into sections (optional)

One of Mexico's most famous *aguas frescas*, this beautiful, ruby-red drink beguiles with its flowery, cranberry-like tartness. It's a wonderfully refreshing foil to any Mexican dish.

When I think of *Jamaica* flowers, I remember my mother when she was exactly my age in Mexico City. She would be busy cooking enormous, elaborate meals on the weekends and would set out a huge blanket in the yard for my sisters and me to sit on, along with a big pitcher of *agua de Jamaica*. While she was indoors, we'd be playing with spoons and pots and sticks and stones, mixing those same bright red hibiscus blossoms into magical elixirs for fairies and elves.

I'm still charmed by *Jamaica*, and as an adult, I appreciate it even more, since it's packed with vitamin C. For a grown-up twist, try it Guatemalan-style and add a splash of rum.

In a large pitcher, stir the *Jamaica* concentrate together with the water. Chill in the refrigerator before serving, or serve right away. Either way, pour into glasses filled with ice and garnish with the sections of citrus fruit, if desired.

❋ MEXICAN COOK'S TRICK: If you'd like an even cooler version of *agua de Jamaica*, freeze it into ice pops. My kids love them with chunks of mango, and we sometimes toss in chocolate chips and shredded coconut as well.

JAMAICA FLOWER CONCENTRATE

∾ CONCENTRADO DE JAMAICA ∾

❋ MAKES ABOUT 5 CUPS ❋ PREPARATION TIME: 5 MINUTES, PLUS STEEPING TIME ❋ COOKING TIME: 10 MINUTES ❋
CAN BE COVERED AND REFRIGERATED FOR UP TO 1 MONTH ❋

8 cups water

3 ounces (about 2 cups) *Jamaica* (hibiscus) flowers (see page 183)

1½ cups sugar, or to taste

2 tablespoons freshly squeezed lime juice, or to taste

The most traditional way to use *Jamaica* flowers is to make a concentrate and use it as the base for an *agua fresca* (see page 268). But don't stop there. You can use it in myriad other ways: Consider it an exotic flavoring for Jell-O or ice pops, reduce it to a syrup to drizzle over cheesecake or brownies, or use as a marinade for a modern spin on tacos, as in my Steak Tacos with Jamaica-Jalapeño Sauce (page 182).

1. In a medium saucepan, bring the water to a boil over high heat. Add the *Jamaica* flowers, reduce the heat to medium, and simmer for 10 minutes. Turn off the heat and let steep for at least 10 minutes.

2. Strain the liquid into a heatproof jar or container. Add the sugar and lime juice and stir well to dissolve the sugar. Let cool, cover, and refrigerate.

LIME AND MINT WATER

∾ AGUA FRESCA DE LIMÓN CON MENTA ∾

❋ SERVES 4 ❋ PREPARATION TIME: 10 MINUTES ❋ CAN BE MADE UP TO 12 HOURS AHEAD, COVERED, AND REFRIGERATED (STIR BEFORE SERVING) ❋

1 **lime, quartered and seeds removed**

½ **cup freshly squeezed lime juice**

6–8 **fresh mint leaves**

¾ **cup sugar, or to taste**

6 **cups water**
Ice cubes

This limeade is like no other and is as refreshing as it sounds. I learned how to make it in the small town of Valle de Bravo, where Señora Ninfa Sánchez, a savvy cook I've known for fifteen years, disappeared into the backyard just before lunch to pick a bunch of fresh wild mint and some limes from a big old tree. By using the lime almost in its entirety, along with whole mint leaves, you get the most from both.

1. Place the lime, lime juice, mint, sugar, and 2 cups of the water in a blender or food processor and puree until smooth. Strain the mixture through a sieve into a pitcher.

2. Return the strained mixture to the blender or food processor, along with 2 cups of the water, and puree again until smooth. Strain again into the pitcher, then add the remaining 2 cups water and give it a good stir. Chill the drink before serving or serve it immediately. Either way, pour into glasses filled with ice.

❋ MEXICAN COOK'S TRICK: Mexican limes have thinner skins than their American cousins. They also tend to be rounder and juicier (and much gentler on your blender and food processor). Look for limes that give a bit when you squeeze them—that means they're mature and have more juice.

ORANGE AND ANCHO CHILE CHASER

∾ SANGRITA ∾

✳ MAKES 10 TO 12 SERVINGS ✳ PREPARATION TIME: 25 MINUTES ✳ COOKING TIME: 10 MINUTES ✳
CAN BE COVERED AND REFRIGERATED FOR UP TO 5 DAYS (STIR BEFORE SERVING) ✳

2–3 **ancho chiles (1 ounce), rinsed, stemmed, and seeded**

1 **cup boiling water**

1 **ripe tomato**

3 **cups freshly squeezed orange juice**

¼ **cup coarsely chopped white onion**

1 **tablespoon freshly squeezed lime juice**

1 **tablespoon kosher or coarse sea salt, or to taste**

Ice cubes (optional)

Sangrita is a chaser, something to sip after fortifying yourself with a shot of tequila. In Mexico you take a sip of tequila, then a sip of *sangrita*, and alternate until you've finished both. It's so much a part of Mexican culture that you can buy ready-made *sangrita* in stores, each brand with its own unique taste. They will do in a pinch, but for me, the best is always homemade.

My *sangrita* gets its attitude from the combination of charred tomatoes, ancho chiles, and citrus. It doesn't contain any alcohol and it is delicious on its own, chilled or served on ice.

1. Heat a *comal* or dry skillet over medium-low heat until hot, at least 10 minutes. Toast the ancho chiles until they have softened and have begun to lightly toast, change color, and release their aroma, 10 to 15 seconds on each side; take care not to burn them, or they will taste bitter.

2. Place the chiles in a bowl, cover them with the boiling water, and let soak until rehydrated and soft, 10 to 15 minutes. Drain, reserving ½ cup of the soaking liquid; set aside.

3. Meanwhile, roast the tomato on the *comal*, turning it a couple of times to get even charring, 9 to 10 minutes. Alternatively, you can char it under the broiler or on a grill for the same amount of time, turning it halfway through.

4. Place the chiles and the reserved soaking liquid in a blender or food processor, along with the orange juice, tomato, onion, lime juice, and salt. Puree until smooth. Strain through a sieve into a pitcher or container, cover, and refrigerate.

5. Serve chilled, on the rocks, or in a *caballito*, alongside tequila.

Caballito A *caballito* is a narrow shot glass, taller and thinner than the ones you find in an American bar. *Caballo* is the Spanish word for "horse," and a *caballito* is a smaller, cuter horse, much as a shot glass is a smaller version of a drinking glass.

CREAMY PEANUT AND VANILLA APÉRITIF

∾ TORITOS ∾

* SERVES 6 TO 8 * PREPARATION TIME: 10 MINUTES * CAN BE MADE UP TO 24 HOURS AHEAD, COVERED, AND REFRIGERATED (STIR BEFORE SERVING) *

2 12-ounce cans evaporated milk

1 14-ounce can sweetened condensed milk

6 ounces (¾ cup) *aguardiente de caña* (cane liquor), 99-proof alcohol, or rum

¾ cup smooth peanut butter

1 teaspoon vanilla extract

Ice cubes (optional)

Mexicans adore peanuts: We eat them raw, toasted, fried, candied, salted, or spiced. They are also used as flavor enhancers and thickeners in sauces like red *pipián* (see page 122) and in candy and marzipan. Amazingly, though, I had never had them in a drink until I went to a wedding in Veracruz. There *toritos* were served as a welcoming drink in the heat and humidity. I fell in love instantly.

Toritos are traditionally made with strong *aguardiente de caña* (cane liquor), which translates to "water that burns"—and it feels like it does if you drink it straight up. The strength of the liquor may be why the *torito*, or "little bull," got its name —hinting at the little kick to the head one may feel after the first couple of sips. Although here the *aguardiente* is subdued by the sweet smoothness of milk and peanuts, make no mistake: it's still there!

The locals enjoy this *torito* as an apéritif, but it is equally delicious as an after-dinner drink.

Working in batches if necessary, combine the evaporated milk, condensed milk, liquor, peanut butter, and vanilla in a blender or food processor and puree until smooth. Transfer to a pitcher or a jar, cover, and refrigerate until chilled. Alternatively, you can serve the drink over ice cubes directly from the blender, or add some ice cubes to the blender or food processor along with the other ingredients to make a frappe.

* MEXICAN COOK'S TRICK: Not a fan of peanuts or peanut butter? *Toritos* can also be made with coffee or exotic fruits. To make a coffee *torito*, replace the peanut butter with ¾ cup strong coffee (espresso or dark coffee). To make a fruit *torito*, replace the peanut butter with 1½ cups fresh or frozen guava or mango puree, or any fruit of your choice. Look for exotic fruit purees in the freezer section of your grocery store and in Latin and specialty stores.

TAMARIND MARGARITA

❋ SERVES 1 ❋ PREPARATION TIME: 10 MINUTES ❋ CAN BE MADE UP TO 12 HOURS AHEAD, COVERED, AND REFRIGERATED (STIR BEFORE SERVING) ❋

One of the favorite ways to eat tamarind in Mexico is in the form of a candy that is salty-sour-spicy-sweet all at once. This tequila drink mimics that addictive sweet. The margarita has a captivating, tangy, and earthy taste that goes wild in your mouth as you sip it through the ground chile, sugar, and salt on the rimmed glass. Trust me, this drink is a conversation starter.

Salty, Sweet, and Spicy Chile Powder (recipe follows) or store-bought Tajín for coating the rim of the glass

¼ **fresh lime**

2 **ounces (¼ cup) white or silver tequila**

About ¼ ounce (1 teaspoon) Triple Sec, Cointreau, or Grand Marnier

2 **tablespoons Latin-Style Tamarind Concentrate or Syrup (page 147)**

1 **teaspoon freshly squeezed lime juice**

Pinch of sugar

Ice cubes

1. Spread the chile powder on a small plate. Rub the rim of a margarita glass with the lime wedge and gently dip it into the chile powder to coat.

2. In a shaker, combine the tequila, Triple Sec, tamarind, lime juice, sugar, and 3 or 4 ice cubes. Close the top and shake vigorously. Strain it into the prepared glass and serve. If you are making more than 1 drink at a time, place all the ingredients in a blender, blend, and pour into a pitcher and chill.

❋ MEXICAN COOK'S TRICK: For an extra-icy drink, chill the margarita glass in the freezer.

SALTY, SWEET, AND SPICY CHILE POWDER

❋ MAKES A SCANT ¼ CUP ❋ PREPARATION TIME: 3 MINUTES ❋ CAN BE MADE UP TO 6 MONTHS AHEAD
AND STORED TIGHTLY COVERED AT ROOM TEMPERATURE ❋

Use this lively spice mix to rim the glasses for margaritas (opposite), Spinning Tops (page 276), or other drinks, sprinkle over freshly cut fruit—or use judiciously as a dip for ice pops.

2 tablespoons ground dried chile, such as piquín, or store-bought Tajín

4 teaspoons kosher or coarse sea salt

1 tablespoon sugar

Mix all of the ingredients together in a small jar or other sealable container.

Tequila or Mezcal? Mezcal is a liquor distilled from the heart of the agave plant, which has been shredded and cooked. Rougher-tasting than tequila, mezcal is traditionally made in open-air buildings in the countryside of the Valley of Oaxaca, and increasingly in other regions as well. The distillation is generally a handcrafted process, with recipes and methods handed down from generation to generation. The end product has a strong peaty, smoky, and earthy flavor.

There is a glut of cheap mass-produced mezcal for sale in the United States, often with a worm in the bottle, although the worm isn't required, nor does it mean much. It's definitely worth the effort to find high-quality artisanal mezcal.

Tequila, on the other hand, can be made only from the blue agave plant, predominantly in the state of Jalisco, in the region called Tequila. Production must follow very strict standards. Although it has a wide range of tastes, tequila is usually more subtle than mezcal.

SPINNING TOP

∼ TROMPO ZACATECANO ∼

❋ SERVES 1 ❋ PREPARATION TIME: 5 MINUTES ❋ CAN BE MADE UP TO 12 HOURS AHEAD, COVERED, AND REFRIGERATED ❋

Kosher or coarse sea salt for coating the rim of the glass

¼ **fresh lime**

3–4 **ice cubes**

2 **ounces (¼ cup) mezcal or tequila**

¾ **cup grapefruit soda, such as Fresca**

¼ **cup pineapple juice**

1–2 **fresh mint leaves**

I was introduced to this drink when we took a vacation in Zacatecas, a state in northern Mexico full of old silver mines, cowboys, burnt-red earth, and more couples of all ages kissing in public than I have ever seen in my life.

A waiter in a restaurant enthusiastically delivered the drink to my table after I asked for the most local and traditional thing he could serve. It takes its name from a *trompo*, a spinning toy popular in Zacatecas. Presumably that's because the mezcal can make your head whirl and spin, although I think maybe it's because so many people in Zacatecas are dizzily in love.

1. Spread the salt on a small plate. Rub the lime wedge around the rim of a glass and gently dip it into the salt to coat.

2. Add the ice cubes to the glass, then pour in the mezcal, grapefruit soda, and pineapple juice; stir gently. Tear the mint into several pieces and drop the pieces into the glass, stirring gently so they release their flavor into the drink. Serve.

❋ MEXICAN COOK'S TRICK: You can give the drink a kick as I like to do by rimming the glass with lime and Salty, Sweet, and Spicy Chile Powder (page 275) or store-bought Tajín.

BEER MEXICAN-STYLE

∾ MICHELADA ∾

❋ SERVES 1 ❋ PREPARATION TIME: 5 MINUTES ❋

Kosher or coarse sea salt

1 lime wedge

Ice cubes (optional)

2–3 tablespoons freshly
squeezed lime juice

1 cold 12-ounce beer, preferably Mexican

FOR A MICHELADA ESPECIAL

Dash of hot sauce, like
Tabasco, Cholula, or
Valentina or a combina-
tion

Dash of a salty sauce, like
soy sauce, Worcestershire,
or Maggi

Pinch of kosher or coarse
sea salt

Pinch of freshly ground
black pepper

Picture this: a frosty, ice-cold mug rimmed with tangy citrus and crunchy salt, filled with a mixture of beer and freshly squeezed lime juice. This is the *Michelada*.

There are many versions: some, like the *Michelada especial*, are over-the-top combos of salty, spicy, and sour flavors. In any case, Mexico's dressed-up version of a beer will have you licking the last drops of salty lime juice off the rim of the frozen mug. You may never think of beer in the same way again.

1. Place a beer mug in the freezer for a couple of hours or until chilled.

2. Spread the salt on a small plate. Rub the rim of the mug with the lime wedge and dip the rim gently into the salt to coat. Place a couple of ice cubes, if using, in the mug.

3. Add the lime juice, then pour in the beer. Or, if making a *Michelada especial*, add the optional ingredients to taste, along with the lime juice, to the chilled mug. Stir lightly, then pour in the beer.

BANANA AND CAJETA MILKSHAKE

✳ SERVES 2 ✳ PREPARATION TIME: 5 MINUTES ✳ CAN BE MADE UP TO 1 HOUR AHEAD, COVERED, AND REFRIGERATED ✳

2 ripe bananas, peeled and thickly sliced (fresh or frozen; see the headnote)

3 cups cold milk or vanilla ice cream

1 teaspoon vanilla extract

6 tablespoons *cajeta* (see page 246) or dulce de leche

It's a pain to get my kids to eat breakfast on a weekday, as I try to pack them up and get them to the bus stop on time. You too? Play to their sweet tooth and make this healthy morning milkshake. I always have bananas in the house, and they ripen faster than we can eat them, so I've gotten into the habit of peeling, slicing, and freezing them. Pair those frozen bananas with the delicious deep caramel taste of *cajeta*, and breakfast is a snap to pull off.

A splash of rum takes this decadent dessert into adults-only territory.

Place the bananas, milk, vanilla, and *cajeta* in a blender or food processor and puree until smooth. Serve chilled.

SPICED SWEET MEXICAN COFFEE

∾ CAFÉ DE OLLA ∾

❋ SERVES 4 TO 6 ❋ PREPARATION TIME: 5 MINUTES ❋ COOKING TIME: 10 MINUTES ❋ CAN BE MADE A COUPLE OF HOURS AHEAD AND KEPT, COVERED, IN THE POT; REHEAT BEFORE SERVING ❋

This coffee gets extra flavor from the raw sugar, *piloncillo*, combined with the warmth of true cinnamon. This is the coffee you'll find in the countryside of Mexico, typically brewed in a clay pot known as an *olla de barro* (see below) and served in tin mugs.

Café de olla used to be found mostly in low-end restaurants, but it has become trendy and is now found in highbrow coffee shops. I like its humble origins and its down-to-earth taste.

8 cups water

6 tablespoons coarsely ground dark-roasted coffee beans

8–9 tablespoons grated or finely chopped *piloncillo* (see page 262) or dark brown sugar, or to taste

1 Ceylon cinnamon stick (see page 238)

1. Bring the water to a rolling boil in a pot. Reduce the heat to low and add the coffee, *piloncillo*, and cinnamon stick. Simmer for about 10 minutes, stirring occasionally, then turn off the heat and let sit, covered, for 5 minutes.

2. Strain through a fine sieve or cheesecloth and serve. Alternatively, remove the cinnamon stick and pour the drink into a French press; press down on the plunger and serve.

Mexican Clay Cooking Pots (Ollas de Barro) Mexicans often cook in clay vessels, which bring authentic flavors with a lot of presence to dishes from Simple Beans from the Pot (page 216) to Spiced Sweet Mexican Coffee. They are great fun to use if you know a few things.

First, a new clay pot is very porous and must be cured before using so the inner surface seals and doesn't leak. I've found what works best is to fill the pot with water to about 1 inch below the rim, bring the water to a boil over medium-low heat, and let it simmer for 15 minutes or so. Remove it from the heat and let it cool thoroughly. Drain the water, and the pot is cured. Although you can boil liquid over high heat in a clay pot, it must be heated gradually to prevent cracking. There is no need to worry about lead poisoning, as modern Mexican clay pots are lead-free.

ACKNOWLEDGMENTS I am eternally indebted to Mexico, where I was born and bred, for its warmth, generosity, and richness. I am equally indebted to my second home, the United States, where I've been able to share what I know and where I am learning so much.

To my agent, Peter W. Smith, I cherish your steady hand, your wise perspective, and your willingness to wear many hats on my behalf.

To my editor, Rux Martin: You've guided my message with such care and thoughtfulness. It's been an honor to work with the entire team at Houghton Mifflin Harcourt. Thanks especially to Melissa Lotfy and Rebecca Springer for production support and to Judith Sutton for your keen eye; you made everything better.

To Sally Swift, I thank the strong winds that moved you to this city. You have my gratitude for helping me distill my writing into this book. Judy Graham, you have the most fabulous pair of eyes any copy editor could wish for; thank you for your hard work. To the oh-so-lovely Carrie Bachman, thank you for all your efforts in spreading the word about this book.

To Penny De Los Santos, who knows how to capture the Mexico in America: I was thrilled to work with you. I love what you did to my food. Thanks to Christine Albano, the food stylist, and Sarah Cave, the prop stylist, for your efforts and beautiful work. Melissa's Produce, thank you for providing gorgeous produce and spices. Kim Steele and Sybil Street, you are a delight, and your work is beautiful. Thank you both for helping me look decent while cooking and posing for this cover.

To Design Army, Jake and Pum Leferbure and designer Charles Calixto, for the perfect web design and logo. To Cade Martin, for those gorgeous photos for my website's banners.

To former Mexican ambassador to the United States, Arturo Sarukhan, and his wife, Veronica Valencia, whose work on behalf of Mexico I deeply admire, a long-lasting thank-you for supporting my work at the Mexican Cultural Institute and beyond, and mostly for your friendship.

A deep thank-you to the entire team of the Mexican Cultural Institute in Washington, D.C.: You've become my Mexican home away from home. To Juan Garcia de Oteyza, who helped my life take a crucial turn by asking me, "What do you do?" and then saying, "Come do it at the MCI." To Alejandra de la Paz, for supporting the continuation of the program and pushing me to improve it with your devotion to excellence. To Elsa Borja, for your lovely personality, professionalism, and support. A heart-swelled thank-you to Angel López and Nazario Mendoza and to my cooking team at the

institute: Doña Rosa Arroyo, Manuel Hernandez, Maricruz Morales, Isabel Solano, and Julio Torres—for six years, you've inspired me and put up with my wild menus.

To WETA, coproducers of my television series: Dalton Delan, Suzanne Masri, Karen Fitz, Jim Corbley, Michael Holstein, John Potthast, and the rest of the team, it is delightful to work with you. And to Anne Kaufman, whose fateful first phone call with my agent planted a seed for all of us. It is an honor to be part of your inspiring programming.

To the entire team of Cortez Brothers production company, coproducers of my television series, *Pati's Mexican Table*, I treasure your positive attitude, hard work, and creativity. A special thank-you to Bernadette Rivero for your ongoing enthusiasm.

To my friends at ASERCA-SAGARPA, who are dedicated to promoting and supporting Mexico's agricultural exports, Froylán Gracia, Gabriel Padilla Maya, and Carlos Vázquez and the whole team in the United States and Mexico, for seeing the potential for our collaboration and giving me the support to move forward.

To the Mexico Tourism Board in Mexico and the United States, thank you for your support. To Rodolfo López Negrete, for allowing me to collaborate with the outstanding

Mexican Tourism team. To Eduardo Chaillo, for your joy for life, positive attitude, strong values, and mostly for being there throughout. Gabriela Ibarra, thank you so much for your ongoing support.

To the Ogilvy team, who does such wonderful work: Andy Kochar, Jennifer Risi, and Josh Levin. Bob Lear, I feel so lucky that we met.

I am proud to be able to collaborate with companies whose products I grew up with and love: Mission Foods, Avocados from Mexico, Tajín, AMHPAC, Omaha Steaks, and your entire teams. Thank you for believing in my work.

To Tamara Belt, Debra Eichenbaum, Marina Feldman, Ceci Kennary, Jeanie Milbauer, Diana Moss, Monika Pamp, Cecilia Ramos, Michael Shifter, Mimi Strouse, and Jessica Wellisch, longtime dear friends: You were at my first classes and I know you will be at my last.

To all of my friends, old and new, who have come to my classes, read my stories, and shared their time with me, thank you for your loving support.

To Bonnie Benwick, Tim Carman, Joan Nathan, and Joe Yonan, thank you for your friendship, tips, stories, and time.

A loud thank-you to Gordon Elliott, for seeing the value in my work; I so admire yours. Every single time we have worked together has been an incredible treat.

To my father, Miki: You've taught me to get up *cuando me tropiezo* ("when I trip") countless times. You also enlightened me as to what a sprinkle of salt can do to any taco or torta. To my mother, Susana, for showing me the exquisite side of almost everything we taste. And now that I am a mother too, I realize how wise you were the times you remained silent. To Karen, Alisa, and Sharon, I am lucky to have you as sisters, but even more so as friends. I couldn't have asked for more, except maybe that we live in the same city as we grow old.

To my in-laws, Carlos and Perla Jinich, for being so enthusiastic about and supportive of what I do.

To my husband, Daniel, for pushing me to do what I love and for reminding me of the things that *valen la pena* ("are worthwhile") when I worry too much. To Alan, Sami, and Juju, for making it hard to go to sleep at night and easy to wake up in the morning. I love you so.

INDEX

A

achiote paste, 166
agua fresca de Jamaica, 268–70
agua fresca de limón con menta, 271
aguas frescas:
    Jamaica, 268–70
    lime and mint water, 271
aioli:
    jalapeño, 128
    lime, 187
albóndigas con chipotle, 153–55
almond-chipotle pesto, creamy, 133
alphabet soup, 80
amarillito, 148–50
ancho chile(s), 13, 73
    burgers with lime aioli, 186–87
    dried chile crisps, 72
    and orange chaser, 272
    orange sauce, shredded pork in, 174–76
    pickled, vinaigrette, 56
    salsa, pickled, 32
apéritif, creamy peanut and vanilla, 273
apple, chorizo, pecan, and corn bread stuffing, 167
apricot(s):
    -lime-glazed mini pound cakes, 242–44
    sticky chicken with tamarind, chipotle and, 146–47
arroz rojo, 224–26
arroz verde, 221
avocado(s), 9
    chunky guacamole, 38–39
    cut, storing, 64
    dressing, 50
    and hearts of palm salad, 46–47
    how to buy, 65
    red leaf, and grapefruit salad with olive-mint vinaigrette, 45
    ripening at home, 65
    soup, classic, 64–66
Aztec chicken casserole, 160–62

B

baby back ribs, honey-chipotle, 172–73
El Bajio, Mexico City, 103
banana and *cajeta* milkshake, 278
banana leaves, 178
bean(s), 9
    black, and tortilla casserole, 110–12
    black, sauce, scrambled egg packets with, 98–99
    canned, 217
    charro, 218
    and cheese heroes, grilled, 113
    cooking, 217
    pinto, soup, hearty, 70–72
    from the pot, simple, 216
    refried, *see* refried bean(s)
beef:
    ancho chile burgers with lime aioli, 186–87
    brisket in pasilla and tomatillo sauce, 193–94
    picadillo, 192
    picadillo empanadas, 190–91
    steak and cheese in pita bread, Mexican, 185
    steak tacos with *Jamaica*-jalapeño sauce, 182–84
    tenderloin, spiral-cut, 188–89
beer Mexican-style, 277
beet, jicama, orange, and caramelized peanut Christmas salad, 54–55
Bellinghausen, Mexico City, 131
berries with lime syrup, 262
bitter orange juice, 166
black bean:
    sauce, scrambled egg packets with, 98–99
    and tortilla casserole, 110–12
Boston lettuce salad with avocado dressing, candied pineapple, and spicy pumpkin seeds, 50–51
breakfast or brunch:
    chilaquiles in red salsa, 105
    divorced eggs, 92–93
    frittata with poblanos, potatoes, and feta, Mexican, 100–101
    poached eggs in chunky poblano-tomato salsa, 97
    scrambled egg packets with black bean sauce, 98–99
broth, chicken, Mexican, 87

burgers, ancho chile, with lime aioli, 186–87
burritas, 175

C

caballitos, 272
café de olla, 279
cajeta, 246
    and banana milkshake, 278
    crepes with toasted pecans, 245–47
    impossible chocoflan, 259–61
cakes:
    guava cheesecake, 256–58
    impossible chocoflan, 259–61
    pound, apricot-lime-glazed mini, 242–44
    pound, marbled, Alisa's, 251–53
    tres leche, 254–55
caldo de pollo, 87
camarones en pipián rojo, 122–23
Camino Real Hotel, Puerto Vallarta, 118
caramel, *see cajeta*
caramelized pecans or peanuts, 49
carne enchilada, 193–94
carrots, pickled jalapeños and, 34–36
casseroles:
    chicken, Aztec, 160–62
    tortilla and black bean, 110–12
cassia, 238
cazuela azteca, 160–62
cebollas encurtidas a la Yucateca, 35, 37
ceviche tostadas Puerto Vallarta, 118–19
charring, 19
charro beans, 218
chaser, orange and ancho chile, 272
chayote, 59
    pickled, salad, 58
cheese:
    and bean heroes, grilled, 113
    feta, Mexican frittata with poblanos, potatoes and, 100–101
    feta, watermelon and tomatillo salad with, 52–53
    goat, spinach salad with caramelized pecans and *Jamaica* vinaigrette, 48–49

cheese (*cont.*)

    melty, tomato-zucchini soup with, 78–79

    mozzarella and tomato salad with pickled ancho chile vinaigrette, 56–57

    and mushroom quesadillas, Oaxaca-style, 106–9

    steak and, in pita bread, Mexican, 185

    tortilla and black bean casserole, 110–12

cheesecake, guava, 256–58

chicken:

    breasts, flattening, 158

    broth, Mexican, 87

    casserole, Aztec, 160–62

    enchiladas in *salsa verde*, 145

    meatballs with mint and chipotle, Mexican, 153–55

    Milanesa, crispy, 156–58

    potato salad, smoky, 159

    red pozole, 84–86

    sautéing in oil, 146, 158

    shredded, in ancho-orange sauce, 176

    sticky, with apricots, tamarind, and chipotle, 146–47

    Thanksgiving, Mexican, with chorizo, pecan, apple, and corn bread stuffing, 163, 164

    tinga, 140–43

    à la trash, 144

    white pozole, 81–82

    yellow mole with masa dumplings, 148–52

chilaca chiles, 194

chilaquiles en salsa roja, 105

chilaquiles in red salsa, 105

chile(s), 12–13

    charred, removing skins vs. leaving them on, 18

    controlling heat of, 30

    dried, crisps, 72

    powder, salty, sweet, and spicy, 275

    puree, 84

    soothing heat in mouth from, 36

    wearing gloves when working with, 36

    see also specific varieties

chile(s) de árbol, 214

    citrus sweet potatoes with, 213–14

chilorio, 174–76

chipotle(s):

    in adobo sauce, 141

    almond pesto, creamy, 133

    creamy corn soup, 68

    and fresh tomatillo salsa, 24

honey ribs, 172–73

mashed potatoes, 212

meatballs with mint and, Mexican, 153–55

sticky chicken with apricots, tamarind and, 146–47

chips, tortilla, 66

    chilaquiles in red salsa, 105

chochoyotes, 152

chocoflan impossible, 259–61

chocolate:

    impossible chocoflan, 259–61

    marbled pound cake, Alisa's, 251–53

    scribble cookies, 239–41

chorizo:

    charro beans, 218

    guajillo-soaked crusty bread stuffed with potatoes and, 179–81

    Mexican, 219

    pecan, apple, and corn bread stuffing, 167

Christmas salad, jicama, beet, orange, and caramelized peanut, 54–55

cilantro, 23

    my favorite green rice, 221–22

cinnamon, Ceylon (Mexican cinnamon), 238

    spiced sweet Mexican coffee, 279

citrus:

    bitter orange juice, 166

    sauce, sweet, pork tenderloin in, 177–78

    suprêmes, cutting, 45

    sweet potatoes with chile de árbol, 213–14

clay cooking pots, 279

cochinitos, 236–38

cocoa powder, adding to batter, 252

coctel de camarón del Pacífico, 120–21

coffee:

    spiced sweet Mexican, 279

    torito, 273

Cohen, Flora, 146

colache de calabacitas, 215

comales, 111

concentrado de Jamaica, 270

cookie(s):

    crust, 256, 258

    Maria, 257

    piggy, 236–38

    scribble, 239–41

    triple orange Mexican wedding, 234–35

corn:

    Aztec chicken casserole, 160–62

bread, chorizo, pecan, and apple stuffing, 167

crazy street, 202–3

soup, creamy, 68

squash blossom soup, 74–76

torte, blissful, 204–6

tortillas, *see* tortilla(s), corn

corn masa flour, 149

    corn tortillas, homemade, 94–96

    Oaxaca-style mushroom and cheese quesadillas, 106–9

    yellow mole with masa dumplings, 148–52

crab cakes with jalapeño aioli, 127–29

crazy street corn, 202–3

creamless cream of zucchini soup, 67

crema, Mexican, 135

crema de calabacita, 67

crema fresca, 135

crepes, *cajeta*, with toasted pecans, 245–47

crisps:

    dried chile, 72

    tortilla, 66

croquettes, shrimp, in tomato broth, 124–26

cucumbers, in crunchy radish pico, 31

D

D'Elvis, Mexico City, 239

desserts, 230–63

    apricot-lime-glazed mini pound cakes, 242–44

    berries with lime syrup, 262

    cajeta crepes with toasted pecans, 245–47

    chocoflan, impossible, 259–61

    guava cheesecake, 256–58

    marbled pound cake, Alisa's, 251–53

    piggy cookies, 236–38

    plantain fritters, sweet, 248–50

    scribble cookies, 239–41

    tomatillo and lime jam, 263

    tres leches cake, 254–55

    triple orange Mexican wedding cookies, 234–35

divorced eggs, 92–93

dressings:

    avocado, 50

    see also vinaigrettes

dried chile crisps, 72

drinks, 264–79

    banana and *cajeta* milkshake, 278

    beer Mexican-style, 277

    caballitos (narrow shot glasses) for, 272

    Jamaica water, 268–70

lime and mint water, 271
orange and ancho chile chaser, 272
peanut and vanilla apéritif, creamy, 273
salty, sweet, and spicy chile powder to rim glasses for, 275
spinning top, 276
tamarind margarita, 274–75
dulce de leche, 245, 246
see also cajeta
dumplings, masa, yellow mole with, 148–52

E
egg(s):
blissful corn torte, 204–6
divorced, 92–93
frittata with poblanos, potatoes, and feta, Mexican, 100–101
poached, in chunky poblano-tomato salsa, 97
scrambled, packets with black bean sauce, 98–99
elotes callejeros, 202–3
empanadas:
freezing, 190
picadillo, 190–92
empanadas de picadillo, 190–92
enchiladas:
chicken, in salsa verde, 145
two forms of, 145
enchiladas verdes, 145
ensalada de navidad, 54–55
epazote, 107
everyday green salad, 44

F
faroladas, 185
El Farolito Taquería, Mexico City, 185
feta cheese:
frittata with poblanos, potatoes and, Mexican, 100–101
watermelon and tomatillo salad with, 52–53
fideo seco, 228–29
fish, see seafood
flan:
in impossible chocoflan, 259–61
frijoles charros, 218
frijoles de olla, 216
frijoles refritos, 220
frittata with poblanos, potatoes, and feta, Mexican, 100–101
fritters, plantain, sweet, 248–50
fruit(s), 9
torito, 273
see also specific fruits

G
galletas Maria, 257
garabatos, 239–41
garapiñados, 49
garibaldis, 242–44
garlic and guajillo pasta, 227
garnishes:
caramelized pecans or peanuts, 49
spicy pumpkin seeds, 51
El Globo, Mexico City, 242
goat cheese spinach salad with caramelized pecans and Jamaica vinaigrette, 48–49
grapefruit:
red leaf, and avocado salad with olive-mint vinaigrette, 45
soda, in spinning top, 276
green beans with orange and pistachios, 207
green pipián, lamb chops in, 195–97
green rice, my favorite, 221–22
green salad, everyday, 44
green salsa, cooked, 22
chicken enchiladas in, 145
grilled cheese and bean heroes, 113
guacamole, 17
chunky, 38–39
guajillo chile(s), 12, 86
and garlic pasta, 227
–soaked crusty bread stuffed with potatoes and chorizo, 179–81
guava:
cheesecake, 256–58
paste, 257
torito, 273

H
habanero chiles, 12
crab cakes with jalapeño aioli, 127
hearts of palm and avocado salad, 46–47
heat (of chiles):
controlling, 30
in mouth, soothing, 36
herbs, fresh vs. dried, 227
heroes, grilled cheese and bean, 113
hibiscus, see Jamaica flower
hoja santa, 150
hominy, 83
dried, cooking, 82, 83
red pozole, 84–86
white pozole, 81–82
honey-chipotle ribs, 172–73
huevos divorciados, 92–93
huevos envueltos bañados en frijol, 98–99
huevos rabo de mestiza, 97

I
impossible chocoflan, 259–61

J
jalapeño(s), 13, 29
aioli, 128
Jamaica sauce, 182–84
pickled carrots and, 34–36
smoked, see chipotle(s)
jalapeños y zanahorias en escabeche, 34–36
jam, tomatillo and lime, 263
Jamaica (hibiscus) flower, 183
concentrate, 270
jalapeño sauce, 182–84
vinaigrette, 48
water, 268–69
jicama, 54
beet, orange, and caramelized peanut Christmas salad, 54–55

L
lamb chops in green pipián, 195–97
leek(s):
cleaning, 77
and potato soup, weeknight, 77
lime(s):
aioli, 187
-apricot-glazed mini pound cakes, 242–44
beer Mexican-style, 277
Mexican vs. American, 271
and mint water, 271
syrup, berries with, 262
and tomatillo jam, 263
Loredo, José Ines, 188

M
mackerel, in ceviche tostadas Puerto Vallarta, 118–19
Maggi, 211
mahimahi, creamy poblano, 134–35
mango:
pico, 30
torito, 273
marbled pound cake, Alisa's, 251–53
margarita, tamarind, 274–75
Maria cookie(s), 257
crust, 256, 258
Marmolejo, Doña María Rosa, 64
marranitos, 236–38
masa, see corn masa flour
meat, 168–97
ancho chile burgers with lime aioli, 186–87
lamb chops in green pipián, 195–97
picadillo, 192

meat (*cont.*)
  picadillo empanadas, 190–91
  see also beef; pork
meatballs with mint and chipotle,
    Mexican, 153–55
mermelada de tomate con limón, 263
mezcal:
  spinning top, 276
  tequila vs., 275
Michelada or *Michelada especial*,
    277
Michoacán-style:
  beef brisket in pasilla and tomatillo
    sauce, 193–94
  hearty pinto bean soup, 70–72
Milanesa de pollo, 156–58
milkshake, banana and *cajeta*, 278
minguichi, 78–79
mint:
  and lime water, 271
  meatballs with chipotle and,
    Mexican, 153–55
  olive vinaigrette, 45
molcajetes, 154
mole(s), 150
  red *pipián*, shrimp in, 122–23
  yellow, with masa dumplings,
    148–52
mole amarillito con chochoyotes,
    148–52
molletes, 113
mozzarella and tomato salad with
    pickled ancho chile vinaigrette,
    56–57
mushroom and cheese quesadillas,
    Oaxaca-style, 106–9

N
nixtamalization, 149

O
Oaxaca-style:
  mushroom and cheese quesadillas,
    106–9
  yellow mole with masa dumplings,
    148–52
olive-mint vinaigrette, 45
ollas de barro, 279
Olvera, Enrique, 263
onions:
  red, pickled, Yucatán-style, 35, 37
  white, 33
orange:
  and ancho chile chaser, 272
  ancho sauce, shredded pork in,
    174–76
  green beans with pistachios and,
    207

jicama, beet, and caramelized pea-
    nut Christmas salad, 54–55
  triple, Mexican wedding cookies,
    234–35
Our Lady of the Immaculate Concep-
    tion, 190

P
pambazos, 179–81
panela or *panocha*, 262
panque marmoleado, 251–53
pasilla chile(s), 13, 194
  dried chile crisps, 72
  and tomatillo sauce, beef brisket in,
    193–94
pasta:
  alphabet soup, 80
  guajillo and garlic, 227
  Mexican-style, 228–29
pastel tres leches, 254–55
peanut(s):
  caramelized, 49
  caramelized, jicama, beet, and
    orange Christmas salad, 54–55
  and vanilla apéritif, creamy, 273
pecan(s):
  caramelized, 49
  chorizo, apple, and corn bread stuff-
    ing, 167
  toasted, *cajeta* crepes with,
    245–47
pepitas, *see* pumpkin seeds
pepitas enchiladas, 51
pescado Rodrigo, 130–31
pesto, creamy almond-chipotle, 133
picadillo, 192
  empanadas, 190–91
picadillo de carne, 192
pickle(d)(s), 17, 34–37
  ancho chile salsa, 32
  ancho chile vinaigrette, 56
  chayote salad, 58
  jalapeños and carrots, 34–36
  red onions, Yucatán-style, 35, 37
pico de gallo salsas, 17
  mango, 30
  radish, crunchy, 31
  tomato, traditional, 28
piggy cookies, 236–38
piloncillo, 262
pineapple:
  candied, Boston lettuce salad with
    avocado dressing, spicy pump-
    kin seeds and, 50
  juice, in spinning top, 276
pipián:
  green, lamb chops in, 195–97
  red, shrimp in, 122–23

pipián verde con costillitas de cordero,
    195–97
pistachios, green beans with orange
    and, 207
pita bread, steak and cheese in,
    Mexican, 185
plantain(s), 250
  fritters, sweet, 248–50
  and refried bean quesadillas, 102–4
poblano chile(s), 13, 76
  anchos and, 73
  Aztec chicken casserole, 160–62
  charring or broiling, 27
  frittata with potatoes, feta and,
    Mexican, 100–101
  mahimahi, creamy, 134–35
  my favorite green rice, 221–22
  rajas, creamy, 208–9
  sautéed zucchini with, 215
  squash blossom soup, 74–76
  and tomato salsa, chunky, 26
  and tomato salsa, chunky, poached
    eggs in, 97
pollo a la basura, 144
polvorones de naranja, 234–35
pork:
  ancho chile burgers with lime aioli,
    186
  picadillo, 192
  picadillo empanadas, 190–91
  ribs, honey-chipotle, 172–73
  shredded, in ancho-orange sauce,
    174–76
  tenderloin in sweet citrus sauce,
    177–78
  white pozole, 82
  see also chorizo
potato(es):
  baby, with lime and parsley, 210
  chicken salad, smoky, 159
  chipotle mashed, 212
  frittata with poblanos, feta and,
    Mexican, 100–101
  guajillo-soaked crusty bread stuffed
    with chorizo and, 179–81
  and leek soup weeknight, 77
poultry, 136–67
  see also chicken, turkey
pound cakes:
  marbled, Alisa's, 251–53
  mini, apricot-lime-glazed, 242–44
pozole:
  red, 84–86
  white, 81–82
pozole blanco, 81–82
pozole rojo, 84–86
prunes, in chicken à la trash, 144
puerquitos, 236–38

pumpkin seeds (pepitas), 51
  chicken à la trash, 144
  pipián verde, 195
  red *pipián*, shrimp in, 122–23
  spicy, 51

Q

quesadillas:
  mushroom and cheese, Oaxaca-style, 106–9
  plantain and refried bean, 102–4
queso fresco, 9, 99

R

radish pico, crunchy, 31
rajas con crema, 208–9
red leaf, avocado, and grapefruit salad with olive-mint vinaigrette, 45
red *pipián*, shrimp in, 122–23
red pozole, 84–86
red rice, 224–26
red salsa (charred tomato salsa), 18
  chilaquiles in, 105
refried bean(s), 220
  and cheese heroes, grilled, 113
  divorced eggs, 92–93
  guajillo-soaked crusty bread stuffed with potatoes and chorizo, 179–81
  and plantain quesadillas, 102–4
ribs, honey-chipotle, 172–73
rice:
  cooking the Mexican way, 223
  green, my favorite, 221–22
  red, 224–26
  soaking in hot water before cooking, 226
rice flour, 206
Rodrigo-style fish, 130–31
rum, in creamy peanut and vanilla apéritif, 273

S

salads, 40–58
  avocado and hearts of palm, 46–47
  Boston lettuce, with avocado dressing, candied pineapple, and spicy pumpkin seeds, 50–51
  chicken potato, smoky, 159
  green, everyday, 44
  jicama, beet, orange, and caramelized peanut Christmas, 54–55
  pickled chayote, 58
  red leaf, avocado, and grapefruit, with olive-mint vinaigrette, 45
  spinach goat cheese, with caramelized pecans and *Jamaica* vinaigrette, 48–49

tomato and mozzarella, with pickled ancho chile vinaigrette, 56–57
  watermelon and tomatillo, with feta cheese, 52–53
salmon, sweet and salty, 132
salsa roja, 18
salsas, 9, 17–32
  green, chicken enchiladas in, 145
  green, cooked, 22
  mango pico, 30
  pickled ancho chile, 32
  poblano and tomato, chunky, 26
  poblano-tomato, chunky, poached eggs in, 97
  radish pico, crunchy, 31
  red, chilaquiles in, 105
  tomatillo, fresh, and chipotle, 24
  tomato, charred, 18
  tomato pico de gallo, traditional, 28
salsa verde, 22
  chicken enchiladas in, 145
salty, sweet, and spicy chile powder, 275
sandwiches:
  ancho chile burgers with lime aioli, 186–87
  grilled cheese and bean heroes, 113
  guajillo-soaked crusty bread stuffed with potatoes and chorizo, 179–81
  steak and cheese in pita bread, Mexican, 185
sangrita, 272
sauces:
  almond-chipotle pesto, creamy, 133
  cajeta, 245–47
  jalapeño aioli, 128
  Jamaica-jalapeño, 182–84
  lime aioli, 187
  pipián verde, 195
  tres leches, 254–55
  yellow mole, 148–50
scrambled egg packets with black bean sauce, 98–99
scribble cookies, 239–41
seafood, 114–35
  ceviche tostadas Puerto Vallarta, 118–19
  crab cakes with jalapeño aioli, 127–29
  mahimahi, creamy poblano, 134–35
  Rodrigo-style fish, 130–31
  salmon, sweet and salty, 132
  snapper with creamy almond-chipotle pesto, 133
  see also shrimp
serrano chiles, 12, 29

shrimp:
  cocktail Pacífico, 120–21
  croquettes in tomato broth, 124–26
  frozen, 120
  in red *pipián*, 122–23
sides, 198–229
  beans, *charro*, 218
  beans, refried, 220
  beans from the pot, simple, 216
  chorizo, pecan, apple, and corn bread stuffing, 167
  corn, crazy street, 202–3
  corn torte, blissful, 204–6
  green beans with orange and pistachios, 207
  pasta, guajillo and garlic, 227
  pasta, Mexican-style, 228–29
  poblano rajas, creamy, 208–9
  potatoes, baby, with lime and parsley, 210
  potatoes, chipotle mashed, 212
  rice, green, my favorite, 221–22
  rice, red, 224–26
  sweet potatoes, citrus, with chile de árbol, 213–14
  zucchini, sautéed, with poblano peppers, 215
Sinaloa-style:
  sautéed zucchini with poblano peppers, 215
  shredded pork in ancho-orange sauce, 174–76
smoky chicken potato salad, 159
snapper with creamy almond-chipotle pesto, 133
Solis, Alfredo, 127
sopa de aguacate, 64–66
sopa de flor de calabaza, 74–76
sopa de letras, 80
sopa de poro y papa, 77
sopa tarasca, 70–72
soups, 60–87
  alphabet, 80
  avocado, classic, 64–66
  chicken broth, Mexican, 87
  corn, creamy, 68
  pinto bean, hearty, 70–72
  potato and leek, weeknight, 77
  squash blossom, 74–76
  tomato-zucchini, with melty cheese, 78–79
  zucchini, creamless cream of, 67
spareribs, honey-chipotle, 172–73
spiced sweet Mexican coffee, 279
spinach goat cheese salad with caramelized pecans and *Jamaica* vinaigrette, 48–49
spinning top, 276

squash blossom(s):
preparing, 76
soup, 74–76
steak:
and cheese in pita bread, Mexican, 185
tacos with *Jamaica*-jalapeño sauce, 182–84
sticky chicken with apricots, tamarind, and chipotle, 146–47
stuffing, chorizo, pecan, apple, and corn bread, 167
sunflower seeds, in chicken à la trash, 144
suprêmes, cutting citrus fruit into, 45
sweet and salty salmon, 132
sweet potatoes, citrus, with chile de árbol, 213–14
Swift, Sally, 110

T
tacos, steak, with *Jamaica*-jalapeño sauce, 182–84
tamarind, 147
concentrate or syrup, Latin-style, 147
margarita, 274–75
sticky chicken with apricots, chipotle and, 146–47
tampiqueña, 188–89
tequila:
mezcal vs., 275
orange and ancho chile chaser for, 272
spinning top, 276
tamarind margarita, 274–75
Thanksgiving turkey with chorizo, pecan, apple, and corn bread stuffing, Mexican, 164–67
tilapia, in Rodrigo-style fish, 130–31
tinga, chicken, 140–43
tingadillas, 142
tiritas, 66
tiritas de chile seco, 72
Titita, Carmen, 103
tomatillo(s), 25
cooked green salsa, 22
fresh, and chipotle salsa, 24
and lime jam, 263
and pasilla sauce, beef brisket in, 193–94
pipián verde, 195
and watermelon salad with feta cheese, 52–53

tomato(es):
alphabet soup, 80
broth, shrimp croquettes in, 124–26
charred, salsa, 18
and mozzarella salad with pickled ancho chile vinaigrette, 56–57
pasta, Mexican-style, 228–29
pico de gallo salsa, traditional, 28
poblano salsa, chunky, poached eggs in, 97
and poblano salsa, chunky, 26
red rice, 224–26
salsa, in chilaquiles in red salsa, 105
zucchini soup with melty cheese, 78–79
toritos, 273
torrejas de plátano macho, 248–50
tortas, 142
torte, corn, blissful, 204–6
tortilla(s), corn, 9
Aztec chicken casserole, 160–62
and black bean casserole, 110–12
chips, crisps, or tostadas, 66
chips, in chilaquiles in red salsa, 105
comales for, 111
consistency of masa dough for, 96
crisping before cooking with, 162
divorced eggs, 92–93
flour tortillas vs., 176
homemade, 94–96
scrambled egg packets with black bean sauce, 98–99
steak tacos with *Jamaica*-jalapeño sauce, 182–84
tortillas, flour, 176
tortillerias, 94
tostadas, 66
ceviche, Puerto Vallarta, 118–19
chicken tinga, 142, 143
totopos, 66
tres leches cake, 254–55
triple orange Mexican wedding cookies, 234–35
trompo zacatecano, 276
turkey:
meatballs with mint and chipotle, Mexican, 153–55
Thanksgiving, Mexican, with chorizo, pecan, apple, and corn bread stuffing, 164–67

V
vanilla, 69

creamy corn soup, 68
harvesting, 255
and peanut apéritif, creamy, 273
tres leches cake, 254–55
veal:
ancho chile burgers with lime aioli, 186–87
picadillo, 192
picadillo empanadas, 190–92
vegetarian dishes, 10, 88–113
chilaquiles in red salsa, 105
divorced eggs, 92–93
frittata with poblanos, potatoes, and feta, Mexican, 100–101
grilled cheese and bean heroes, 113
mushroom and cheese quesadillas, Oaxaca-style, 106–9
plantain and refried bean quesadillas, 102–4
poached eggs in chunky poblano-tomato salsa, 97
scrambled egg packets with black bean sauce, 98–99
tortilla and black bean casserole, 110–12
vinaigrettes, 44
Jamaica, 48
oils for, 58
olive-mint, 45
pickled ancho chile, 56

W
watermelon and tomatillo salad with feta cheese, 52–53
wedding cookies, triple orange Mexican, 234–35
weeknight potato and leek soup, 77
white pozole, 81–82

Y
yellow mole with masa dumplings, 148–52
Yucatán-style:
Mexican Thanksgiving turkey with chorizo, pecan, apple, and corn bread stuffing, 164–67
pickled red onions, 35, 37

Z
zucchini:
creamless cream of, soup, 67
sautéed, with poblano peppers, 215
squash blossom soup, 74–76
tomato soup with melty cheese, 78–79